THE LIMITS OF AGRARIAN RADICALISM

Western Populism and American Politics

PETER H. ARGERSINGER

UNIVERSITY PRESS OF KANSAS

FOR ALLAN G. BOGUE

Published by the University Press of Kansas (Lawrence, Kansas 66049), which
was organized by the Kansas Board of Regents and is operated and funded by
Emporia State University, Fort Hays State University, Kansas State University,
Pittsburg State University, the University of Kansas, and Wichita State
University

Library of Congress Cataloging-in-Publication Data

Argersinger, Peter H.
    The limits of agrarian radicalism : western populism and American
Politics / by Peter H. Argersinger.
        p.   cm.
    Includes index.
    ISBN 0-7006-0702-1 (alk. paper)
    1. Populism—West (U.S.)—History.   2. West (U.S.)—Politics and
government.   I. Title.
    F595.A74   1995
324.2732 '7—dc20   94-23556

British Library Cataloguing in Publication Data is available.

Printed in the United States of America

10 9 8 7 6 5 4 3 2 1

CONTENTS

v

PREFACE

With its dramatic personalities, important challenges to economic, social, and political orthodoxies, and alternative visions of democratic fulfillment and equal rights, Populism has always drawn the attention of historians. This book is not a narrative history of Populism but a collection of essays that I have written over a quarter century that examine a variety of the political aspects of the movement, ranging from electoral and legislative behavior to organizational issues of party management and the structural factors of election laws. These pieces vary in their focus, sources, methodologies, origins, and objectives, but they all explore in some fashion the ways in which western Populism interacted with and was limited by the features of the American political system. In stressing the interactive nature of political constraints and political decisions, these selections frequently draw from the "new institutionalism" of political scientists, the mobilization theories of sociologists, and the fertile insights of more empirical historians in attempting to explain the contours of Populism and the course of the People's party in the context of American politics.

The first chapter, written expressly for this book, develops the organizing construct and provides the framework for the following, more specialized, studies. The latter do not always explicitly engage the interpretive motif, but they do demonstrate that it is a central theme that explains much about the twists and turns in the Populist experience. Several of the chapters examine the Populists' involvement in popular electoral politics, from creating a party, mobilizing support, and running a campaign in a hostile external environment to their internal dilemmas in balancing the aspirations of a popular movement with the requirements of a party organization. One chapter examines the additional pressures and obstacles Populists encountered in the process of electing a U.S. senator, then accomplished through legislative rather than popular elections. Two of the chapters analyze the ways in which particular election laws and procedures restricted the Populists' ability to participate fully in politics. Two more explore their behavior in western state legislatures, especially in attempting to enact laws to implement their reform principles despite external opposition and internal factionalism. The last chapter reveals how the procedural and institutional features of Congress frustrated Populists in that important political arena.

All of the chapters stress the limits of Populist political success, but I have tried to suggest as well how the Populists were themselves political agents. They evaluated their environments and made decisions about mobilizing support, developing party structures and procedures, organizing campaigns, and promoting policy innovations. They recognized, for example, that legislatures were not mere fixed institutions but political bodies with changing rules and opportunities, and the Populists' typical partisan voting on roll calls constituted an attempt to impose their own goals. Even the infrequent voting cleavages among Populist legislators reflected party decisions adopted in the electoral realm, a clear demonstration of the dialectical interplay of constraints, decisions, and consequences. Similarly, rather than regarding the electoral structure established by election laws as given and impartial, as exogenous to political activity, Populists realized both that it influenced election results and stemmed itself from previous political decisions. Accordingly, they attempted to change the rules of the electoral game, suggesting again the importance of the interaction between the institutional structure and political agents. This dynamic relationship was highlighted by the political volatility of western states in the 1890s, for as parties alternated in power they also alternated in revising election laws and procedures. In short, Populists saw all of politics as contested terrain, and they actively struggled not merely within and against their political environment, but also to transform it.

Another consistent theme in these chapters is the issue of fusion, which itself is perhaps the classic example of interaction between structural constraints and political decisions in American politics. Nevertheless, fusion appears in this book in a variety of ways, reflecting my own changing understanding of its role, function, and effects. At first I held the simple view corresponding to what I have termed the political arithmetic of fusionists: the assumption that the combined votes of minority parties would defeat a party that won by a plurality and the conclusion that fusion was therefore a sound policy. In subsequent work on internal party management I saw a much more complicated picture in which fusion arithmetic involved division as well as addition, in which the whole could frequently be less than the sum of its parts if the act of fusion itself alienated some of the participants. Then in studying election laws and their political origins I came to realize that fusion, though perhaps disruptive for some minority parties, played a larger structural role in preserving a third-party tradition and permitting minorities some access to political influence and public policy. Finally, as I studied legislative behavior, I recognized again how limited was that influence and how little interest many fusionists had in substantive policy innovations. The result of these shifting perspectives is perhaps to leave me somewhat more sympathetic to the concept of incremental change, but that goal does not motivate men and women to form third parties.

Publishing these various essays together should permit the reader to see such substantive relationships in the history of Populism and also to understand some of the currents of Populist historiography. The chapters are reprinted in the order in which they were written, reflecting not only my own evolving interests but often the shifting focus of historical scholarship generally, from a traditional study of a single political campaign to more varied and complex analyses of political organizations, legislative behavior, and government institutions. Because these pieces have appeared over the years in many different publications, their varying focus and format also reveal their often distinctive origins. One, for example, was written for a conference on the significance of quantitative research in history, one in response to an invitation to join a collaborative project analyzing the institutional history of Congress; another began simply as a book review and gradually took on a life of its own. In preparing this collection I have made no substantive revisions in the original articles, but I have made a few minor editorial changes to correct typographical errors and to standardize citations.

Essays written over such a lengthy period invariably benefit from the assistance of many people. My greatest debt, both personal and professional, is to Jo Ann E. Argersinger, who has always and generously given me needed encouragement, valuable criticism, profound insights, and welcome inspiration. She has also tried valiantly to make me see the opportunities in what I have persistently regarded as limits.

My single oldest debt is to the late George L. Anderson. By showing me a complete run of an 1890 small town newspaper he introduced me to the joys and limits of studying Populism, though I fear he was always amazed at what I found when I looked for myself.

My most enduring debt is to Allan G. Bogue. As a scholar, mentor, and friend he has consistently provided useful suggestions, kind advice, and welcome opportunities. His own work has often generated models and insights that I have appropriated to my advantage. My obligation to him is inadequately suggested in the dedication.

I am also obliged for the repeated and generous support of James E. Wright, who has over the years shared research with me, critiqued my work, and provided encouragement and assistance. Many other scholars gave me the benefit of their suggestions, comments, and even reassurance on one or more of the articles collected here. Among those who have tried to refine my thinking and sharpen my arguments are Michael J. Brodhead, Ballard Campbell, Gene Clanton, David Danbom, J. Morgan Kousser, Robert C. McMath, Jr., James D. Norris, Martin Ridge, James Shideler, David P. Thelen, and Philip R. VanderMeer.

For their professional typing and their remarkable patience I am indebted to Linda M. Hatmaker and Nafi Shahegh. I have also benefited from the interest and encouragement shown for this project by Cynthia Miller of the University Press of Kansas. Like an old Populist, I appreciate the good work of a committed editor.

1

THE POLITICAL LIMITS
OF WESTERN POPULISM

For a century Populism has been an absorbing subject of study. From widely different perspectives, and often with conflicting assumptions, analysts have attempted to explain its origins, development, decline, failures, implications, and tragedies. Different features of the movement, real or imagined, have received particular emphasis, depending upon the geographic locale, time frame, or social group examined or the focus, method, or objective of the observer. It seems increasingly clear, in fact, that the traditionally discrete ways in which Populism has been studied have tended to obscure a central theme that provides coherence to many of its seemingly disparate tendencies and clarifies much of its tortured course.[1]

Populism developed in a dynamic relationship with its political context, interacting both with an existing political culture defined by partisanship, sectionalism, moral rhetoric, and distinct ideas of political economy and with a political structure shaped by election laws, federalism, and party and government institutions. The People's party evolved within the opportunities and obstructions of particular political situations that varied by state, and its course represented efforts to negotiate the shifting possibilities of independent political action, complicated as well by the dilemmas of balancing the aspirations of a popular movement with the requirements of a party organization. As Populists mobilized their resources and adopted strategies and revised them in response to their conse-

1

quences they engaged in what Robert McMath has so aptly described as "wars of maneuver," in which they confronted not only
cultural and structural constraints but also existing—and en-
trenched—major parties determined to use their own power to exploit and if necessary to destroy the People's party for their own advantage. Within such a situation, Populist decisions and actions, if
not completely determined, were definitely limited.[2]

That political context consisted of cultural and structural compo-
nents, although the two themselves often interacted in their own dynamic. The prevailing political culture had several features immediately relevant to Populism. Its ideology emphasized limited
government, which inhibited the appeal and prospects of a movement seeking an activist state to correct economic injustices. In challenging such political orthodoxy Populism drew from different cultural traditions, those of rural protest and religion, to mobilize
support for its program. Framing their appeals in evangelical language, Populists invoked moral imperatives to attack industrial capitalism and an unresponsive polity for producing and permitting injustice and to justify their own program as a means of establishing
an equitable society. Indeed, for many Populists their party displaced the church as an institution of moral vision and expression.
One fervently announced, "The *only* pulpit where Christ is truly and
wholly preached today is THE PEOPLE'S PARTY PLATFORM. The *only*
movement pervaded by His spirit is the movement represented by
that party. . . . The poor, the naked, the hungry, the oppressed, the
wandering have *only one champion*—the People's Party." Conversely, of course, as another Populist noted, the opposition party
was the "headquarters for Satan."[3]

The tactic of mobilizing support—and justifying their cause—in
moral and religious terms, however effective at first, carried its own
political risks for Populist leaders, for such a strategy often made
practical political compromises unacceptable to segments of the
rank and file thus engaged and left them susceptible to disillusionment and withdrawal. The moral imperatives of Populism required
faithful and selfless leaders pursuing policies of integrity and independence; the politics of Populism would often include calculating
or self-seeking politicians making deals and compromising principles.

There were other important characteristics of the late nineteenth-century political culture that shaped the course of Populism as it emerged. The era's intense partisan loyalties, forged in bitter cultural and sectional conflict, had several different consequences. First, these allegiances often impeded or delayed the very formation of a third party since many farmers were loath to leave their traditional parties. Most leaders of the Iowa Farmers' Alliance, for example, were closely linked to the Republican party, objected to Alliance indictments of the GOP, and opposed plans to launch a third party. Even Alliance members not so compromised hesitated at the prospect of political action, fearing that their organizations could be destroyed by the conflicting pulls of partisanship. In both Nebraska and South Dakota, Alliance leaders who would eventually become prominent Populists initially hoped the Farmers' Alliance would restrict its political involvement to pressure-group activity, concerned that partisan action would divide the Alliance membership. In Kansas, too, a group of Alliance officials in 1889 urged members "to avoid all political action or discussion of partisan politics within the Alliance, as we regard such action as valueless to us politically, a certain element of discord in our order, which would prove ruinous to the most promising organization of farmers the world has ever known."[4]

Second, the strong party ties of the past affected the course of the third party, once organized, by hampering the creation of an effective coalition of former enemies. Many Republicans who joined the new party carried with them their traditional hostility to Democrats—what one called their "hereditary foe." Estrangement from Republican politicians did not itself diminish their antagonism to Democrats and their programs. Mary E. Lease, for example, always harbored what she called "an intense hatred" of Democrats and was never comfortable cooperating with them within the People's party even as she begged her listeners to "forget party affiliations of the past . . . in this great struggle for our homes." Similarly, Democrats who left their party to help form the People's party often felt a lingering antipathy toward the former Republicans with whom they now worked. Moreover, with their more traditional ideas and local perspective, they sometimes rejected as "paternalism" the interventionist government favored by their new colleagues.[5]

Tensions also accompanied the Populist affiliations of former Greenbackers, Union Laborites, Prohibitionists, Socialists, and other members of previous third-party efforts. Some Populists from the major parties regarded these veteran reformers as eccentric malcontents whose radical ideas would subject the party to ridicule or rejection. Populists of third-party antecedents naturally had their own reservations about their new associates arriving belatedly from the major parties. One reporter, for instance, described "the suspicion" held by former Union Laborites that some of their new allies in the People's party had "too much Republican blood in their veins to be up to the wild-and-wooly standard of reform." Indeed, press reports of party conventions commonly depicted factional struggles in terms of the former party affiliations of the Populists involved: "After the meeting adjourned the Greenbackers and Union Laborites were very jubilant, the Republicans looked careworn, and the Democrats were not as jubilant as they have been in times past." Mutual distrust also encouraged vote trading and scratched tickets.[6] Thus the People's party was more an uneasy coalition of former opponents temporarily united through dissatisfaction, distress, hope, and hard politics than a unified and cohesive political party. Its hopes of substantial success depended in part upon suppressing divisive issues and partisan traditions and muffling the attempts of old-party leaders to activate the jealousy, suspicion, and distrust that they had carefully encouraged for decades and that now lurked within the People's party.

Leaders of the major parties indeed tried to exploit these emotions of the political culture to limit or constrain agrarian radicalism. With their constituencies aligned along sectional and ethnocultural divisions, the major parties were unable to deal effectively with crosscutting economic issues. Their leaders accordingly invoked partisan sentiments to block Alliance movements toward political analysis and action. One Kansas newspaper, for instance, announced that it would support farmers as long as they debated "the best methods of raising cabbage . . . [or] how many rows of corn should be on a cob" but that if they raised economic or political issues it would "denounce the farmers' organization as breeding discontent and treason to the republican party."[7]

Major parties also appealed to existing strong sectional prejudices in efforts first to divert the Alliance from independent political

action and then to disrupt the People's party. The political sectionalism of the party system complicated particularly the Populists' task
of building a national party. That effort required bringing together
contrasting regional political minorities, which in turn enabled both
major parties to incite sectional and partisan prejudices to prevent
defections to the new party. As one Populist complained, "In the
south, people are told that this movement is of northern origin, a
Republican device to disrupt the Democratic party, strike down
white rule, and establish black supremacy instead, while in the
north, politicians tell us the movement is a southern institution, devised by southern Democrats . . . and designed to destroy the Republican party of the north . . . and thereby abrogate all the results
of the war."[8] Western agrarians who had abandoned the Republican
party were particularly vulnerable to such pressures. If southern
farmers refused to leave their traditional party the consequence of
Populism in the West was to benefit the Democratic party nation-
ally. Confronted with that reality in 1892, one Populist editor
showed the tenuous effects of third-party conversion efforts among
old Republicans steeped in years of partisan and sectional prejudice:
"Right here we foreswear all allegiance to the People's Party. We
must be honest with ourselves. Hereafter we shall be found battling
for square-toed, stalwart Republicanism. We would rather belong to
the Republican plutocrats than the Southern brigadiers."[9]

The residual effects of previous party allegiances not only impeded building a new coalition but also then established within the
People's party what Walter Nugent has called "a permanent threat
of instability." The possibility that Populists might be persuaded to
return to their former parties complicated campaign and policy tactics for the People's party and drove the strategy of the major parties
as well. Republicans in particular tried to lure their former members back to the fold by appealing to partisan traditions, blatantly
waving the bloody shirt, and warning that radicals were turning the
People's party toward unacceptable socialism. They also adopted the
reliable tactic of selectively endorsing Populist issues and then suggesting it was time to return to the obviously regenerated old party.
In 1892, for example, Kansas Republicans adopted a reform platform "as wild and visionary as that of the People's party" and nominated a state ticket of agrarian reformers.[10] To the degree that such

tactics were successful in reclaiming former Republicans for the GOP, the People's party of the West became increasingly composed of former Democrats. This changing composition had its own reinforcing effects on the party, for it caused party leaders to dodge cultural issues that offended Democrats, such as prohibition, but that strategy alienated Republican-Populists even more and threatened the party with further losses in membership.

Indeed, the ethnocultural divisions that underlay the party system in the nineteenth century also complicated the task of creating and maintaining a new political coalition. In Kansas, Populist officials deployed Swedish and German speakers, distributed appeals to Russians and Norwegians, and subsidized foreign-language newspapers in efforts to draw ethnic voters from their traditional major-party allegiances. F. W. Frasius urged the Populist state committee to "strengthen the people's party numerically by getting after the GERMAN VOTE" and launched the *Topeka Volksblatt* to champion the party among Germans. The state committee urged party candidates to underwrite ethnic appeals and asked county committees to compile lists of ethnic voters to receive campaign literature in their own language. Such efforts were not especially successful — Frasius himself was defeated in a campaign for the legislature — but when the party suppressed prohibition as a campaign issue it often did attract important ethnic support.[11]

Retaining that support, however, was often difficult. South Dakota Populist governor Andrew E. Lee found the competing claims of ethnic groups for political recognition and patronage one of his greatest problems in holding together the Populist coalition in his state. Norwegian immigrants, a large segment of the state's voters, particularly demanded attention and complained when they felt neglected. Germans, Irish, and Czechs also insisted upon recognition through nominations and appointments. Lee realized the political need to accommodate each group in order to maintain the party coalition and often lamented the insufficient patronage he had at his disposal. Moreover, the major parties moved firmly to blunt the Populist efforts and to retain the allegiance of the various ethnic groups. South Dakota Republicans, for example, appealed to their party's national committee for funds to subsidize foreign-language newspapers and to employ political agents in ethnic communities.

Democrats in the region, heavily dependent upon ethnic voters, also made strenuous and usually successful efforts to retain their loyalty.[12]

Given these constraints within the political culture, then, third parties were not inevitable, regardless of economic grievances. Independent political action required the discrediting or failure of alternative strategies, political as well as economic, and the clear recognition that the existing party system would not, or could not, function to satisfy popular demands for remedial action. Had voters been able to control their parties effectively or had existing political leadership developed responsive policies there would have been no need for the People's party.[13] But in a dialectical process, the political decisions and failures of the major parties caused the creation and development of third parties.

In Kansas, the defiant refusal of Republican legislators in 1889 to enact reform measures to which they had pledged themselves in the preceding campaign was the crucial factor in the launching of the People's party in 1890. An important contributing determinant, which provoked the righteous character of the Alliance cause, was a notorious speech by Republican senator John J. Ingalls ridiculing those who favored reform, which he sneeringly referred to as an "iridescent dream."[14] Similarly in South Dakota, a Republican legislature elected upon a pledge to enact Alliance reforms ignored the farmers' demands, prompting the Alliance first to condemn this betrayal and then to establish a third party. Contributing to the Alliance's decision were efforts by Republican regulars to exclude Alliance members from party conventions and even to hold party meetings without public notice.[15] Clearly the concept of working within the party in such circumstances was meaningless or, worse, self-defeating. Agrarian reformers thus broke from the two-party system only when convinced that politicians were promoting their own rather than the public interest. This conviction would shape the course of the new party because it left the Populist rank and file disposed to be suspicious of even their own politicians and their motives.

Once farmers broke from their cultural constraints to form third parties, they immediately encountered a new and daunting set of limits in the structural features of American politics: modes of representation, ballot and voting systems, election laws and procedures, party organizations, legislative and judicial institutions of government. Moreover, in manipulating these elements against the People's party—while continuing to exploit cultural issues to its disadvantage—the major parties were themselves a significant component of the political structure that the Populists confronted. In an additional complication, federalism meant that all such forces operated in different mixes in different states, which helps explain some of the diversity so characteristic of Populism. The relationship between the new party and its political context was a dynamic one, a war of maneuver in which Populists devised strategies to counter obstacles and then dealt with the effects of their decisions. These structural limits were more important and influential than the cultural barriers: By helping establish the two-party system they underlay (and could further exploit) the cultural limits and imposed serious constraints of their own.

Perhaps no structural feature of the political system was more basic, with more serious consequences for political parties, than the mode of representation, which affected party decisions from nominations to campaign tactics. Several different representation systems operated simultaneously in the nineteenth century, but virtually all shared two significant characteristics. First, they were spatially defined; that is, the unit of representation was a geographic district rather than a political party or interest. Second, they employed the plurality method of voting, under which a candidate wins an election by gaining a plurality of the district's votes, effectively disfranchising the minority in the district by leaving them without any representation. Basing elections on this winner-take-all principle rather than on a proportionate-representation rule favors the dominant party because it exaggerates that party's representation relative to its popular vote. The single-member district/plurality-vote system also has a bipolarizing effect on political parties. Since only one candidate can win in each district, this electoral form encourages coalitions and discourages multiple parties. It discriminates against smaller parties (unless their voting strength is geographically concentrated, as was that of some agrarian protest parties of the 1870s) to the point of virtually eliminating them. And by encouraging the tendency for the defeated major party to gain a monopoly of the opposition, such an electoral mode guarantees that party's perpetuation even in defeat and thus establishes the two-party system, one of the most prominent and enduring features of American politics.[16]

One practical response to the disfranchising and bipolarizing effects of the representation system was the practice of fusion, the nomination of a single set of candidates by two or more parties. Fusion constituted a significant feature of late nineteenth-century politics and customarily involved a temporary alliance between a third party and the weaker of the two major parties in the hope of sharing political influence that would otherwise be denied to both parties acting separately in an electoral system based on single-member districts and plurality victories. The strong partisan identifications of the time, however, made the tactic a tenuous one; voters insisted on their own party's ticket, candidates, and principles and did not want to vote directly with another party, which often represented antagonistic groups and values. Fusion was thus an imperfect and often divisive tactic for minority parties, but it was often their only realistic method of achieving fair representation, and it became a continuing objective of third-party leaders seeking personal advancement or limited, tangible goals.[17]

Fusion plans were generally undertaken, nevertheless, to promote the needs of the major party and initiated or avoided according to the calculations of its politicians rather than to those of the leaders of the evanescent third parties. In the West, Democrats at times even pursued fusion to thwart the dominant Republicans despite the opposition of third-party members.

The Populists encountered this situation in the presidential election of 1892. By producing a winner-take-all result, the general ticket for electors transformed each state into the equivalent of a single-member district, maximizing the influence of its leading party and effectively disfranchising voters in the minority. Unable to carry any state in the region for their candidate, Grover Cleveland, the Democrats faced the prospect of wasting their ballots and seeing western electoral votes provide the margin to elect a Republican president. The Democratic National Committee thus urged party officials in western states to withdraw their nominees for the electoral college and to fuse on the Populist nominees pledged to James

B. Weaver, thereby denying Republicans the electoral votes that
Cleveland would be unable to capture for himself.

Democrats in Idaho, Minnesota, Oregon, and other states responded, replacing some or all of their nominees with candidates
nominated by the Populists. Many Populists denounced the Democratic maneuver, worrying that, as one Minnesota Populist elector
said, the tactic "will hurt the People's Party rather than help it, as a
great many in that party were formerly Republicans, and . . . will
have a tendency to drive them back to the old party." Indeed, the
Democrats' scheme, while promoting their party's interests, injured
the Populists by giving currency to the Republican attempt to woo
Republican-Populists back to the GOP by arguing that "a vote for
Weaver is a vote for Cleveland." Populists desperately countered that
they had not fused with the Democrats: "The populists neither
asked, nor could they if they wished, prevent the democratic
action." This tactic demonstrated the ability of other parties to set
the political context for the Populists regardless of their own wishes,
and it left many Populist voters distraught over having their votes
contribute to the election of Cleveland, who opposed everything
their own party stood for.[18]

The larger question of fusion became the great political issue that
determined the direction and success of Populism. It activated several overlapping fault lines, one dividing Populists according to
their previous party identifications, one separating Populists determined to preserve the moral integrity of their movement from Populists entrusted with the institutional responsibilities of directing a
party, and another splitting Populists who disagreed over the simple
efficacy of fusion. Some Populists of third-party antecedents, for example, believed that fusion with a major party had brought their
earlier third party to ruin; others such as Iowa's James B. Weaver,
thrice elected to Congress as a Greenbacker with Democratic fusion,
saw in fusion their only hope for success. More important, fusion
plans aroused the partisan hostilities embedded in the Populists' political culture. As one South Dakota Populist maintained, "We did
not leave the corrupt Republican party to hobnob with the rotten
Democratic party." One Montana Populist conceded that such
strong partisan prejudices were politically irrational, but "we must
take people as they are, not as we would have them. . . . Most men

vote on prejudice instead of principle." Therefore, fusion had to be avoided, lest "our weak friends who have formerly been members of the Republican party . . . , owing to the blind prejudice which they hold against the Democrats, reobligate themselves to their [old] party and blindly shut their ears and eyes to the appeals of reason."[19]

Complicating the prospect for such Populists, fusion arrangements often required them to narrow their reform agenda in order to make cooperation acceptable to more conservative Democrats. Many Populists, of course, would have stayed with their old parties had such a plan been acceptable; instead they had justified joining a third party precisely on the moral basis that certain reforms were absolutely necessary and major parties could not be trusted to support them. Populist John Willits articulated the moral position on the issue: Fusion "is simply a compromise with wrong. It is an agreement with death and a covenant with hell. If our immortal declaration of principles is just and right, in the name of God let us stand by them and go down if need be, fighting for God, home, and humanity instead of disgracefully surrendering to the common enemy."[20]

But many Populist leaders championed fusion as an immediate campaign tactic for limited but tangible ends. Party officials, of course, focused on the short-term goal of nominating candidates and winning elections and were well aware of the bipolarizing and disfranchising effects of the representation system. Using a political arithmetic, they calculated that the combined votes for separate Populist and Democratic candidates surpassed that of the Republican candidate who won with a plurality and concluded that fusion was a logical policy. As one Oklahoma Populist insisted, "In unification there is strength, the result, power." These party officials defended fusion arrangements as simply practical politics, "the only road to success," and dismissed their opponents within the party as "cranks" who had not "the least particle of political sense."[21]

To overcome rank-and-file opposition to fusion, party officials often adopted devious practices and manipulated the party's committee and nominating machinery. In Kansas, for example, the fusionist majority of the state central committee refused to notify antifusion members of committee meetings. In Nebraska, the party chairman dismissed antifusionists as "kickers" and promised to exclude them from party meetings. And although popularly elected delegates to the 1894 Idaho state convention resolved as "our final determination that we will not, now or at any future time, form any fusion or coalition with any party whatever, in any state, county, or municipality," party officials promptly arranged fusion campaigns, sometimes by replacing duly nominated Populist candidates with Democrats on the Populist ticket. One such betrayed Populist nominee refused to cooperate and, declaring his opposition to any dealings with "the old harlot" Democratic party, continued to campaign in his own behalf. Party managers had more success with such tactics in Kansas in 1892 when they rigged conventions, lied to their rank-and-file members, and overturned duly nominated candidates in their pursuit of fusion.[22]

Naturally, the methods party managers adopted as they pursued fusion activated the persistent Populist distrust of politicians and party organization, a force that continually constrained Populist political development. Many people had joined the People's party because they had been repulsed by the manipulations, expediencies, and indifference of the major parties. The new party, wrote one, "started out as a great uprising of the people for reform, a crusade against the evils of which both old parties were alike guilty." And Annie Diggs described the origins of Populism as "a protest against the dangers and tyranny of permanent party organization." Such Populists had justified their break from the two-party system — an act of cultural apostasy — by referring to the necessity of justice, morality, and honesty in politics. For them Populism was a democratic movement based on popular participation and autonomy, and they were determined that it not degenerate into hierarchical politics as usual. They vehemently objected to the party officials' cynical disregard of the concept of popular control and their defiance of the limits of their proper authority. In a refrain that echoed across the West, one original Populist lamented that his party's state chairman had become "a dictator, whose power is absolute; who in practice of corrupt and disreputable political methods has out done all other political managers that have ever risen."[23]

This hostility to politicians emerged in an early Alliance doctrine: "The office must seek the man, not the man the office." It reached its apogee in the adoption by the 1892 Populist National Convention of a unique resolution repudiating politics in favor of Populism. The Omaha Ordinance for the Purification of Politics established as "fundamental party law" the principle that "no person holding office . . . federal, state, or municipal . . . including senators, congressmen, and members of legislatures . . . shall be eligible to sit or vote in any convention of this party." Populists were determined that the people and not the politicians should control their movement.[24]

In the West, Populists in their local meetings assumed they had the right to instruct their legislative representatives on how to vote on pending measures and senatorial candidates, and they did so frequently. After several Populists in the 1897 Kansas legislature failed to support bills to implement important party principles, local Populists summoned the legislators to appear before their respective county committees to explain their votes and demanded that at least one resign. Idaho Populists adopted a state platform calling for the removal from public office of politicians who violated their campaign pledges. In another state, Populists in one county convention threatened to enforce that principle themselves, warning their legislator that "if he betrays his pledge . . . he had better abandon all idea of returning home." The National Reform Press Association, the organization of Populist editors, so consistently acted to oversee the party hierarchy that a minority complained, "It is not the function of a press association as a body to go into the business of . . . deposing the regularly constituted political authorities or organizations of the party."[25]

Dissident Populists also commonly held rump conventions in opposition to party meetings they regarded as machine-controlled. In 1897, for example, some Iowa Populists, convinced that their state committee had adopted new rules to pack the state convention in favor of fusion, called their own convention to nominate a separate ticket.[26] Similarly, in Colorado in 1896 radical Populists reassembled in convention to nominate their own ticket after the majority of the regular convention approved fusion nominees. Davis Waite maintained that bolting the regular ticket was necessary in order *not* to "abandon the Populist party and its principles." An especially dramatic schism occurred in Idaho. In an irregular meeting, a few members of the state committee, claiming to hold proxies for most of the state's counties, decided to force a fusionist campaign upon the party. They rescheduled the time and place of the state convention to coincide with those of the Democrats and Silver Republicans, reapportioned delegates to reduce the strength of the mid-road areas and inflate that of the fusionist counties, and ousted party officials who opposed fusion. These arbitrary and unauthorized actions plunged the party into chaos and recriminations and ultimately into two competing state nominating conventions, one for the fusionist Populists and the other for "the middle-of-the-trail Pops—the genuine longhaired, dyed-in-the-wool, fire-eating, greenback inflation element."[27]

The disruptive effects of fusion politics often extended into the voting booth. Some Populists refused to vote for fusion candidates, and conservative Democrats also knifed Populist fusion nominees, so rarely did a fusion candidate get the full vote of the two fusing parties, undercutting the calculus of party managers pursuing what they saw as practical politics. Yet fusion with Democrats also undermined Populist politics in the long run, for in Kansas, Minnesota, and other western states it drove some Republican Populists back to the GOP. As one reporter paraphrased their explanation: "They did not leave the Republican party to go body and soul over to the Democracy; that if it has to be one of the old parties they will return to the one they naturally belong to." Over time, fusion thus made the People's party in the West less Republican and more Democratic in composition. This was a self-reinforcing tendency, for the more dependent the party became upon Democratic sources, the more congenial fusion appeared. And unfortunately for Populist arithmetic, a Republican-Populist returning to the GOP carried two votes with him, one from the Populists and one for the Republicans; a Democratic convert brought but one. Any policy that threatened to drive former Republicans from the Populist ranks, even if directly replaced by Democrats thereby attracted, was suicidal, not practical.[28]

These tensions and conflicts over party tactics and policy not only played themselves out in every western state, but they also characterized the party's course in national politics. Herman Taubeneck and J. H. Turner, the party's national chairman and secretary, together with important members of the Populist National Committee, such as Marion Butler, John Breidenthal, and James B. Weaver, were convinced that practical politics required fusion on the basis of a plat-

form trimmed to silver to attract the largest possible number of allies. Accordingly, party leaders moved to eliminate the radical
objectives of the 1892 Omaha Platform and to undercut those impractical Populists committed to the party's creed. With Taubeneck
defending this approach as "cold-blooded, practical politics," they
repeatedly attempted to manipulate party committee meetings and
conventions to promote such a course, used their influence to undermine editorial opponents and to subsidize sympathetic newspapers,
established a news bureau to doctor information for the rank and
file, and conspired and cooperated with Silver Democrats in arranging fusion campaigns.[29]

Of course, antifusion or middle-of-the-road Populists opposed this
course of the party oligarchy. Montana Populists complained, "Our
self-constituted leaders, Weaver, Taubeneck & Co. have no right to ask
us to abandon or curtail our principles. They are traitors to the principles which have raised them from obscurity." Davis Waite of Colorado
similarly condemned "the desertion of principle by those who were put
in charge of party affairs on account of their presumed loyalty to the
Omaha platform" and attacked the party officials who had "assumed
supreme control of the party and exercised that control without consulting the popular will and without appeal."[30]

These critics understood the political context better than their
practical party managers. One dissident noted that in imposing the
silver/fusion policy the party leaders were ironically manipulating
"our party machinery . . . in the interests of the enemy." Indeed, the
bankruptcy of the party's fusion politics became evident in 1896
when its silver emphasis led to the party's absorption by the Democrats in a classic case of selective endorsement of reform issues by a
major party. Despite fusing on the Democratic presidential nominee, William Jennings Bryan, Populists attempted to preserve their
party's separate identity by nominating Tom Watson rather than the
Democrats' Arthur Sewall for vice-president. This futile tactic only
plunged Populists into more complicated and self-defeating fusion
arrangements, varying according to the specific political situation in
each state. In Iowa, Minnesota, Nebraska, and other states, Democrats and Populists divided the presidential electors, thereby potentially saddling Bryan, if elected, with a Republican vice-president.
In Colorado and Kansas, Populists repudiated their party's vice-

presidential nominee by fusing on Democratic electors in exchange for Democratic fusion on Populist state candidates. Such contradictory arrangements left party leaders quarreling and confused, prompted mid-roaders to put out their own separate tickets, and contributed to the rank and file's disillusionment and demoralization.[31]

The conflicts over fusion and party management continued after the 1896 campaign, formally splitting the party and assisting its demise. Mid-roaders demanded the reorganization of the national committee to ensure independent action in the future. "Abolish the bargain counter, repudiate the fusion leaders, reorganize the party, oust the office-holders from our National Committee," wrote one, "and Populism yet has a future." When party officials rejected the demand, mid-roaders called their own conferences in 1897 and 1898 "to save the party," as Sen. William A. Peffer approvingly put it, by capturing "the party machinery." Indeed, one such conference established the National Organization Committee as a counterweight to the regular national committee. In June 1898 the two bodies reached an agreement, the Omaha Contract, prohibiting the national chairman from trying to use his power to promote fusion. But disintegration was too far advanced; the factions held separate national conventions and nominated separate presidential candidates for 1900, and then both withered away.[32]

Fusion and an oligarchic party had been practical responses to the structural context of the representation system, however much they incited the party's cultural divisions. Yet other important aspects of the electoral structure also had developmental consequences for the People's party and help to explain the behavior of its officials and its rank-and-file voters. Moreover, these aspects demonstrate other means by which the major parties shaped the political context within which Populists maneuvered and an obvious way in which Populist prospects — and ultimately even their existence — were limited.

Of crucial significance in this regard was the question of ballots and the method of voting. At the time the People's party was organized few states had a secret ballot.[33] State ballot laws generally specified only that ballots be paper ones and otherwise made few provisions for their shape, size, or color or for their distribution at the polls. Nor were there effective legal provisions to ensure secrecy in voting. In the absence of official machinery and legal regulations, political parties assumed the task of preparing and distributing ballots. The consequence was the party ticket, a strip of paper on which were printed the names of the candidates of only the party that issued it. Eager to identify their followers and maintain their loyalty, party managers differentiated their tickets from those of other parties by size, color, or other characteristics, and the voter's use of a ballot clearly revealed his choice of party. The tickets were distributed to the party's supporters by party workers who crowded the polls and pressed their tickets on prospective voters. Receiving the party tickets under such circumstances, the voter had little chance to examine his ballot before being hustled to the ballot box, where he deposited it in view of all interested observers.

On the one hand, by imposing no procedural obstacles, this system made it fairly easy to launch a new, third party. It also facilitated fusion, for the individual voter could remain ignorant of the nominees of other parties; he merely had to deposit his party ticket in the ballot box, without studying or, in some states, even marking it. Thus partisans of fusing parties could cast their votes without explicitly acknowledging their shared behavior or its significance, and a party could pursue fusion with an unwilling partner. On the other hand, this ballot system imposed financial and other burdens on small parties, restricting their possible success. The printing and distributing of ballots were expensive, eliminating many poor farmers from seeking nomination and political influence; the system also required an organization in all election districts — something that few third parties had — if every voter were to have an opportunity to vote his principles. In Nebraska, for example, the People's party at times had no party workers at some polling places to distribute their tickets, limiting the party's possibility of attracting votes. Too, the party-ticket system facilitated voting intimidation and fraud, important issues to Populists who already believed the political system corrupt. Like their third-party predecessors, the Greenbackers and Union Laborites, then, Populists pushed for ballot reform as a way to secure legitimate and responsive government.

This effort was but part of a consistent Populist search to democratize and make more open the political system. Throughout the western states they also sought such electoral reforms as the popular election of senators, woman suffrage, proportional representation, and direct legislation. In Idaho, for instance, the 1894 Populist state platform endorsed woman suffrage, demanded a corrupt-practices act to limit and regulate campaign expenditures, and called for the removal from public office of politicians who violated campaign promises.[34] Populists had some success in several of these areas, but electoral reform seemed most completely achieved in the Australian ballot. Populists were not alone in pushing for this reform, but they often were instrumental in its enactment, as in Minnesota, Nebraska, Kansas, and other states.

Three features of this new voting system attracted reformers. First, it provided an official ballot, prepared and distributed by public authorities, theoretically benefiting independent organizations and candidates by minimizing their election costs. Second, it mandated secret voting and therefore presumably discouraged vote buying and intimidation. Finally, it provided a consolidated or blanket ballot, listing all candidates instead of merely those of one party. This provision permitted more independent and split-ticket voting than was possible under the party-ticket system.

But in enacting the Australian system to ensure secrecy and an official ballot, legislators also had to consider other subjects, such as the format of the ballot, the question of who could be listed, the rules for registering nominees, and other questions that previously had been left up to the parties. In establishing these procedures, politicians often responded to their political context and contrived rules to achieve partisan ends. Many of the new procedural rules were designed to promote the interests of the two major parties, particularly the dominant GOP, and thus ballot reform had the ironic effect of restricting or injuring the Populists. In short, election legislation was contested terrain in the political war of maneuver: While Populists fought to remove structural limits, major parties counterattacked to restrict and disrupt third parties, the Populists in particular.

Major-party politicians sought to prevent equal access to the electorate by giving their own parties preferential treatment on the ballot, making it difficult or impossible for third parties to appear before the electorate, or by placing them under discriminatory conditions. In detailing the procedures by which candidates could gain a place on the ballot, for example, the laws generally provided that a party securing a certain percentage of the popular vote in the preceding election could have its nominees listed on the official ballot by the relatively easy method of filing certificates of nomination. Populists responsible for passing Nebraska's 1891 Australian ballot placed that figure at a low 1 percent; but in its 1891 ballot law Colorado's Republican legislature demanded 10 percent — high enough to exclude the Alliance-backed Independent party, which had polled 7 percent in the 1890 election on a platform demanding ballot reform.[35]

A second method under the Australian system by which candidates could gain a place on the ballot was by petition of voters. Reformers had expected that this provision would enable their groups to overcome the crippling obstacles of preparing and distributing tickets and to appear before the electorate on equal terms with the major parties. But in many states major-party politicians framed the law to require large numbers of signatures for nomination by petition in order to protect the privileged ballot positions of the major parties, limit the voters' options, and promote partisan regularity. The 1891 California law required a prohibitive 5 percent of the total popular vote in the preceding election, and Nevada in 1893 required an astonishing 10 percent of the voters to sign nominating petitions.[36]

It was by the petition method that third parties had to make their nominations when their age, size, or previous strength excluded them from nominating by certificate, explaining their anxiety and determination to have an automatic ballot placement. The chairman of Minnesota's Alliance Labor Union Party complained of the great "expense of labor and money" required in meeting "the formalities imposed upon a new party by the law of the state relating to the Australian ballot system." In Illinois Populist state chairman A. L. Maxwell had to borrow money on his personal credit to cover the huge costs of circulating and filing nominating petitions. Indeed, petition costs constituted the major expense of the state party and left it with virtually no funds for printing campaign literature, paying speaker expenses, or other mobilizing efforts new parties particularly needed.[37]

The election laws of several states also strengthened the position of the major parties by denying new parties ballot headings for straight-ticket voting. This partisan restriction particularly handicapped the People's party in California, already struggling with the task of securing the petition signatures of 5 percent of the voters to be listed on the ballot. Finally, Populist Thomas V. Cator successfully argued before the state supreme court that the provision was unconstitutional because it denied parties equal treatment on the ballot and subjected some voters to "partial disfranchisement."[38]

A far more important legal restriction had the same discriminatory effects on parties and voters and devastating consequences for Gilded Age politics. Although the use of separate party tickets had facilitated fusion, the new ballot system provided the means to disrupt and destroy it. Beginning in South Dakota in 1893, Republican-dominated legislatures in the Midwest and West modified the Australian ballot to take advantage of voters' partisan attitudes by simply prohibiting a candidate's name from being listed more than once on the official blanket ballot. This stipulation resulted either in splitting the potential fusion vote, by causing each party to nominate separate candidates, or in undermining the efficacy of any fusion that did occur by requiring some partisans to vote under the heading of another party. In this time of intense partisanship many Populists refused to vote for a fusion candidate designated as a "Democrat," and many Democrats were equally reluctant to vote for a "Populist." Given the closely balanced elections of the period, the elimination of even a small faction of their opponents in this fashion helped guarantee Republican ascendancy. This simple prohibition against double-listing became the basic feature of the practice that the Nebraska Supreme Court described as a Republican effort to use the Australian ballot as a "scheme to put voters in a straight jacket." Other related and complex procedures increased the effectiveness of this prohibition and threatened the legal existence of fusing parties.[39]

Antifusion legislation also undermined the People's party by aggravating the existing fratricidal split between mid-roaders and fusionists. The usual arguments against fusion, based on the necessity of maintaining the party's identity and organization, acquired new and intense meaning in a legal situation that, as one judge phrased it, "says to the party, and through the party to the electors composing it: 'You shall not endorse candidates of any other party, except on condition that you surrender your existence as a party and lose your right of representation upon the official ballot in the future.'" Antifusion laws thus impelled those Populists intent on preserving their party's integrity to battle fusion ever more forcefully. But fusionist Populists countered that the mid-road position, in combination with the Republican "ballot law plot," would itself "disfranchise Populists and aid the monopoly and gold standard power." Believing that ballot laws blocked the traditional fusion coalitions that had given third parties their practical importance, the fusionists saw no choice but to merge the People's party into the Democratic ranks. Limited to a ballot choice between Democrats and Republicans, some Populists voted Republican and others dropped out. The mid-roaders, though legally a bolting minority, issued their own Populist ticket, which after lengthy court battles between the two Populist factions invariably failed to gain enough votes to ensure the party a position on the ballot in the future. In either case the People's party ceased to exist.[40]

By preventing effective fusion, the antifusion law not only secured Republican electoral success but also ended the importance and even the existence of significant third parties and discouraged voter turnout among their traditional constituencies. Unwilling either to vote as a member of the "corrupt" old parties or to cast a futile ballot for a symbolic third party, they were citizens legislated out of the effective electorate. Such use of the Australian ballot system convinced Populists that it had become, as one maintained, "a means for the repression instead of the expression of the will of the people." Feeling betrayed, some Populists campaigned to amend the ballot law; others argued for its repeal. "If 'amendment' is insisted upon," wrote one Iowa Populist, "let it be in the style of the farmer who amended his worthless dog's tail by letting the cleaver fall just behind the cur's ears." Ballot "reform" had limited the Populists' influence while providing the major parties with privileges and protection.[41]

Other factors also constrained Populism and contributed to its failures and demise. Some were imposed by its opponents in the war of maneuver, but others were of the Populists' own making. Too often when Populists gained office, they seemed to produce records marred by incompetence, conflict, and even corruption. Much of this image was inaccurate, distorted by a partisan Republican press seeking to discredit Populists in order to improve Republican prospects of returning to power. Some of the Populist failure was produced by political limits beyond their control. And, certainly, the Populists' performance generally surpassed that of their Republican predecessors. Yet just as surely, Populist governors and legislators did not establish the millennial polity their followers had expected.[42]

South Dakota Populist governor Andrew Lee suffered numerous troubles and embarrassments, attributable in part to his political inexperience and to the absence of reliable advisers and sources of information that established major-party politicians could draw upon. Assessing his administration, he concluded, "I have had many things to contend with and one of the greatest troubles of all was we were almost all strangers to on[e] another and worked to great disadvantage." Such limitations produced some woeful patronage decisions, including several in which Lee's appointments were charged with the same corrupt practices for which Populists had condemned their Republican predecessors.[43]

Even worse for the Populist image and appeal were patronage and policy decisions of the administration of Kansas governor L. D. Lewelling. The governor's appointment as adjutant general, for instance, had been disbarred by the Colorado Supreme Court after he was accused of perjury and bribery. Lewelling finally removed him after an investigation revealed irregularities in his accounts. The selection of municipal police commissioners proved still more damaging as some evidence indicated that the administration took money from Kansas City gambling interests in return for naming acceptable officials. Other scandals or charges of corruption tainted Lewelling's appointments to the State Board of Charities, the School for the Deaf, and other agencies, and members of the governor's personal staff were implicated in questionable financial schemes.[44]

Such improprieties dismayed Populists mobilized by the righteous crusade and convinced at least some party members that their own politicians were as corrupt as those of the major parties they had denounced. Mary Lease arraigned the "corrupt men" of the Lewelling administration and charged them with accepting bribes from railroad companies. Many other prominent Populists joined Lease to form a virtual party in exile, devoted to attacking the administration for sins of both commission and omission. Such disaffection contributed to a Populist defeat in 1894 — a defeat that Populist pamphleteer Percy Daniels at least described as a repudiation of party leaders, not a rejection of Populist principles. The party had been organized to purify political life, he wrote, and Populists would "not deserve success until their leaders show they have resumed their allegiance to this purpose, and are governed by the same spirit of uprightness and candor as inspires the men in the ranks."[45]

Political aspects of Populist governors' patronage policies also disrupted the party. Some Populists complained that in awarding offices these governors slighted agrarian radicals in favor of party newcomers from the very ranks of town and village political leaders against whom the early movement had often been directed. When Nebraska Populist governor Silas Holcomb, himself a Democrat until 1891, denied an appointment to veteran Alliance activist Walter Wright, one of the latter's supporters complained to an Alliance leader: "Old men like him who have done the work & elected a young man to office have got to stand back and see men young in years & young in the party get all the places. . . . I never heard one of them say he [Wright] wasn't honest or truthful, they only say he is an old crank." Wright himself believed that "the Alliance of Nebr is sold out to Lawyers & dudes so far as the Party is concerned." Such appointment policies fed into an increasingly important split within the party. As the movement became more institutionalized and as townspeople — especially former Democrats — moved into the party, farmers felt unfairly displaced and even betrayed. One Nebraska Populist leader, for example, disavowed the party because "the middleman, the jackleg lawyers, and the town loafers are more influential in controlling the People's Party than the farmer." These often overlapping concerns about the increasing influence of village politicians and former Democrats created bitter dissension and weakened rural support for the party. This, too, was a self-reinforcing tendency, for the newcomers often opposed many of the original Alliance reform goals, especially those dealing with mortgage and railroad issues, and thereby further alienated farmers.[46]

Still another feature of Populist patronage policies proved divisive. Governors Lewelling and John Leedy in Kansas, Holcomb of Nebraska, Lee of South Dakota, and John Rogers of Washington, elected through fusion, angered Populists when they naturally distributed patronage to Democrats and Silver Republicans. Because fusion was an instance of "practical politics," it required tangible rewards for its participants, who agreed to it only in that spirit. But Populists frequently complained that the governors slighted their own party while excessively rewarding their allies. Lee clearly gave too much to the Democrats, as he himself came to regret. One disappointed Populist complained to him, "I deplore the fact that the majority of the honors justly earned by our party, should be relinquished to the Democrats." The patronage and other policies of North Dakota Populist governor Eli Shortridge convinced another disgruntled Populist that "the only aim the governor has in view seems to be to turn the Independent party over to the democrats."[47]

For Kansas governors Lewelling and Leedy, the attempt to preserve fusion coalitions with Democrats influenced not only their patronage decisions but also their attitudes toward the state's prohibitory legislation. To satisfy Democrats, who objected fervently to prohibition, they made little effort to enforce the law; but many Populists were ardent prohibitionists and the failure of their party's government to uphold the law — indeed its obstruction of the law — infuriated and at times even alienated them. A prominent Populist ran for governor on the Prohibition ticket against Leedy when he sought reelection, suggesting the divisive effect of cultural politics on the People's party and the tactical dilemma prohibition posed for Populist politicians.[48]

The performance of Populist legislators in the western states, itself circumscribed by political factors, also had repercussions for the party. This was particularly true when Populists participated in electing U.S. senators, a process then accomplished through legislative elections and that almost invariably resulted in disaster for the Populists. It activated all the fault lines in their unstable coalition, provoking divisions according to previous party affiliation, reform ideology, rural-urban tensions, personal interests, and divergent political calculations. Those divisions were further complicated by the Populists' legislative inexperience, intense public scrutiny, frantic lobbying, and their own conviction that such elections were inherently corruptible, which encouraged them even to exaggerate the very real pressures and to distrust the motives for decisions as well as to campaign for direct election of senators. Finally, Populists rarely held full control of legislatures and thus had to debate whether, how, what, or with whom to negotiate.

Ironically, the Populists' first participation in a senatorial election was their most successful and satisfying. This contest involved the defeat of the hated symbol of Republican arrogance and reaction, John J. Ingalls, by the Populist farm editor, William A. Peffer, in Kansas in 1891. The goal of defeating Ingalls had been in many ways the mobilizing agent and unifying force of the great popular rebellion in 1890 that created the People's party, and Peffer had clearly emerged as the logical choice to replace Ingalls. And yet, the senatorial election in the legislature was tense. Other Populist leaders, representing the various partisan, ideological, and geographic elements in the state's party, challenged Peffer for the honor. Democrats and Republicans tried to manipulate Populist legislators, who were so anxious about the task and the opponents they confronted that they traveled with bodyguards, avoided reporters, and closeted themselves behind locked doors. But they managed to coalesce behind Peffer in the face of great public attention and thereby give their party a symbolic leader who would represent its principles before the nation better than they dared hope.[49]

Yet in nearly all other senatorial elections, the Populists failed to master these divisive elements and made poor selections that injured the party, elected non-Populists, or had imposed upon them candidates that the majority did not want. One complicated scenario, also in 1891, involved senatorial elections in Illinois and South Dakota. In Illinois, legislators were so evenly divided between the major parties that three agrarian independents held the balance of power in the senatorial election. Populist leader Jerry Simpson helped to persuade the farmers to elect the Democratic candidate, John M. Palmer, in exchange for Democratic support for the election of James H. Kyle in South Dakota. Neither result significantly helped Populists or their cause, however. The Populists' belief that Palmer's election was "at least a partial victory for them" was quickly shattered. In the Senate, he consistently opposed their reform plans; in 1896 he became the presidential candidate of the Gold Democrats. Moreover, by gaining prominence in the 1891 senatorial election, one Illinois independent legislator, Herman Taubeneck, acquired an unwarranted reputation for integrity that catapulted him into the national chairmanship when Populists organized their national party three months later. He was wholly unfit for the position and pursued policies that disrupted the party and led to catastrophe in the 1896 election. As for Kyle, as a senator he was so indifferent to many Populist goals that the party's other senators once denied that he was a Populist at all. He was soon despised by most leading South Dakota Populists, but he was reelected in 1897 despite their opposition when Republicans supported him in exchange for his pledge to support the McKinley administration, an indication of his relatively conservative and expedient career. Kyle's election left Governor Lee "heartsick and enraged," and Kyle's own hometown Populist paper denounced him as "the miserable thief who robbed the people's party of the opportunity to elect a United States senator, and of the right to be represented by one who was free of the stigma of dishonor, of bribery, of treachery, and of miserly selfishness."[50]

Tactical maneuvering for political advantage characterized other Populist senatorial elections, and many of these contests were tied to the question of fusion in popular elections. Sometimes party legislators selected Populist senators in order to facilitate or reward fusion. Peffer himself was a victim of this practice. Although universally regarded as a "faithful, tireless worker" for Populist principles, Peffer was not reelected in 1897 when, in order to ensure subsequent fusion and to placate Democratic demands for recognition, Populist legislators elected his polar opposite in the party: William A. Harris, a former Democrat opposed to basic Populist principles but a leading fusionist championed by Democrats as one of their own. This election sharply indicated how the People's party had been transformed by interacting with the dynamics of the two-party system over the previous six years. In 1891 both Democrats and Republicans had urged Harris's candidacy, the first seeking to control, the second to destroy, the People's party, while some Populists had doubted Peffer's commitment. Peffer had then demonstrated his constancy; the party had lost its. Harris himself would renounce the party before the end of his term.[51]

In Idaho, too, Populist legislators chose a party colleague as senator largely in response to fusion politics and Democratic wishes. In 1896 Democrats had agreed to support a Populist for senator in ex-

change for Populist endorsement of Democrats as presidential electors and governor. In the 1897 legislature Democrats manipulated
their promise by voting for a Populist — but not for the candidate selected by the Populist caucus. William H. Clagett, the Populist
choice, accordingly fell just short of the votes necessary for election.
Reluctantly, Populist legislators endorsed a series of other candidates, but the Democrats kept pace, always redistributing their votes
to other Populists to prevent any election. To break the impasse, the
Democrats then announced *their* list of acceptable candidates,
nearly dictating the choice to the Populists, who had lost their independence despite their greater numbers. As a result, the legislature
elected the obscure Henry Heitfeld. But Heitfeld's election produced
widespread dismay, one Populist reporting that party members "in
all parts of Idaho are down-hearted and filled with aches, pains,
and deep regret." Worse still, a legislative committee soon uncov-
ered evidence of extortion and bribery in Heitfeld's election and recommended expulsion of two Populist legislators. This often lurid fiasco convinced Populists of the necessity for direct popular elections
of senators. As a senator, moreover, Heitfeld was notoriously reticent
and inactive, and he soon switched to the Democratic party, proposing that the People's party be officially disbanded. Referring to his
"accidental election," the Populist state committee excoriated him
for "neglecting his duties at Washington and parading up and down
the state in an effort to seduce the membership of the party and
cause them to become, like him, traitors to the principles so long
urged by us."[52]

In other senatorial elections Populists did not even elect members
of their own party but chose candidates from other parties for practical political reasons, again often involving fusion considerations.
In Colorado in 1897, for instance, Populists, although the largest
partisan group of legislators, voted unanimously for Silver Republican leader Henry Teller.[53]

More dramatic and disruptive was the 1893 decision of Kansas
Populists to elect a Democrat as senator. John Martin had been instrumental in gaining Democratic endorsement of Populist candidates in 1892 and in exchange received their support when he
sought election by the 1893 legislature in which Populists had a clear
majority on joint ballot. Other Populists, of course, logically de-

manded that their party elect a Populist. The decisive factor involved a controversy over control of the lower house, claimed by both Republicans and Populists. Each party organized its own legislative body, producing a "legislative war" with heavily armed partisans on the capitol grounds and great public anxiety. Structural considerations of constitutional restrictions and political realities limited Populist options. The U.S. Senate was the final judge of the election of its members, and its Democratic majority seemed likely to refuse to seat a member of a third party elected in these circumstances. Reluctantly, a majority of the Populist caucus therefore agreed to support Martin, whose party standing would guarantee Senate acceptance regardless of the ultimate legal resolution of the legislative dispute. Nevertheless, Martin's election hurt the Populists. Some of their legislators refused to vote for him, one complaining that he had entered "a Populist caucus, but found he had been entrapped into a Democratic stronghold." Party members outside the legislature were also appalled by the spectacle of Populists electing a Democrat who had "never said anything in favor of the success of Populist ideas," in the words of Senator Peffer. Mary Lease decried Martin's election as "a death blow to the People's Party, both state and national. It will drive 100,000 Populists in the South back into the Democratic party, and in Kansas and the North thousands will return to the Republican party." A Populist in the state of Washington testified to the wide impact of Martin's election when he lamented that it seemed to verify the contention that Populists had been struggling to deny—the Republican assertion that the People's party was but an adjunct of the Democracy. The nation's Populists, he wrote, had watched Kansas for another senator like Peffer "only to have their fond hopes dashed to pieces."[54]

But four years later Washington State Populists also elected a non-Populist to the U.S. Senate and without the restricting circumstances that had limited the Kansans. Again, however, fusion, factionalism, and intrigue were involved. Populists, Democrats, and Silver Republicans had fused in the 1896 campaign, carrying the state. Populist governor John Rogers declared the success of the Populist cause at issue in the subsequent senatorial election and urged harmony. Populists had a majority of the legislators without Democratic or Silver Republican support and could have chosen a straight

Populist but immediately fell into squabbling. More than forty Populist legislators caucused on January 19 to discuss the situation, but after passing a motion excusing all candidates, so many left that no quorum remained. Amid frantic lobbying, balloting began January 20, with fusionists splitting their votes among more than a dozen candidates, and continued day after day with only slight shifts in the vote. Finally, Populists agreed to enter a fusion caucus; after a stormy session and despite their great majority, they elected a Silver Republican, George Turner. As in Idaho, the senatorial contest was accompanied by charges of manipulation, corruption, and bribery, implicating both Populist legislators and Turner himself. Legislative committees investigated the allegations but despite suggestive testimony took no action. The disintegrating effect of the senatorial election disrupted the Populists' prospects of enacting their legislative program and produced considerable popular disgust and alienation. Turner did promise that henceforth he would act as a member of the Populist party and declared that "as long as I live I never expect to cast another Republican ballot so long as God helps me." Indeed, he soon turned to the other major party and became a Democrat.[55]

In other legislatures, Populists were often no more than a small minority, but in a closely divided body they sometimes faced a choice of standing by their principles or cooperating with a major party to determine the election. In both Montana and Wyoming in 1893 a few Populists held the balance of power and refused to support the candidate of either major party for senator. Their determination prevented any election by the legislature, leaving each state with only one senator for two years.[56] In California in 1893, eight Populist legislators similarly held the balance of power and were subjected to great pressure to align themselves with one of the major parties in voting for a senator. Initially the Populists faithfully rejected such pressure and stood as a unit for Populist leader Thomas V. Cator, earning for themselves the nicknames of the "solid eight" and the "immovable phalanx." National Populist leaders provided encouragement, declaring "millions of true hearts expect the eight to stand by their guns and receive the fire of the plutocrats without a quiver." Eventually, however, one Populist legislator voted to help elect Democratic candidate Stephen White, prompting the remain-

ing Populist legislators and the party's state central committee to denounce the "traitor" and recommend that he "be spurned and cut
off from fellowship in the party." Populists also charged that bribery
had purchased the miscreant's vote, leading to a legislative investigation.[57] In Idaho, too, Populists held the balance of power in the 1895
senatorial contest and hoped to prevent the election of a Republican. But after holding together for several weeks, the Populist bloc
broke down when one Populist absented himself, allowing a Republican to gain election by a single vote. After investigating the legislator's absence, Populists censured and formally expelled him from the
party.[58] Such pressures, disappointments, and animosities were virtually inherent in the vulnerable situation in which third-party members were placed by senatorial elections, and they continually disrupted the Populists and disillusioned their followers.

Populist legislators not only participated in the election of senators but also attempted to enact laws to implement their reform
principles. They were not without significant achievements in several western states, but in this political arena, too, they encountered
a variety of political obstacles that clearly limited their success, leaving their supporters disappointed and discouraged.

In a small measure, perhaps, the Populists' legislative prospects
were hampered by their relative inexperience. In both the 1891
Kansas House and the 1893 Colorado legislature, Populists were only
half as likely as Republican and Democratic members to have had
any previous government experience, a differential perhaps supporting the Populist contention that they sought to reclaim the government from the politicians. Some Populist newcomers found their
legislative career hampered by the very intensity of their convictions,
which had caused them to break free of the shackles of past party
ties and join a third party in the first place. In Oregon, for example,
a reporter described Populist legislator J. H. Upton, "the wild-eyed
and eccentric member from Coos," whose frequent speeches always
"created a sensation in the house" as he charged "up and down the
aisle, sometimes gyrating as a double-back action turbine water
wheel." Conceding that there was "no more industrious or faithful"
representative, the reporter noted that Upton's "powerful efforts,
however, failed somewhat of the effect intended, from the fact that
he was hardly understandable" in his fervor.[59]

Inexperienced Populists were sometimes unfamiliar with, and vulnerable to, legislative proceedings. In Idaho's 1893 senate, one Populist attempting to discuss railroad legislation was so blocked by points of order raised against him that he finally abandoned his speech and sat down, sputtering that "to tell the truth in this house is like throwing pearls before swine." More extreme, and certainly idiosyncratic, was the action of a Populist in the Oklahoma legislature. Frustrated at his inability to gain the floor, he drew a revolver to demand recognition from the speaker at gunpoint. Of more consequence politically, Populists in Nebraska's 1891 legislature elected as speaker a man whose apparent ignorance of his official prerogatives seriously obstructed Populist legislative plans.[60]

Many Populists, of course, were well acquainted with legislative rules and procedures but still found in them obstacles to the realization of their reform agenda. Idaho Populists, angered that their bills were killed in committee, attempted in 1895 to reform legislative rules to restrict the authority of committees. Rules that violated the right of a minority party to have its proposals considered by the legislature, they declared, effectively precluded democratic government.[61]

Far more important in limiting Populist legislative success than either their relative inexperience or the effects of legislative rules were the basic realities that legislatures were partisan arenas reflecting and continuing the divisions of election campaigns and that Populists rarely controlled the legislature in any western state. Republicans, and to a lesser extent Democrats, consistently opposed Populist reform initiatives in state legislatures.[62] One reporter observing Oregon's 1895 legislature suggested the reflex rejection of Populist proposals by major-party legislators. After describing one Populist's excellent speech on a major reform issue, the reporter concluded, "Of course, he fails of any great influence by reason of the populistic principles he embodies within himself." Another legislative reporter in neighboring Washington noted the same partisan barrier: "The Populists may introduce, but the Republicans will not pass any measure" that promoted Populist ideals. In Kansas such knee-jerk opposition to all Populist proposals, regardless of the subject, was so invariable as to alarm even a conservative Republican editor who complained that Republican legislators had mindlessly killed "a quiet, inoffensive and necessary appropriation bill" simply because of its Populist authorship.[63]

Such resolute opposition was particularly effective because of the Populists' usual minority status in western legislatures. In Colorado, Idaho, Iowa, Oregon, and of course in California and other states, Populists never had a majority in either house and were unable to overcome the hostility of major-party legislators to their leading reform objectives. In some states they were able to form temporary legislative coalitions with Democrats, but these rarely brought success. In Minnesota in 1891, for example, Populists and Democrats combined to organize the legislature, but the two groups differed so sharply in their policy objectives that little was accomplished. The result left Populists disappointed and enabled Republicans, effectively if unfairly, to construct an image of Populist incompetency that became part of Minnesota's campaign mythology.[64]

When Populists did control one house of a legislature, hostile Republicans usually controlled the other and blocked Populist proposals. In the 1891 Kansas legislature, for instance, Populists dominated the lower house after their 1890 landslide, but thirty-nine of the forty senators, all holdovers from the 1888 election that preceded the creation of the People's party, were Republicans. The Populists pointedly indicated how their efforts at reform were hamstrung by divided legislative control when they carefully spelled out in their 1892 state platform the bills that they had passed in the house but that the Republicans had rejected in the senate—bills for an Australian ballot, an elective railroad commission, maximum freight rates, a weekly wage system, the abolition of labor blacklisting, restrictions on the use of Pinkertons, and other reforms.[65] The effectiveness of divided control emerged even more dramatically in 1893 when Populists controlled the senate and Republicans and Populists organized separate and competing houses of representatives. The Populist senate and house passed nearly all the measures promised by the Populists during the 1892 campaign, but these acts were invalidated when the partisan state supreme court ended the "legislative war" by ruling in favor of the Republican house.[66]

A different form of divided control often frustrated Populists even in legislatures in which Republicans were reduced to a minority in each house. As a consequence of the 1896 campaign, fusionists captured several western legislatures. Sometimes these fusion coalitions were nominally Populist, as in South Dakota and Washington, where antifusion laws had required the adoption of a single party name by opponents of the GOP. But Populists were merely one group in the coalition, did not constitute a majority of legislators, and could not impose their will or principles on their campaign allies. Partisan factionalism among the fusion partners easily thwarted the Populists, as one hostile observer gloated, "in any attempt to revolutionize existing conditions by fantastic legislation." In Washington a reporter found that fusionist legislators "represented political principles entirely at variance with each other" and that "on nearly every fundamental proposition that came up the fusionists were divided and the hostile factions fought each other bitterly." The resulting defeat of reform proposals, lamented one Populist representative, was a "pitiable and humiliating end to a movement that promised so much good for the people." The fusionist-controlled Idaho legislature, where important Populist reforms were likewise killed by campaign allies now voting with Republicans, was nearly as disappointing and adjourned to virtual unanimous condemnation. "A damnable disgrace," concluded one Populist newspaper. "Of all the pig-headed, pusillanimous, dirty and damnable outfits that ever got together, the present legislature of Idaho takes the cake." A Republican newspaper, perhaps pleased by the failure to enact most Populist legislation, was more restrained, declaring the session "perhaps no worse than some others," but it cruelly pointed out that "if anybody thinks it fulfilled the hopes of those who expected it to inaugurate an era of legislative reform he has not kept track of its performances." In short, Populists learned that fusionists from other parties might help them win elections but were rarely willing to help them enact reforms.[67]

Factionalism among Populists themselves also limited their success in western legislatures. This dissension was most painfully apparent in the 1897 Kansas legislature where Populists, not mere fusionists, controlled both houses. Although they did enact a number of important reforms, many others were defeated when some Populists betrayed their party's principles and voted with the intransigent Republican minority. These divisions within the ranks of Populist legislators reflected the often overlapping lines separating farmer from merchant and lawyer Populists, former Republicans from former Democrats, and especially mid-roaders from fusionists. The "Judases of Populism," as one editor described the relatively conservative Populists who made possible the defeat of promised reform legislation, at times resembled Republicans and Democrats more than their own party colleagues in their occupational origins, economic attitudes, and political cynicism. Their prominence within the party often represented Populist attempts to appeal to a wider constituency and thereby achieve electoral success. As one Populist newspaper observed of such legislators, "These 'conservative' Populists are largely composed of men whose political status was a matter of considerable doubt—who had been nominated because of their supposed ability to get votes." The Populist tragedy, then, was that the methods by which the Populists created a political coalition powerful enough to win elections often limited its ability to enact the promised reforms. A despondent Populist recognized this sobering restraint: "We were successful at the polls but defeated in the legislative halls."[68]

In one last political arena Populists encountered significant limitations on their opportunities to promote—or even to espouse—their party's program. With their focus on national legislation, Populists naturally looked to Congress and expected their many representatives and senators to secure necessary reforms. To their dismay, however, they found that by the 1890s Congress had institutionalized the two-party system and adopted procedures and norms that simultaneously obstructed Populist policy objectives and promoted the power of the very political and economic interests against which their party had been organized. The organizational attributes of Congress—ranging from the great powers of partisan presiding officers and committee chairs to the rules for debate and for reporting legislation—promoted institutional conservatism and virtually excluded Populists from real participation. Populists challenged such rules and procedures and valiantly tried to democratize the internal workings of Congress, paralleling their attempt to democratize the external electoral arena. Defeated in this effort, the Populists had "no rights on this floor," in the words of Nebraska congressman Omer Kem, and they gradually sank into frustration and resignation, unable to promote their party principles or effectively to represent their popular constituencies.[69]

With courage and imagination, and sometimes desperation, Populists consistently attempted to negotiate within and even to change the political limits they encountered in their struggle for reform. They denounced partisanship and sectionalism, even while ultimately falling victim to the continuing effects of those strong emotions. They mobilized supporters with evangelical appeals that often raised expectations to unrealistic levels and threatened disappointment. They attempted to counter the limitations of the representation system first by pursuing fusion, which itself activated the crippling forces of prejudice, and then by campaigning for proportional representation, an alternative that failed because the major parties were determined to preserve the structural advantages they enjoyed under the existing system. Populist leaders adopted forceful tactics to manage their campaigns but thereby alienated those members who viewed the movement as a popular protest against "the dangers and tyranny" of party organization. Populists pushed for ballot reform to make it easier for third parties and their constituents to participate effectively in politics, only to have the major parties seize the issue and use it to undercut political challenges, limit democratic opportunities, and entrench themselves in authority. Frustrated by the obstacles encountered in the legislative elections of senators, Populists campaigned for direct popular elections but without immediate effect. They proposed changing legislative and congressional rules and procedures in order to facilitate new ideas and policies and to promote equal participation, only to run into a hierarchical system designed to secure the very things Populists opposed and to prevent the democratic possibilities they sought. Frustrated by the limits of representative government, they proposed to bypass unresponsive institutions with systems of direct legislation. South Dakota Populists did manage to establish the initiative and referendum in 1897, but it proved as ineffectual as other Populist efforts in reversing the inertia of a political system that limited popular and institutional innovation. By the turn of the century, the structural limits of politics were in many respects more powerful than before the Populists emerged, though by challenging orthodoxy, devising new ideas, and criticizing partisan loyalties Populists had at least weakened some of the cultural constraints of politics. That modest achievement had scarcely been their objective. Looking back years later on his Populist career, Henry Vincent sadly concluded that Senator Ingalls's notorious statement that "the purification of politics is an iridescent dream" had contained "more truth than poetry."[70]

2

ROAD TO A REPUBLICAN WATERLOO: THE FARMERS' ALLIANCE AND THE ELECTION OF 1890 IN KANSAS

Kansas was proclaimed "the banner state" of the Republican party after the elections of 1888 when that political party swept all national, state, and local contests in Kansas and gave a greater majority to Benjamin Harrison than did any other state. In 1890, just two years later, the November election was "a Waterloo to the Republican party" as the Grand Old Party retained only two of seven congressmen, lost its famous U.S. senator of eighteen years, and was nearly overwhelmed by the opposition in a state legislature previously considered a private club.[1] What success the party was able to achieve in "the most intense and spectacular,"[2] "the most angry and stormy,"[3] campaign in Kansas history was due not to its own merits but to the mistakes of the opposition, a new political force in existence only a few months. The fantastic and, to the old order, the disturbing success of the People's party in Kansas in 1890 was to serve as a prelude to the coming Populist storm on the national scene.

The Populist movement was rooted in the economic situation of the farmer in the decade that began in 1885, and the self-proclaimed aim of the People's party was to relieve those conditions that had placed him in such an unfavorable position. Kansas in the early 1880s entered a period of exceptional prosperity based primarily on the high prices for corn and wheat. The peak prices for both grains in the interval from the Civil War to the end of the century came in

1881. From 1880 to 1885 the Kansas population increased by 37 percent, or by more than 300,000 individuals, and the value of property more than doubled. Accordingly, it was nearly inevitable that land prices should increase rapidly and that there would be land speculation on the rising markets. The healthy and potentially helpful development thereby deteriorated into a boom, "created and artificially maintained for its effect on land values" and encouraged and spurred on by the widespread activity of the boomers.[4] Newspapers, railroads, speculators, and even official state agencies joined hands and voices to boom. The *Tenth Biennial Report* of the State Board of Agriculture admitted that earlier reports of the board had been propaganda instruments intended "to persuade millions of less fortunate strangers that the mere fact of coming hither with unalterable, ready-made views of Kansas people and Kansas agriculture means a life of ease, perpetual June weather, a steady diet of milk and honey" (p. vii).

Accompanying the boom was excessive railroad construction. The decade of the 1880s saw in Kansas an increase in railroad mileage second only to that in Texas, and by 1888 there was one mile of railroad track for every nine-and-one-third square miles of land or one mile of track for every 181 people in the state. The rapid increase in land prices made it necessary for the new arrival with limited means to borrow in order to purchase a farm. Kansas was unable to provide this credit, but eastern capital was eager to supply it.

The boom collapsed in the winter of 1887–1888 for three general reasons. The boom in the city had been largely based on unwarranted optimism and an artificial demand, and the first sign of wavering in that confidence revealed the shaky character of the entire development. The prosperity in rural areas had resulted from the inflated prices for agricultural products of the first years of the 1880s, but by 1885 that foundation had broken down. Adverse weather conditions contributed to the collapse in western Kansas.[5]

The price for farm products declined steadily from 1881 to 1895. Corn sold for 83 cents per bushel in 1881 and 28 cents a bushel in 1890; wheat dropped from $1.19 in 1881 to 49 cents per bushel in 1894. The United States Department of Agriculture reported in 1893 that corn and wheat, among other crops, had for the last ten years been selling regularly for less than the cost of production.[6] The

sharp drop in prices for agricultural products was such that a read-
justment of land values was not only proper but a practical necessity.
Moreover, the eight-year period of unusually heavy rainfall was followed after 1886 by a period of unusually dry weather.

The creation of an overwhelming debt, public and private, was
another consequence of the Kansas boom settlement. It was taking
an ever-increasing amount of the farmer's products to pay his debts;
a mortgage worth 1,000 bushels when contracted now required
2,000 bushels to be retired. Too, with the drop in prices the value of
the farm itself fell, and a farm that five years previously had been
ample security would not now sell for enough to pay the mortgage.
The census of 1890 reported the total mortgage debt of Kansas to be
over 27 percent of the actual value of all Kansas real estate. Sixty
percent of the taxed acres of Kansas was mortgaged, a figure un-
matched by any other state. The per capita private debt was nearly
four times that of the nation as a whole. The state auditor's *Report*
for the same year set the assessed value of all property in Kansas at
$348,459,943 and the total indebtedness, both public and private,
at $706,181,627.[7]

In response to these depressing conditions some political opposition
developed, and the third-party vote more than doubled from 16,000
Anti-Monopoly in 1884 to 37,000 Union Labor in 1888. Although it
attracted more voters and more disparate groups of voters than had
any other third party of the 1880s, the Union Labor party still received less than 12 percent of the total vote cast in the election of
1888. Twelve percent was valuable, but neither it nor all the appeals
and work that had gone into it apparently would ever really accomplish anything.[8] The inertia of a history of Republicanism proved
too strong. Moreover, Union Labor was obviously only a repetition
of the two decades of the Greenback party. The old call of "the
Crime of '73" needed to be replaced by newer, more appropriate,
and pressing questions. The political base of reform had to be en-
larged.

The Union Labor party had introduced into Kansas in 1888 the
secret, oath-bound "National Order of Videttes," an organization
frankly and purely political in nature. However, the ritual of this se-

cret society, an auxiliary to the Union Labor party, was stolen and published by the Republicans, and the society disbanded after the 1888 election. Only in its own demise did this order accomplish something: It appointed an executive committee that was "to select some existing organization, or to organize a new one into whose ranks the reformers and farmers and laborers of Kansas could be enlisted as members."[9] The executive committee recommended the Farmers' Alliance, and three committeemen, C. Vincent, J. R. Rogers, and W. F. Rightmire, left for Texas to be initiated into the secret organization.

The Farmers' Alliance had been born in 1874 in Lampasas County, Texas. Its operations were confined to Texas until 1887, when it began to expand rapidly. Only two states, Texas and Louisiana, were represented at its first national convention, held in Waco, Texas. Its second, in Shreveport, Louisiana, was held October 12, 1887, and attended by delegates from nine states. The third, in Meridian, Mississippi, on December 5, 1888, had representatives from twelve states. The fourth, in St. Louis in December 1889, attracted nineteen states; and the fifth convention in Ocala, Florida, in December 1890, recognized delegates from twenty-seven states. Within these four years the Farmers' Alliance joined with, federated with, or absorbed farmers' organizations in three-fourths of the states.

After the three Kansans introduced the Alliance to Kansas, the organization spread quickly throughout the state. The conditions resulting from the collapse of the boom after 1887 made of the Farmers' Alliance "a messianic call to economic redemption," and its appeal to the hard-pressed farmers of Kansas was virtually irresistible.[10] The progress of organizing the suballiances in Kansas was such that the presidents of the county Alliances called for their first state convention, in Newton, August 14, 1889. Eighty delegates from twenty-seven counties were present, and the convention ratified the constitution of the National Farmers and Laborers Union of America. The state secretary reported that 470 suballiances had already been organized with a total membership of 25,000. The amazing growth of the Alliance in Kansas in 1889 even included the absorption of the state Grange.[11]

In these early months, entering politics apparently figured little in the Alliance plan. In 1882 the Texas Alliance had adopted the following resolution as the law of the Alliance: *"Resolved,* that it is contrary to the spirit of the constitution and by-laws of our order to take part in politics; and further, that we will not nominate or support any man or set of men for office as a distinct political party."[12] Even before the formation of the state Alliance, the directors of the Kansas State Alliance Exchange Company, the business branch of the many-sided Farmers' Alliance, adopted and proclaimed on October 2, 1889, a resolution "that we earnestly entreat our brethren of the Alliance to avoid all political action or discussion of partisan politics within the Alliance, as we regard such action as valueless to us politically, a certain element of discord in our order, which would prove ruinous to the most promising organization of farmers the world has ever known."[13]

On November 16, 1889, the presidents of the county Alliances met in Newton again and organized the state Alliance. Benjamin H. Clover, a former Greenbacker, was elected state president. The Southern Farmers' Alliance had for its plan of action to agree upon a needed reform and then attempt to convince each political party to aid by supporting appropriate legislation. Accordingly, the first action of the newly formed state Alliance was to send a circular letter to each of the suballiances of the state suggesting that they submit the Alliance platform, drawn up at the Newton meeting, to their individual representative in Congress, requesting an answer of approval or disapproval. Most of the members of the congressional delegation, being veterans of several terms and originally elected long before the Alliance entered Kansas, were hardly sympathetic to the Alliance program and were "unable to adjust themselves to the new conditions."[14] All but Sen. Preston B. Plumb, who wholeheartedly approved of the program, were evasive in their replies. Sen. John J. Ingalls, after great delay, said through his secretary that he would present his position in a speech shortly. That speech was never given.

The second step taken by the Alliance after the November meeting in Newton was to submit the platform to William A. Peffer, the editor of the *Kansas Farmer.* He then wrote the pamphlet, "The Way Out," and became a traveling lecturer supporting the principles of the Alliance. This was but another stimulus to the growth of the Alliance in Kansas, and by March 6, 1890, the *Farmers' Advocate* claimed a membership for the Alliance in Kansas of 100,000. Moreover, it stated that from twenty-five to fifty new organizations were being established each week by the fifty-two Alliance organizers.[15]

The increasing strength of the Alliance in nonpartisan political circles was augmented when on March 5, 1890, committees of the Farmers' Alliance, the Grange, the Farmers' Mutual Benefit Association, and the Knights of Labor adopted mutual political platforms in Emporia. Of these organizations, however, only the Alliance had a strong following in Kansas, but when Benjamin H. Clover was interviewed in Topeka on March 13, 1890, he said that the Kansas Alliance had doubled its membership since the St. Louis national convention just two months earlier, and he admitted that even with two assistants he was unable to send out supplies to the newly formed suballiances as fast as they were formed.

Clover assured the interviewer that the Alliance would not enter politics "as an order" but would merely support the best candidates nominated "on the various tickets."[16] This statement was supported but expressed more forcibly by the resolutions of the County Farmers' Alliance and Industrial Union of Atchison County, organized by the farmers on March 18, 1890. It declared that it would support no one for Congress or the legislature who did not pledge to uphold the principles of the Alliance platform.[17]

The growth of the Alliance in an election year was bound to cause some political speculation. The very fact that Clover denied the possible entrance of the Alliance into the arena of political parties indicates that the possibility had occurred to some observers. One widespread rumor was that the Alliance lecturer, William A. Peffer, would seek the Senate seat held by John J. Ingalls. Finally, the editor of the *Kansas Farmer* denied that he would be a candidate for the Senate in opposition to Ingalls. To the Republican *Lawrence Daily Journal*, "Such generous refusing of the unattainable savors of vainglory. . . . [Peffer] does not belong to the class of men who get such plums." Peffer, the *Journal* surmised, would apparently consider himself the candidate of the farmers, but, as with all "farmer politicians," he would be unable to secure the full support of the Kansas farmers. The conservative editor declared any senatorial ambitions on Peffer's part to be absurd and closed by stating flatly that "Mr. Peffer will never be a senator from Kansas."[18]

Two days later, state Alliance president Clover called for a state convention of the presidents of the Kansas county Alliances to meet in Topeka on March 25, 1890, just over four months after the organization of the state Alliance, to consider the affairs of that body. The short period before the March convention was to become of crucial significance in the campaign of 1890.

W. L. Jennings, the state organizer for the Alliance, completed a trip through the state in the middle of March. Nearly every county in the state was organized, with a central organization in the county seat and township Alliances subordinate to that body. The county central organization, in turn, was instructed from the state Alliance headquarters. The Wilson County Alliance, for example, met with high attendance in Fredonia beginning March 20. State lecturer Van B. Prather was present, and President Clover was scheduled to speak at an open public meeting in Fredonia in conjunction with the Alliance meeting. The Wilson county organizer, George H. Anthony, reported that there were forty suballiances with a total membership of 2,000 in the county.[19]

This thorough organization made the Alliance stronger than its membership lists, no small consideration in themselves, indicated. On the local level most Alliances had already decided "to support only those candidates who coincide with their views and adopt their principles."[20] But for the Alliance to function only as a pressure group, making independent endorsements, would create suicidal splits in the organization, composed as it was of Republicans, Democrats, and old-third-party men. As the realization of the doubtful success of the nonpartisan method of seeking its ends grew among the Alliance leaders, it was only natural that a movement to create a separate political party founded on Alliance support should attract interest and consideration among the same men. The idea appealed particularly to the old-third-party men, many of them active in the Alliance since its introduction into Kansas at their possible instigation; and, since the Emporia convention earlier in the month, they were becoming increasingly influential.

The shift toward more active participation in politics can be seen in the March meeting of the two county Alliances of Douglas and Shawnee counties. The first meeting, that of the Douglas County farmers, was held at the courthouse in Lawrence on the first Saturday of the month. The first topic discussed concerned the possibility of withholding their products from market until the prices were better. A committee was formed to investigate the matter. Then the special report for the month was given. J. M. Shepherd indicated by market reports that the prices received by the county farmers for both corn and cattle were well below their cost of production. As the meeting progressed and the accounts of economic injustices mounted, so did the resentment of the farmers. By the end of the meeting the Douglas County farmers declared themselves in earnest and determined to discover the reasons for the great depression in agriculture and "to find out and apply the remedy."[21] Judge Peffer was then announced to be the speaker at the next meeting. Thus, the meeting of a county suballiance, like the development of the Alliance in Kansas, began with concern strictly for economic circumstances and moved toward a wider sphere of action.

At their March meeting the Shawnee County farmers discussed at great length the political situation in which they found themselves. The unanimous decision of the group was that the farmer was being slighted by the legislator, who used him only as a voting tool so that he, the politician, could serve the interests of other classes. The principal speaker said that it was the fault of the farmers themselves for allowing the wrong kind of men to be placed in positions of such influence, and he criticized the farmers' inattention to machine politics. It was admitted that there must be careful watching to undo the harmful legislation and to nominate the right men to protect the farmers' interests. As Annie L. Diggs, later one of the most prominent Populist leaders, wrote in her "Farmers' Alliance Department" of the *Lawrence Daily Journal* in describing the meeting, "It is more than probable that there will be little cause in the future to complain of the over trustfulness or gullibility of the farmer. He is awake and there is a good many of them."[22]

This change in the Alliance outlook was becoming increasingly widespread and apparent in a very short period of time. Not much more than a week after its editor derided "Senator Peffer," the *Lawrence Daily Journal* admitted that the Farmers' Alliance had grown so rapidly as to become a "disturbing faction" in politics and that "indications of the determination of the alliance to enter politics are troubling the politicians and they are becoming decidedly nervous."[23] The *Atchison Weekly Times* declared that "the old political shysters who have been running the affairs of the city and county to suit themselves for years are 'skeered.' . . . The farmers in the county have them . . . trembling in their boots"; the newspaper promptly announced its support of the Alliance movement.[24]

The meeting of the presidents of the county Alliances began on March 25, 1890, in Representative Hall in Topeka. Sixty-two counties were represented at the convention, and, although the transactions of the first day were temporarily secret, the *Lawrence Daily Journal* "learned that they devoted the time largely to the discussion of political matters."[25]

The convention asked Republican governor Lyman Humphrey to call a special session of the legislature to enact laws giving more time for the farmers to pay mortgages and forcing the railroads to reduce rates.[26] A second resolution passed was the demand that farmers be represented on the Board of Railroad Commissioners. It was suggested that P. B. Maxson of Emporia replace Commissioner Greene. These or similar resolutions had been expected and had become characteristic of any meeting of farmers. The final two resolutions dropped the bombshell. By a vote of 44 to 19 the convention adopted the following:

> Notwithstanding the fact that John J. Ingalls has represented Kansas for eighteen years in the United States senate, it is a difficult matter for his constituents to point to a single measure he has ever championed in the interests of the great agricultural and laboring element of Kansas; and we will not support by our votes or influence any candidate for the legislature who favors his reelection to the United States senate.[27]

Formulating other propositions as "demands," the convention called for the direct election of U. S. senators and railroad commissioners, the exemption of homesteads from taxation, a congressional investigation on a word change revising U. S. bonds, and the application of the old "rule of three" to farm mortgages: Mortgages should be shrunk in proportion to the shrinkage of the farm value.[28] The adoption of the final resolution anticipated some form of direct political action: "*Resolved,* that we will no longer divide on party lines, and will only cast our votes for candidates of the people, for the people, and by the people."[29]

The *Lawrence Daily Journal* acknowledged that the Alliance convention was generally concerned with methods of political work but attempted to reassure its Republican readers by adding that the discussion was carried out "not with a view of organizing a political party, but to determine the best methods of influencing political sentiment."[30] In the same issue the *Daily Journal* declared that in the Republican state convention, probably to be held in June, only the offices of state treasurer, auditor, and printer would be contested; the present (Republican) governor, lieutenant governor, secretary of state, attorney general, superintendent of public instruction, and adjutant general would be renominated "and consequently re-elected."

In a very real sense, the campaign of 1890 had begun. From the sudden flurry of Alliance activity just preceding the March convention until the polls closed in November there was no true letup in the political struggle between the Republicans and the recalcitrant farmers. On the day the convention assembled in Topeka, the farmers of Scott County met in Scott City and organized a branch of the Farmers' Alliance.[31] Three days later in Fort Scott a convention of the Farmers' Alliance, the Farmers' Mutual Benefit Association, and the Knights of Labor met and discussed politics "with more than usual interest," declaring their intention to support "only such candidates as will represent our interests."[32] The following day, March 29, 1890, "was a gala day for Osborne," as some 3,000 Osborne County Alliance members assembled to listen to speeches by Benjamin Clover and William Peffer. In the morning the procession of farmers and their families was "fully 200 wagons," each carrying appropriate banners and signs. The *Fort Scott Daily Monitor*, certainly not friendly to the Alliance cause, declared that Osborne County "is now thoroughly organized, and the farmers are presenting a solid and determined front."[33]

As the political activity of the farmer increased, the heavily Republican Kansas press leaped to the attack. It was reported that President Clover had informed the Kansas delegation in Congress, in a none too polite or refined letter, that the farmers were suffering a depression "due to vicious legislation."[34] Benjamin Clover, interviewed at the Topeka convention in March, denounced the alleged letter as a "miserable fake," originating "in the imagination of an ir-responsible newspaper correspondent."[35]

A second rumor, more pernicious than the first, linked Clover in particular and the Alliance in general with the movement to resub-mit the state liquor prohibitory amendment to a popular referen-dum, a movement with a certain minority following and limited fu-ture in the dry state. The "official" Alliance newspaper, the *Farmers' Advocate,* declared that this attempt to associate "Brother" B. H. Clover with the resubmission movement was aimed to divert the at-tention of the people from the real and pressing issues of the time. The rumor was "as conscienceless as Satan" and "too absurd to be dignified by a denial."[36] The joint convention in Fort Scott adopted a resolution that "this convention of farmers and laborers assem-bled, look upon the question of resubmission that is now being agi-tated as being for the purpose of misdirecting the minds of the people from what is of more vital importance."[37]

The *Daily Monitor,* a newspaper that was to prove a master of smear tactics and innuendo in this election year, editorialized after the resolutions of the Topeka March convention were announced that it was in sympathy with the Alliance as long as that organiza-tion was "content" to discuss

> the best methods of raising cabbage . . . how many rows of corn should be on a cob. . . . But when the farmer transcends that sphere of action and undertakes to discuss economic ques-tions, [e.g.] the causes that lead to the price of farm products which are now below the cost of production, . . . then the *Mon-itor* will denounce the farmers' organization as breeding discon-tent and treason to the republican party.[38]

Such newspaper attacks hit the Alliance movement in its vulnerable spot, old party loyalties. With the monthly suballiance meetings in April came a small wave of strong disagreement with the Topeka convention of March, despite the Alliance's constitutional provision for majority rule.[39] The Jackson County Farmers' Alliance met in Holton on April 10, 1890, and, even with Judge Peffer present, de-nounced "as partisan and out of order" the resolution condemning

Ingalls.[40] The following day the Haskell County Farmers' Alliance repudiated the anti-Ingalls resolution and the Dickinson County Farmers' Alliance, meeting in Abilene, censured the action of the Topeka convention in opposing Ingalls, after a lengthy discussion of politics.[41] A week later the Pottawatomie County Alliance rebelled against the anti-Ingalls resolution.[42] The Farmers' Alliance of Logan Township, Smith County, went one step further in its next meeting, denouncing on May 24 the anti-Ingalls resolution and resolving "to vigorously oppose the alliance party movement by all legitimate means within our power."[43]

On the other hand, there were some suballiances that felt the To-peka meeting had not gone far enough. The Leavenworth County Alliance, meeting in Tonganoxie, declared that none of its members would support anyone for Congress who was either an officer of any national bank or a lawyer. Notice of this example of increasing dissatisfaction was given to both the Republican and the Democratic parties.[44]

The relatively sudden shift in the Alliance's apparent destination seemingly caught the older parties unprepared. It was unusual to open the political guns so early in an election year, and this tradition, like others, was hard to overcome. The Republican state central committee, however, did meet in late spring in Topeka at the Copeland Hotel, and there was a large attendance. It was decided to hold the state convention in Topeka on September 3, 1890.[45] The feeling that the convention would merely be a rubber stamp for the renomination of Republican state officials apparently was one reason for the late date. A second reason was expressed by the *Daily Monitor:* Though the farmers constituted two-thirds of the state's voters, most were Republicans and would do little that might hurt Republican candidates on state and congressional tickets. "The politicians express great confidence in the re-election of Senator Ingalls [for example]. . . . The movement against him among farmers is limited and scattered."[46] The Democratic state central committee met in Leavenworth in late April to consult with a committee of the resubmissionists "with a view to uniting upon a state ticket for the coming campaign."[47] The apparent sentiment among the seventeen members of the Democratic committee who were present, however, was against fusion and in favor of a straight Democratic ticket.

The resubmissionists, mainly from Wichita, then met in Topeka in May. Governor Humphrey refused to appear before the convention, and the group adjourned after doing little.

These early stirrings of the older parties passed nearly unnoticed as "the Farmers' Alliances are holding daily demonstrations throughout the state."[48] The demonstrations were semipolitical in character and resulted in demands for the support of the movement in the interests of the farmers and laborers. It was at last becoming apparent to all, even to the *Daily Monitor,* that the farmers were opposed to both of the old political parties and in favor of breaking from them.

On June 3, 1890, the Farmers' Alliance of Barber County declared its intention to vote only for farmers for the office of judge. On June 4 a meeting in St. Mary's attracted 5,000 farmers "in parade" who were addressed by William Peffer. This joint meeting of the Alliance and the Farmers' Mutual Benefit Association decided to put forth a farmers' ticket for all local offices and then voted to have a full Alliance ticket for both state and congressional offices as well. The same day, Farmers' Alliance meetings in Harper and Johnson counties nominated entire county tickets and resolved to vote against John J. Ingalls. The Harper County Alliance even required a pledge from its nominees certifying their opposition to Senator Ingalls. The Rosevale Alliance of Clay County followed suit the next day, resolving not to support any candidate for the state legislature who favored the reelection of Ingalls. On June 6, the Farmers' Alliance in Augusta placed a full county ticket in the field and adopted the national platform. On June 10, the Farmers' Alliance of Sedgwick County met in convention in Wichita with members of the Union Labor party and, after President Clover addressed the meeting briefly, selected a full county ticket.[49]

By early summer, then, the majority of the Alliance membership had decided that the benefits to be gained outweighed the risks involved in entering politics as a separate party. Peffer, earlier one of the more cautious souls, wrote that the Alliance had concluded that the farmers were entitled to "at least a fair share in the benefits of legislation." However, the Alliance had found that the machinery of the present political parties was controlled by town-dwellers and connected to the railroads or corporations lending Eastern money. These elements, moreover, were interested in matters "directly and continually and powerfully in opposition to the interests of farmers." The natural conclusion to which the Alliance men came was that "the best way out of their troubles was through an independent political movement."[50]

Accordingly, Benjamin Clover, the state president of the Alliance, after some consultation called for another meeting in Topeka on June 12, 1890, of all reform organizations to determine the appropriate action to follow in the political campaign. The response to the call was excellent, and the Alliance proposition was supported by several distinct elements.[51] The older farm-protest organizations, although they had declined in strength and importance during the 1880s, had retained a hardcore following and formed a basic component in the convention. The Grange felt committed to its older and more conservative program and never merged with the Alliance, but it did cooperate and did vote the Alliance ticket straight down the line at the decisive time. The "single-taxers" added to the "solid reform front" by their presence in the movement although they were never numerous. The ideas of Edward Bellamy and his "nationalist" followers were also expressed in the June convention in Topeka.

More important as a contributor, both of men and ideas, was the Knights of Labor. This organization had gained strength in the late 1880s among the miners and railroad men of Kansas, partially as a result of their desire to offset the direct competition of imported Italian contract laborers and partially because of several wage and mine-safety disputes. Moreover, the Knights favored land reform, antimonopoly, and inflationist policies and believed that primary producers, whether agricultural or mechanical, had the same basic interests. The Knights also had a considerable rural membership.

The Union Labor and Greenback element had been totally absorbed into the Alliance movement even before it became a political vehicle. W. H. T. Wakefield, the Union Labor vice-presidential candidate in 1888; W. F. Rightmire, the former Union Labor candidate for state attorney general; and Union Labor presidential electors John

Davis, Cyrus Corning, J. L. Shinn, and P. B. Maxson early became prominent Alliance men.

The June 1890 Topeka convention was composed of forty-one Alliance men, twenty-eight Knights of Labor, ten members of the Farmers' Mutual Benefit Association, seven Patrons of Husbandry, and four single-taxers.[52] The Federation of Labor may also have been represented.[53] The assembled delegates unanimously decided that full state and congressional tickets, supporting the principles of the St. Louis platform, should be nominated. Moreover, the suballiances should lead in nominating legislative and county tickets responsive to their interests. The convention, however, decided that it would be better to create a separate organization from the Farmers' Alliance in order to avoid the transformation of the Alliance directly into a partisan organization. Still, good Alliance men would naturally give their support to the new organization, and in effect, the membership of the two groups came to be practically identical. It was decided that the name of their new party should be the People's party, and a state nominating convention was called to meet in Topeka on August 13, 1890.

The platform adopted was, in effect, the national Alliance's St. Louis platform of December 1889 and comprised seven principal demands: (1) the abolition of national banks and the substitution of legal tender notes, (2) legislation to suppress speculators in grain futures, (3) "free and unlimited coinage of silver," (4) the prohibition of alien ownership of and railroad restrictions on land; (5) equal taxation, (6) the issuance of fractional paper currency, and (7) government ownership of "the means of communication and transportation."[54]

The convention itself was secret, and journalists were excluded by the use of secret grips and passwords. A committee of one member from each congressional district was appointed "to issue an address to the people of the state." J. F. Willits of Jefferson County was selected as president of the committee, and S. W. Chase of Cowley became secretary. This committee called for the August delegate state nominating convention and would manage the subsequent campaign for the People's party: "Campaign material, including songs, will be scattered broadcast, and a great effort be made to enthuse the people and preserve a strongly centralized and effective organization."[55]

The first district convention held by the People's party was at Hill City in the Sixth Congressional District. Journalists were excluded and a guard was stationed at the door. An informal ballot taken to determine the candidates for the congressional position was followed by ten-minute speeches by each aspirant concerning his position on the issues of the day. A formal ballot was then taken. A former Republican, William Baker, a farmer and a preacher, was chosen as the nominee, the first time he ever ran for any political office. This procedure, with the exception of the exclusion of journalists, was typical of the early conventions of the People's party.[56]

On July 17, 1890, Albert F. Allen, a resident of Vinland and Douglas County for twelve years, was nominated as the congressional candidate for the People's party in the Second District. Seventy-five delegates composed the voting convention but five hundred Alliance members were present at the Ottawa meeting. Allen, a graduate of the Michigan agricultural college, was a lifelong Republican until just nine months before his nomination. Since that time of conversion he had been a lecturer for the Douglas County Alliance.[57]

The Seventh District convention was held in Great Bend on July 22, 1890. After some confusion due to lack of planning, Jerry Simpson of Medicine Lodge, Barber County, was nominated for the congressional office. His only previous office had been the nonelective one of city marshal of Medicine Lodge, which he had held for the preceding six months, after he had failed as a farmer because of the hard times.[58] The People's party, now generally called the Populists, also nominated L. C. Clark for the First District congressional position, Benjamin Clover for the Third, John G. Otis the Fourth, and John Davis the Fifth.

The practical transference of the Farmers' Alliance into the People's party did of course cause some stir in some of the suballiances in the state. However, there were no wholesale repudiations. Bradford Miller and Thomas Buckman, two lifelong Republicans, after being voted down in the July meeting concerning political action of the Shawnee County Farmers' Alliance and Knights of Labor, declared that they "would no longer affiliate with an organization which was officered by southern brigadiers and run in the interest of the democratic party."[59] There were few such individual desertions, however, and a more common news story was the announcement of a suballiance voting overwhelmingly for separate political action.

Indeed, there were also many Kansans living in the towns who expressed a desire to join the new party. The Farmers' Alliance, however, required its members to be rural residents of Kansas, and the popular equating of the Alliance with the People's party led to the formation of a new organization composed of these sympathetic town-dwellers.[60] Although begun only at about the time of the formation of the People's party, the Citizens' Alliance, a supplementary movement to the Farmers' Alliance, had 10,000 members when it met in Topeka August 12, 1890, to create a state organization. Delegations were sent from Johnson, Kingman, Chase, Shawnee, McPherson, Wyandotte, Jewell, Pottawatomie, Phillips, Lyon, Logan, and Osage counties. J. F. Willits, the chairman of the Populist state central committee, assisted with the organization of the convention. Delegates from the Citizens' Alliance were admitted to the nominating convention of the People's party the following day in Topeka.[61]

Willits called the state nominating convention to order in the morning. There were 250 delegates from the Farmers' Alliance, Citizens' Alliance, Union Labor party, Knights of Labor, and other groups present. Most were farmers. Mary Elizabeth Lease of Wichita spoke to the convention for half an hour urging both prohibitionists and resubmissionists to unite "to stamp out this unhealthy monster, the money power. Forget party affiliations of the past, forget moral issues of the present, in this great struggle for our homes. Let the old political parties know that the raid is over and that monopolists, trusts and combines shall be relegated to hades."[62]

Despite this plea the convention was something "less than harmonious."[63] Elements of the radical prohibitionist, woman's suffragist, nonfusionist, and Greenback persuasion on one side were arrayed against the more moderate and practical group on the other. In general, the moderate viewpoint had been adopted in regard to the platform — the prohibition question had been sidestepped — but the

Alliance doctrine that the office should seek the man and not the converse stopped the attempt to nominate the well-known and popular former governor Charles Robinson of Lawrence who publicly called for resubmission. Although he apparently had done nothing other than indicate that he would accept the nomination were it offered, his candidacy had been promoted since late spring by the non-Republican elements of the press as the logical gubernatorial choice of the new party, and this was enough to defeat his chances at the August convention.

It was widely known that the Democrats would nominate Robinson for governor, and the radical nonfusionists objected to surrendering "bag and baggage to the democrats"[64] and were "determined to go it alone and avoid all bargaining."[65] The growing sentiment against Robinson because of his strong antiprohibition views guaranteed the nomination of Willits, a prohibitionist, for governor, for there was "no definite strength worked up for any other person for any . . . office."[66] The nomination of Willits, a former Republican farmer, destroyed the possibility of statewide fusion with the Democrats against the Republicans as well as the hope for the support of the Germans.[67]

In addition to Willits, the Populist ticket included A. C. Shinn, a farmer of Franklin County, for lieutenant governor; Capt. R. S. Osborn, a farmer of Rooks County, for secretary of state; W. H. Biddle, a Butler County farmer, for state treasurer; the Reverend B. F. Foster, pastor of the African Methodist Episcopal Church of Topeka, for auditor; Fannie McCormick, a schoolteacher of Barton County, for superintendent of schools; John N. Ives for attorney general; and W. F. Rightmire for chief justice.

The ticket was not particularly strong; the nominees were not well known, one having lived in the state less than a year. A measure of their obscurity was given in a short newspaper article reporting on the nominating convention; the name of John Willits—the head of the ticket—was given as Willetts, Willet, and Willets: three different spellings in one article and not even one of them correct.[68] The *Emporia Republican,* in like manner, corrupted Rightmire into Wrightman.[69] The candidates, moreover, were to demonstrate an inability to create a following and to conduct an effective campaign.

It is significant to note that not one of these 1890 candidates led the Populists in subsequent campaigns.

As the campaign moved through late summer the other parties began to pick up their own tempo. The third-party Prohibitionists had held their state convention in McPherson on July 5, 1890. They denounced the resubmission movement as "a scheme of the brewers" and called for rigid enforcement of the prohibitory laws. It had been expected that this year the Prohibitionists would endorse the ticket of the officially dry Republican party, but the convention, to the chagrin of the Republicans, nominated a full ticket, headed by the Reverend A. M. Richardson and Prof. E. Leonardson.[70]

When the Republican state convention met in Topeka in early September, virtually the same state ticket that had carried Kansas by 80,000 votes only two years previously was renominated. Gov. Lyman U. Humphrey of Independence, Lt. Gov. A. J. Felt of Seneca, Secretary of State William Higgins of Topeka, Attorney General L. B. Kellogg of Emporia, Chief Justice Albert H. Horton of Atchison, and Superintendent of Public Instruction G. W. Winans of Junction City were renominated by acclamation, an action that did not surprise Humphrey.[71] It took another day to nominate C. M. Hovey of Thomas County for auditor, and S. G. Stover of Republic County was not nominated for state treasurer until after a long and hard struggle.

By this time the Republican congressional candidates had already been nominated in their districts. The Sixth District convention met at Colby to nominate Webb McNall and, on August 5, the Republican delegates of the Second Congressional District met in Kansas City and unanimously renominated E. H. Funston for Congress while endorsing the reelection of Senator Ingalls.[72] The other districts nominated Case Broderick (First), Bishop Perkins (Third), Harrison Kelley (Fourth), William Phillips (Fifth), and J. R. Hollowell (Seventh).

The Democratic state convention was held in Wichita on September 9, 1890, and the resubmission Republicans, meeting simultaneously, joined with the Democrats in a coalition ticket described by the Republican press as a "conglomeration of disgruntled politicians."[73] The ticket included John Ives as the nominee for attorney general, but this was the only instance of fusion with the Populists on the state level. As expected, Charles Robinson of Lawrence headed the ticket as the nominee for governor. The Democrats selected candidates for only four congressional districts—Thomas Moonlight (First), J. B. Chapman (Second), P. S. Warren (Fifth), and Tully Scott (Sixth)—but had high hopes of electing some of them as well as their gubernatorial candidate. For county offices and especially for members of the state legislature the Democrats made no nominations in most counties or else publicly supported the candidates of the People's party.[74]

The platforms of the three major parties were substantially the same, for the Republicans drafted a platform nearly as radical on economic issues as that of the Populists.[75] The principal differences occurred over prohibition and John J. Ingalls. The Populists side-stepped the question of prohibition, the Republicans endorsed prohibition, and the Democrats called for resubmission. The Republicans commended the work of Ingalls in the Senate and endorsed his reelection. The Democratic platform asked Kansas to repudiate at the polls the Ingalls who had denounced reform in politics as an "iridescent dream." A principal demand of the Populists, too, was the removal of the hated Ingalls from the U. S. Senate. Despite the surface similarities in the rest of the three platforms, "everyone knew which was the radical party and which party was tied to the Harrison administration and the old guard."[76]

The party lines and campaign tactics were founded on three principal issues. The Democrats revived their old issue of resubmission of the constitutional amendment on prohibition and counted on the personal popularity of Robinson. The Republicans in "a stodginess born of fear" reverted to the tariff and the waving-of-the-bloody-shirt type of campaign in an effort to split the opposition. The Populists struck hard with the appeal of their threefold economic position on land, transportation, and money and turned aside only slightly to denounce Ingalls.

The specific strategy of the Populists seems to have been to get out the large crowd by any means and then harangue it with such speakers as "Sockless Jerry" and "Mary Yellin'." Not uncommonly, speakers from outside Kansas were brought in through the influence of the Farmers' Alliance. Ben Terrell of Texas and Ralph Beaumont of New York addressed in July what was probably "the largest crowd ever assembled in [Marion] county" despite the fact the Alliance meeting was held during a rainstorm.[77]

Perhaps the most famous of these outside speakers was L. L. Polk, the president of the national Farmers' Alliance. He came from North Carolina to Kansas to campaign for the Populist party in the summer and stayed through the autumn. The production in Emporia in early July was typical of a meeting at which Polk spoke. The *Emporia Republican* reported that the Farmers' Alliance and "kindred organizations" staged one of the grandest demonstrations ever seen in Emporia. L. L. Polk delivered a speech to 20,000 people; the streets were literally blockaded. Never before had such a turnout been witnessed in the area. Bands and banners were present and prominent. A parade five miles long was held with the best position to watch being the rooftops: "When the head of the procession was under the equator the tail was coming around the north pole."[78]

Another favorite practice was to hold a picnic or fair. These activities continued well into the fall to keep up the interest of the farmers. An Alliance picnic was held in Salina on September 29, 1890. A 600-team procession led the way to Oakdale Park where Willits, Rightmire, and Davis spoke. About 5,000 men, women, and children were present and many carried banners and signs "throwing slurs" on Ingalls, Humphrey, and others. Popular songs rewritten with Alliance words stimulated "crowd participation."[79]

At such meetings Ingalls was the most obvious target of the Populist speakers. After "savagely" attacking the senator verbally at Beloit, Annie L. Diggs concluded that "I do not speak of John J. Ingalls in a personal manner; I will not deal in personalities. I regard John J. Ingalls as I do Washington, Lincoln or — Benedict Arnold."[80]

Another characteristic of the Populists' campaign was hard work; they left the post first and ran hard all the way. W. F. Rightmire, the Populist candidate for chief justice, delivered his 187th speech of the campaign in Atchison on election eve.[81]

The planning of the People's party was not in vain. *Cosmopolitan Magazine* reported that all the trained "stump speakers" were lecturing for the old parties, but on the old party issues and to small crowds; the farmers, mechanics, and laborers met by the thousands to hear the "new gospel" taught and to discuss the new and pressing issues.[82] The rabble-rousing speakers were most in demand, and their styles were always a favorite topic of the *Topeka Daily Capital:* L. L. Polk "threatened," Mary Lease "raved," and Jerry Simpson "ranted."

In forcing the fight from the beginning, the Populists surprisingly had an efficient party press. Many country editors enthusiastically supported the new party, and others, in all likelihood, had to follow suit to retain their subscribers. The following practice was not uncommon: "The Butler County Alliance has passed a resolution refusing to patronize any and all papers that do not support the principles of the Farmers' Alliance in their editorial columns. Other Alliances are doing the same and demanding that the home papers come out on the side of right instead of party."[83] If a party paper were lacking in an area, it cost little to establish one at the time if a few hundred subscribers and some advertising patronage could be found. Thus as late as September, the *Alliance Gazette* of Hutchinson and the *Farmers' Vindicator* of Valley Falls issued volume 1, number 1.

The newspapers were an integral part of the Republican campaign also. Earlier, many Republican papers had been sympathetic to the Alliance and its demands for reform, but after the movement took political form in the Populist party these papers rapidly changed their positions. The *Chase County Leader* of Cottonwood Falls even declared, "There is not only a difference between the Farmers' Alliance and the People's party, but in principle they are antagonistic" (October 16, 1890).[84] As the campaign approached its climax, it became increasingly bitter. The *Topeka Daily Capital,* strongly anti-Populist, denounced L. L. Polk after he gave the quasi endorsement of the national Farmers' Alliance to the Populist political movement. Under the editorial headline "Who Is Polk?" appearing daily, the paper answered that he was the chief of the "calamity howlers," an outsider who had come to Kansas to dictate to the inhabitants of the state. Making the old-soldier campaign pitch that had always before proved so effective, the *Capital* pictured Polk as a former officer in the Confederacy during the Civil War.[85] The *Fort*

Scott Daily Monitor chimed in with the assertion that "Mr. Polk has the distinguished honor . . . of having murdered in cold blood a number of [unarmed Union] prisoners of war."[86]

Earlier the *Monitor* had reprinted with approval an editorial of the *Emporia Republican:* "Lyman U. Humphrey is the only one of the several candidates for governor of Kansas who went to the defense of his country in the hour of its peril. The others were all old enough, but for some reason they did not answer the call. . . . The old soldier[s] will march to the polls in November in solid phalanx and cast their ballots for Comrade Humphrey regardless alike of party and party issues."[87]

An important element in the use of the Republican press was a bitter and dirty newspaper attack against Willits shortly before the election. Republicans claimed that records and affidavits of Jefferson County District Court and a Mrs. Lincicum, Willits's sister, showed that the Populist candidate for governor was a perjurer, swindler, confidence man, defaulter, and "personally dishonest and corrupt" and "controlled by selfish greed."[88]

The Republican newspapers also devoted time to the Democratic opposition although, realizing the true opposition had become the Populists, the news attack on the Democracy was not as extensive as that on the People's party. There was an attempt in the last week of the campaign to associate the Democrats and resubmissionists with the National Liquor Dealers Association in an effort to buy votes. The hope of the Democrats, a news release said, was in boodle and the divisive effect of the Farmers' Alliance. The conclusion, however, was that the attempt "to buy Kansas" would fail, for money could not buy people of principle and, moreover, the Alliance was a success only so long as it remained a social organization.[89]

The political campaign proper of the Republicans was planned by the state central committee meeting in Topeka on September 12, 1890. The program for the state campaign was devised to open in each of the seven congressional districts on September 20, 1890, when each of the candidates delivered a speech. Attorney General Kellogg was in Holton; Lieutenant Governor Felt in Fort Scott; Higgins, Hovey, and Humphrey in Eureka; Webb McNall in Logan; and J. R. Burton in

Hutchinson. The committee arranged speaking engagements ten days in advance, beginning with about thirty speakers slated to talk.

The Republicans, too, welcomed speakers from outside the state. Pres. Benjamin Harrison arrived in Atchison on October 10, 1890. Governor Humphrey and Chief Justice Horton served as the president's escort from St. Joseph to Topeka. In Atchison, Harrison spoke from the train, expressing his pleasure to be at last in Kansas and in the home of the distinguished Senator Ingalls. Brief stops were made at Nortonville and Valley Falls before the campaign train reached Topeka. In Topeka Harrison spoke to 20,000 people and reviewed a parade of 7,000 soldiers. The Republican press sought to make political hay by inflating the figures to 75,000 and 30,000.[90] Ingalls accompanied the president, and the same article described him as "quite as much the object of popular ovation as the president." A second news release from Topeka declared that the Republican campaign had ceased in the past week so that their candidates and speakers could attend the grand reunion of old Union soldiers in Topeka. With the bloody shirt waving wildly, it noted that Willits and Robinson were conspicuously absent. "They probably felt that they had no business there, having quietly folded their arms during the 'late unpleasantness' and remained at home, although it is a well known fact that both were in perfect health and of suitable age." Doubtless, the report concluded, neither had any sympathy with such reunions, either.[91]

The presidential train moved through Lecompton, Lawrence, and Kansas City before leaving the state. Ingalls then undertook a whirlwind campaign through Kansas in the closing days of the campaign. He spoke in Ottawa on October 21, 1890, Pittsburg on October 22, Hutchinson on October 23, Salina on October 27, Clay Center on October 28, Beloit on October 29, and Fort Scott on November 1. Senator Plumb, "a power on the stump," arrived in Kansas on October 22, and the Republican state central committee, waiting for his arrival "with considerable impatience," had already scheduled him for several speeches. He was to provide fresh energy to the Republican campaign at this important stage.[92]

All three parties forecast victory for their gubernatorial candidates in the last week of October. Chairman Chase of the People's party estimated after a careful poll that Willits would receive 107,000 votes. Republican chairman William Buchan reported a "wonderful change" in favor of his party since the publication of "Willits' record." He estimated Humphrey's plurality as at least 30,000 votes.[93]

Two days later the *Chicago Tribune's* special from Topeka proclaimed that "the reelection of Senator John J. Ingalls is a foregone conclusion." Of the forty state senators, all holdovers, thirty-nine were Republicans. Of the 125 members of the lower house to be elected, the Republicans needed to elect only forty-four to ensure Ingalls's reelection. The Republicans, wrote the *Tribune,* were claiming sixty-five and were certain of fifty. To defeat Ingalls the opposition would have to elect eighty-two members of the house and unite behind another candidate. Such a result did not seem to be among the possibilities.[94]

The Republicans expressed optimism, and even the late withdrawal of Tully Scott did not greatly dampen their spirits. Scott, the Democratic candidate for Congress from the Sixth District, considered his election an impossibility and withdrew so as not to hurt the chances of the Populist Baker against Republican McNall.[95]

"The election in Kansas has been a Waterloo to the Republican party." So wrote the *Kansas City Star* on Wednesday, November 5, 1890. Even the *Topeka Daily Capital,* after having predicted an overwhelming Republican victory, was forced to admit that "the landslide has slid."[96] The Democrats had already conceded Robinson's defeat and the election of Willits. Apparently three and perhaps five Populist congressmen had been elected, and the Republicans clearly would not elect more than thirty legislators. Plumb's own county of Lyon had been carried by the Populists with a 380-vote majority.

The Republicans staggered under the blows of such headlines and were only slightly relieved when the final results at last trickled in on November 19, 1890. The Republicans, in fact, did reelect their state ticket with the exception of Attorney General Kellogg, but their 80,000 vote plurality of just two years earlier was down to barely one-tenth of that figure.

The People's party had become the other major party in Kansas, doubling the vote of the Democrats and nearly matching that of the Republicans. On its own it might have elected three or four congressmen and a strong faction in the lower house of the Kansas legislature. When joined with the Democrats, however, it swept all before it. John Ives, their joint candidate for attorney general, was elected by 48,000 votes even though Kellogg led the Republican ticket. The rest of the Populist state ticket lost by from 5,000 to 9,000 votes. Five congressmen were elected: Clover (Third District), Otis (Fourth), Davis (Fifth), Baker (Sixth), and Simpson (Seventh). The People's party elected ninety-one members of the legislature, the Republicans twenty-six, and the Democrats eight. The imminent retirement of Ingalls was ensured, and his successor was to be none other than William A. Peffer of Topeka.

Peffer himself wrote that "the political complexion of the State was changed in six months to the extent of 100,000 votes."[97] Had the Populists nominated the well-known Robinson rather than Willits, it is likely that they would have captured the governor's mansion. Robinson ran ahead of his party by more than 15,000 votes; Willits ran about 9,000 votes behind his party and only 8,000 behind Humphrey.

The labor counties in southeast Kansas and elsewhere strongly supported the Populists, but the greatest strength of the new party was in the central counties of the state, "where mortgage pressure and Alliance activity were greatest."[98] Because of the close agreement between Populist vote and Alliance membership — 200 of the 521 delegates in the first People's party state convention were old soldiers — the tariff and bloody shirt had lost some of their appeal as campaign issues. Straightforward economic issues appeared quite likely to dominate Kansas politics in the near future.

Many of the Populists talked only of the 90 percent drop in the Republican margin of victory. The more thoughtful reviewed the results of the gubernatorial race. They also saw that fusion congressional candidates had won while Republican candidates received pluralities in the three-ticket districts. The inducements to and advantages of fusion became increasingly obvious to the leaders of both the Democrats and the Populists. The lessons learned in this initial foray into Kansas politics were to come to fruition in the future battle plan of the People's party.

3

PENTECOSTAL POLITICS IN KANSAS: RELIGION, THE FARMERS' ALLIANCE, AND THE GOSPEL OF POPULISM

Students of Kansas Populism have often characterized it as a political movement marked by behavior common to emotional religion. But, as though this were an incidental but requisite obeisance, they have largely neglected any deeper consideration of the subject in their haste to judge whether the farmers were revolting against real or imagined grievances. Yet in this gap between economic conditions and religious behavior lies the key to understanding Kansas Populism, for it was not only a movement of religious people but a religious movement of people.

The act of migration to Kansas shattered the pattern of social relationships that had previously ordered the lives of the new settlers, and most sought to reestablish a social structure that would allow a satisfactory life.[1] Kansas weather, allied with the difficulties of adapting to new crops, techniques, machinery, and work patterns, made the time of settlement in central and western Kansas a transitional period of acute importance. The collapse of the economic boom and the crop failures of the late 1880s and 1890s complicated the process of adjustment. Many recent settlers left the state; but many more remained, in a precarious situation made more critical by debts incurred during the expansive days of the boom, the lack of experience to cope with prevailing conditions, and the absence of any institutional arrangements to effectively aid the social and material maintenance of a discontented people.

On earlier frontiers, organized religion served to facilitate adjustment to new conditions and to aid in the reestablishment of a former society.[2]

In Kansas in the 1880s and 1890s, however, religion failed to fulfill its social role and for many did not respond to its religious role. The churches, failing to develop during the plush boom years, entered a period of retrenchment with the onset of hard times, leaving many Kansans without religious service or solace. James Malin has observed that after the collapse of the boom, "the emotional defense of a disillusioned and nearly desperate people alternated between religion and politics; . . . but in the nineties it settled down to politics pretty much all the year round."[3] The Alliance or Populist politics of the 1890s, however, was a religio-political movement, not only involving demands for major reform but also offering a functional alternative to the missing religious activity. And much of the religious aspect of Kansas Populism can be understood only as a response to the perceived role of organized religion in the crisis of depression and drought.

That the churches recognized their ideal role seems clear. A Kansas minister reported in 1895 that "in case of crop-failure, destructive fires, or monetary troubles, the minister is in demand. He is expected to visit the victims of these disasters with sympathy in his heart, words of comfort on his lips, and means of relief in his hands."[4] It is equally clear, however, that neither ministers nor churches satisfied that expected role. And nowhere have this failure and the reasons for it been expressed more vividly than by a Kansas Presbyterian in 1892: "I have made many long and laborious trips into 'waste places,'" wrote the Reverend S. B. Fleming. "My heart has sunk within me as I have visited the famishing and destitute regions and heard the calls of the people and witnessed their tears, desiring the gospel for themselves and their children, and yet, because of their poverty and the embarrassed state of the [Presbyterian] Board [of Home Missions], I have been compelled to say 'nay.'"[5]

The collapse of prosperity greatly reduced the treasury of the established churches and seriously restricted the work of all denominations. Retrenchment became the order of the day for all church activities in central and western Kansas, including church construction, Sunday school work, and especially missionary services.[6] The Episcopalians instructed their general missionary to "hold the strategic points, and not waste . . . effort on impossible things"; the Presbyterians emphasized "maintaining" their position rather than engaging in active work among the unchurched; the Congregationalists devoted their efforts "to saving the churches" then existing. One minister later explained that the policy was "to sustain hopeful enterprises only," which apparently meant those fields that least needed support, and conceded that "a few churches were allowed to 'die to the glory of God.'" Another clergyman phrased it less euphemistically when he admitted that "39 [Congregational] churches disappeared . . . and 45 ministers fled."[7]

Missionary organizations uniformly reported the disastrous effects of the retrenchment program in the abandonment of churches and the discouragement of the neglected settlers. All religious denominations recorded the denial of endless requests for assistance while admitting that the people were thereby distressed, being without other hope.[8] It was this further discouragement after the onset of material difficulties that disturbed many Kansans, one of whom declared that it was precisely in "such trying circumstances [that] the people all the more need the Gospel, and ought to have the sympathy and help of their abler brethren." Yet a typical clerical response was that of the Episcopalian missionary who acknowledged that he served "a loving, devoted people" but who then discontinued his services because they could not pay his expenses.[9]

The churches further neglected the rural regions because of their policy of "overlapping" as well as "overlooking."[10] Withdrawing their support from the country churches, the religious organizations concentrated their decreased resources in the towns and cities of the state. Served by several competing denominations, these localities witnessed sectarian rivalry that resulted in duplicating churches and wasting clergy, while much of the countryside, left without organized religion, begged unsuccessfully for attention. A Congregational missionary revealed the significance of church competition in the towns: "When I was commissioned and called to this place," he wrote, "I expected to only spend half my time in Longton, for the M. E. only had service every alternate Sunday and I was to fill in the vacant Sunday. But ten days after my arrival here the Presiding Elder of the M. E. Church instructed the pastor to preach every Sunday, so that forced me to the same measure which has kept me from going out to the [rural] school houses to preach."[11]

Thus, not only did the major denominations dissolve their rural churches, but the traveling missionary increasingly restricted himself to the towns. It is hardly surprising, then, that the optimistic accounts of the mid-1880s gave way by the early 1890s to ministerial reports that "there is no more churchless . . . class than a large portion of the rural population."[12] The religious revivals so common in the early days of the bust and depression became much less frequent and were confined more to the major towns and cities.

The *Home Mission Monthly* summarized in 1891 the social consequences of organized religion's general response to hard times in Kansas: "Churches were in large numbers left pastorless, and needy, promising fields had to be abandoned. The results were dissatisfaction and depression, unfriendly criticism and divided counsels." Such "unfriendly criticism" should not have surprised religious leaders, for "in times of commercial distress, as in all other distress," explained a Lawrence minister, "people turn to the church for spiritual strength and consolation."[13] Rural Kansans had indeed turned to the churches for solace and support, but they had been rebuffed when they were unable to pay the institutional costs. No longer relevant to their needs, the churches and ministers remained in the cities, not heeding the call of the rural faithful.

In short, the reaction of institutional Christianity to events in Kansas in the late 1880s and early 1890s was to concern itself with money, not suffering, and with church organizations, not people.[14] Not until the mid-1890s did some church leaders begin even imperfectly to realize the connection they had made between money and religion, the requirement of material ability to receive spiritual assistance.[15] This corruption of the true spirit of Christianity implicit in the actions of organized religion disappointed and angered many Kansans. "Manfully acknowledge that the Presbyterian Church has lost interest in the great cause of extending the Redeemer's Kingdom in our country, and refuses to listen to the *pitiable cry* for the gospel, in all our destitute regions, if we are to judge by the indifference with which these calls are received," cried one Kansas missionary. "The need is as great as ever, nay, greater; and if we cannot as a Church do our part, let us yield to those who will."[16] Though the churches vigorously refused to yield in theory, in practice another organization arose to fill the vacuum, and rural Kansans turned to accept what a major leader of Kansas Populism called "the new gospel."[17]

The Farmers' Alliance entered Kansas shortly after the collapse of the boom of the 1880s. A recent historian has described the appeal of this organization as "a messianic call to economic redemption," but the redemptive properties of the Alliance were not limited to economics.[18] Regardless of any original intentions, the Alliance filled the social and religious void bequeathed to the farming classes by the indifferent and remote churches. And while the neighborhood subordinate alliances functioned on the local level as religious substitutes for the absent or detached churches, the broader movement that grew out of the Alliance, the People's party, made an outspoken and far-reaching attack on the evils that it saw corrupting Christian civilization and oppressing Christian life.

Structurally and functionally the Farmers' Alliance resembled the church in Kansas. An Alliance lecturer reported that the Kansas Alliance was "semi-religious, for every member must be 'a believer in the existence of a Supreme Being,' and all the meetings are opened and closed with prayer"; but this far from exhausted what Alliancewoman Annie Diggs called the "religious tone" of the organization. There were chaplains, though any member could and often would lead prayers in the meetings of the suballiances. Hymns formed a major part of the weekly meetings. Contributions to the Alliance were equated with donations to missionary organizations. Common religious terms were used to describe activities. Organizers had to pass examinations and receive commissions. Suballiances were especially concerned to provide rites of passage for their members, a necessarily religious function. There was a burial service, provisions for the care of orphans and widows, an obligation "to care for the sick and to aid the needy."[19]

William A. Peffer, a somewhat practical mystic who led the Alliance to its greatest success and emerged as one of the first national figures of Populism, indicated the relationship between the Alliance and religion in his writings. In 1891 he described the Alliance in precisely the same words that he had used earlier in envisioning the perfect religion. Speaking of the suballiances, Peffer also declared that "these meetings to a large extent, and in many instances wholly, take the place of churches in the religious enjoyment of the people." The farmers avoided the churches because of poverty and because they were made to feel uncomfortable, Peffer claimed; but at the Alliance meetings "here in these neighborhood assemblies . . . out where the pure air of heaven sweeps over the fields, they meet together upon a plane of perfect equality" and "the highest form of devotional feeling is manifested throughout all the exercises," with all discussion "based upon the fundamental idea which angels sang to shepherds when the Babe of Bethlehem was born."[20]

The Alliance in practice counterbalanced the decline of the Sunday schools by establishing Juvenile Alliances for the children of its members. Benjamin Clover, Alliance state president, explained that "lessons and teachings" would educate the children in the doctrines of the Alliance "to the end that our children may not go out into the world . . . ignorant of the true principles."[21] Alliance women organized their own society to promote the Decalogue and the Golden Rule in politics and to encourage their husbands to act in the cause of their families and their God.[22]

More important than these practical similarities in ritual and structure between churches and Alliances were the broad, sociologically defined, religious functions that the latter served: the integration of the individual with his fellows, the interpretation of events, and the reinforcement of the values of the group.[23] One observer recognized the role of the Alliance in all three areas when he reported that in that organization "some good will be accomplished socially and [in] developing an intelligent inquiry, also to disseminate and propagate the broad principle of the Brotherhood of man."[24]

In the atmosphere of uncertainty, social isolation, and disorganization, the Alliance achieved spectacular success in its integrative function. The *Kensington Mirror* declared that the Alliance in Smith County had "made warm friends of the hitherto rather distant citizens of a neighborhood," and the *Great Bend Democrat* praised the Alliance for allaying "personal animosity between country people." A reporter attending an Alliance picnic perceived a hopeful new spirit among the farmers present: "They address each other as Brother" as they put aside old prejudices to "unite in one common cause" that "will do much towards improving their condition." A sympathetic minister summed it up when he declared that "the true Christian spirit of truth and fraternity, with charity to all, has been developed by the Alliance."[25]

More important, the Alliance mastered the role of interpreting events for its members. Nearly every county maintained an Alliance

newspaper and each of the neighborhood suballiances had its own lecturer, who regularly received literature from the county and state lecturers. Commissioned organizers and itinerant lecturers also served to
provide the discouraged farmers with a rationale for action, a reassurance that their plight resulted from external forces, whether Wall
Street bankers or corrupt legislators in Washington. S. M. Scott, the
"champion organizer" of the Kansas Alliance, disclosed the significance of the interpretive function when he described the inability of
the farmers to focus their discontent before the arrival of the Alliance:
"There seemed to be a disposition on their part to move in some direction, [but] what that direction was they were unable to determine. . . .
They seemed to be going to and fro," he continued, "with apparently
no object in view, only waiting for some theory to be offered to which
they could rally . . . as a common people." The Alliance principles,
Scott found, were quickly accepted "as the first step to the goal for
which they so earnestly hoped."[26]

Those principles provided support for what has since become
known as the agrarian myth. At a time when traditional values ex-
alting the agrarian way of life were being increasingly undermined
in the larger society, when the impersonal price and market system
made the unorganized farmers mere ciphers, when the vagaries of
the weather combined with unsuitable crops actually made life uncertain, through the myth the Alliance reaffirmed the psychologically necessary and meaningful self-images for its members, uphold-
ing the ultimate dignity and importance of the believers, whatever
their status. The agrarian myth reestablished the integrity of their
existence and reasserted in ritual and symbol the essential morality
of their world. Scott declared that with the arrival of the Alliance,
"once more the farmer is proud of his calling."[27]

This was the essential appeal of the Alliance and of Populism to
the Kansas farmers. The situation of being permanently underprivi-
leged was to be replaced with a putative society in the Kingdom of
God where those who followed "the primal mandate—'replenish the
earth and subdue it'"—would be the elite. Denying the world, which
withheld its benefits from them, they awaited its destruction "in a
cosmic cataclysm" that would exalt them and cast down the rich and
powerful. Thus the Alliance members gathered in open fields and
groves ("God's first temples") to sing "the Kingdom of Mammon

shall fall" and to assert that "God hears the cry of the millions / Who labor and toil, who have reaped down the grain, / Their cries saith the Lord of the Sabbath, / Shall not go unheeded, shall not be in vain." And as the Alliance moved to bring about the new world, its state president professed to recognize the coming of "that rejoicing day" when the lame would walk. Frank McGrath then thundered the conclusion: "Then will we be able to say: 'we were hungry, and ye took our bread;' 'we were naked, and ye would not allow us to clothe ourselves,' 'we were sick, but you would not administer to our ailments.' But for all these things, God and not we, will bring you to judgment."[28]

Originally the Farmers' Alliance hoped to work through existing political parties in its attempt to reform society, each member being "a missionary in his own party to spread Alliance doctrines there."[29] As the difficulties of such an approach became clear, the third-party movement gathered strength; and the transition began, as Annie Diggs recalled, when Alliancemen in central Kansas met in Hill City, refused admittance to "unsanctified outsiders, took up the pass word from the brethren and proceeded to nominate William Baker, one of their very own, a tiller of the soil, a non-politician, for their representative to Congress." And what Scott termed "our most sacred order" evolved into "this *Great People's Movement*" to destroy the evils tyrannizing Christian life—a crusading force with its own message.[30]

The Gospel of Populism as propounded by its Kansas advocates derived from the clash between the prevailing practices and values of American society and the ethics of the Christian gospel. Believing that religion, law, and industrial capitalism were ignoring the interests of the American masses, they feared for the continuation of the Republic and ultimately for the preservation of Christian civilization. They demanded the application of the gospel of Christ to existing economic and social conditions to solve the problems of poverty, waste, inadequate distribution, unemployment, and the injustices within the structure of American society. The elemental objective for the leaders of Kansas Populism was the achievement of a correspondence between society and Christianity and of the practical recognition of the fatherhood of God and the brotherhood of man.

The lecturer of the suballiance at Clinton sketched the Populist apprehension of the course of American history: The unjust economic system grinds down the poor while enriching the manufacturers, who become tyrannical and greedy. The poor become hopeless and turn to violence. The frightened rich require the military to suppress the poor. The military chieftain becomes dictator, "and the republic is dead." A. Hollingsworth then put his "honest heart-felt prayer" into words: "May God help this alliance of the American farmers to stop injustice before . . . it will be too late." And as men would not comply with the "law of God without being made to do it," the role of the Alliance/Populists was "to make them do it."[31]

That the nation was not complying with "the law of God" was plain to all Populists. Garnett's *Kansas Agitator* explained that Christ fed the hungry, healed the sick, and clothed the naked, but the nation ignored his example. Others asserted that the courts and the clergy "have been silent to the cry of the weak and unprotected and hence they have been devoured," and they condemned the course of American industrialization and its pernicious consequences as unchristian and immoral. They saw that the nation had solved the problem of production but, in its "denial of Righteousness," had failed to provide *"equitable distribution."* Declaring that money and land monopoly were "the two sins expressly forbidden" by God, Populists felt that their existence in America was "bringing a curse upon the land." "In the economy of God," one Populist announced, "there is no room for a *usurer or a landlord.*"[32]

Though Kansas Populists believed that Americans rejected the precepts of Christianity—for "under competitive life they have, like heathen, strove with one another, and preyed upon their neighbor"—most expected that the introduction of "the ethics of Christ" into political society would correct social and economic iniquities. They foresaw eventual relief because "a just God sits in Heaven," and accepting the continued relevance of "the prophets and apostles," they cited the Bible as providing the necessary guide for social action. The followers of the People's party were to "act the part of missionaries" to restore Christianity to society and thus "right any wrong." The solution for society's problems involved the triumph of Populist policies, so that both the government and the economy would be in the hands of the people and Christianity would finally prevail.[33]

Kansas Populist congressman John Davis stated the Gospel of Populism most succinctly when he declared that "the battle is between

God's people and the worshippers of the golden calf."[34] The struggle was indeed between the faithful and the forces that had corrupted America and threatened the maintenance of the nation. Thus, deeming Christianity to be the basis of their civilization, in God's name the Populists entered the political arena with practical proposals to reform the system.

S. B. Bloomfield, a Populist nominee for Congress, disclosed the relationship between the practical side of the Populist Gospel and its overriding religiosity: "This populist movement which appeals to individual men to correct the wrongs of tyrannical government, is the voice of God preparing the people for the coming of Christ's Kingdom, which is shortly to be set on earth, by which the nations and all combines of capital are to be tried and overthrown, and justice and equity to be set up, through a glorious restitution of all things. A millennium of human glory to which all reformers have pointed."[35]

So believing, Kansas Populists, once they entered political office, sought to align the government and the economy with Christian dictates. Populist advocates likened the cause of free silver and fiat money to Christianity and opposed Grover Cleveland's financial policy in order to save "Christian civilization." They attacked the tariff as "contrary to the fundamental principles of Christianity," denounced arbitrary or unresponsive government as opposed to "the laws of God," and argued that a graduated income tax would merely "enforce God's law." The enactment of these practical policies was important, not only to alleviate depression and restore prosperity but because it meant, wrote one Populist, "a return to the Christian impulses of our fathers, a repudiation of the alliance with Satan, an end to the daily confession at the shrine of the Golden Calf, and the restoration of, and a new lease of life for the American Republic."[36]

Republicans denounced this Populist program as tending to anarchism and communism, but a Topeka minister, the Reverend Richard Wheatley, recognized an important part of the Gospel of Populism: "The end at which the majority of Populists aim is neither Anarchy, nor Communism, . . . but Christian Socialism."[37] Many Kansas Populists did indeed endorse Christian Socialism, seeing in an "integral commonwealth" based on Christian fraternity the only alternative to the evils of the capitalist system. Successful Populist candidates for both governor and Congress advocated Christian Socialism, and a Populist state supreme court justice less explicitly supported the same position. In a reciprocal action, the official organ of the Society of Christian Socialists urged its members to support both the Alliance and the People's party, and H. C. Vrooman, president of the state organization of Christian Socialists, was a prominent Populist leader. Populism in Kansas also absorbed the Bellamy Nationalists, and one of the state's first Nationalists, John Breidenthal, became the state chairman of the People's party. Ezra Yoder of Paola, a Populist writer and an avowed Christian Socialist, represented all positions when he declared that "there is but one way to govern the world in righteousness and that way will be found in obedience to him who commanded men to 'lay not up for themselves treasures on earth.' "[38]

That the People's party followed the dictates of God, in contradistinction to the old parties, was of course an implicit commandment in the Gospel of Populism and a favorite theme of Populist speakers. An orator declared at a Populist rally, "There is only one party in line with the teachings of God and the best result for the common people, and that is the Populist party." State Senator Michael Senn believed that "the platforms and principles of the People's party are directly in harmony with true religion," and a Populist editor saw the opposition party in Kansas as the "headquarters of Satan." The state central committee of the People's party merely followed the logical extension of such thoughts when it gave its blessing to the organization of a People's Church in Topeka, founded in opposition to orthodox churches and staffed and attended by Populist politicians. Populist congressmen helped to establish another People's Church in the nation's capital and then alternated in delivering sermons there.[39]

Mary Lease fully developed this position. She announced that Populists "have sprung into existence to fulfill the 'mandates of God'" and that their positions rested "upon the basic principles of Christianity." That the bitterness of the Populist attacks on the established parties involved more than a desire for their own establishment, Lease demonstrated in her statement that "the old parties have set up statute laws against the natural rights of man, and thus, through his image, they strike at God." The Populists, she felt, demanded "the enactment into law of the truths taught by Jesus; the truths which must prevail before Christ's kingdom can be established," before "the bondage of Christ's children, the poor and lowly for whom he died, be ended forever." Every true Christian, she reasoned, had to believe in Populist principles, which were "religious as well as political."[40]

Confronted with this religio-political movement that based its proposals on the dictates of God and Christianity, organized religion could not remain silent. However, its strong attack on the Kansas Populists and their charges against the churches could finally only be described as amounting to sectarian bickering.

The Reverend J. G. Dougherty of Kansas City denounced Populism as a "disease of lunatics"—"a kind of insanity of the type melancholia. The victim talks only of losses, threatening evils, great disasters, calamities impending over the nation. Every real evil or loss is greatly magnified by his diseased imagination." Though less complacent, a Topeka minister feared the "great evil" he saw in Populism and its "intense anxiety." Other ministers instructed their congregations to vote Republican and warned of religious perils if the Populists gained control.[41]

Episcopal bishop E. S. Thomas attempted to defend intellectually the existing order that the Kansas Populists attacked, but his position represented only a restatement of the old orthodoxy. He sought to counter the Populist appeal for radical economic reform with his caution that in considering "the interests of society upon its economic side, . . . we must never destroy the rights of property." In 1893 Bishop Thomas combated the increasing interest in Christian Socialism and the Populist emphasis upon social salvation by repeating the older Christian emphasis upon individual salvation. And in opposition to the Populist program for collective solutions to the social ills of the day, the bishop sounded an anachronistic note when he counseled "men and women to bear their own burdens strongly and patiently if they would lift the burden of society."[42]

The missionary organizations also criticized Populism, for they were often in direct competition with the suballiance's Gospel of Populism. The Reverend H. C. Bradbury complained from the center of Populist territory that the people had forsaken religion for political salvation. The superintendent for Congregational Missions felt that the discussion of Populist measures absorbed the "spiritual fire" that "ought to be" involved in traditional religious discussion. The Woman's Board of Missions admitted that political life under a Populist state administration "directly affected the progress of our work" and reported that "we are waiting almost breathlessly for the results" of the 1894 election, which turned the Populists out of office. Other clergymen also lamented that "unusual political agitation" checked missionary work.[43]

Significantly but not surprisingly, those people who needed the true gospel, according to the representatives of organized religion, were those classes most strongly supporting Populism. The description of the "interior farming districts" as indifferent and irreligious replaced the laudatory reports of God-fearing farmers of the previous decade. Anxious for the restoration of the status quo *ante Populismum,* Kansas churchmen sought to replace the fervor for the Gospel of Populism with old-time religion. "The agitating events in Kansas," declared the Reverend L. P. Broad, "are God's object lesson to Christians intended to arouse us to undertake to reach both farmers and [i.e., as well as] town people with the Gospel if we would save all that is dear to us." Broad requested special rural missionaries, particularly to the "destitute," and outlined a policy for social and religious action that paralleled the Alliance movement of the past half decade.[44]

Populist antipathy to organized religion was marked, but leaders made it clear that "it was not Christianity but churchianity" that they attacked.[45] Populists felt that the churches distorted Christ, speaking more often in his name than with his voice. That function of religion which provides a radical criticism of the secular present had been lost, and Populists emphasized the transformative thrust and revolutionary character of early Christianity. As a religion of the socially disinherited, Populism showed a greater awareness of the radical nature of the ethics of the gospel and a stronger opposition to the tendency to compromise with the morality of power than did the established religious structure. Strict censure of the prevailing religious sentiment and institutions, then, was a common but now generally overlooked aspect of the Gospel of Populism.

Populists stressed the biblical injunctions against usury and human indifference and the Christ-like admonitions to help the needy and oppose the wicked; they denounced the church for trying "to make peace with the world, especially if the 'world' is clothed in riches." Demanding that "the church . . . return to the original teachings of the founder of Christianity," Populist leaders attacked ministers and churches for their hypocrisy and sycophancy in condoning usury, corruption, and industrial oppression.[46]

The Populist pamphleteer Percy Daniels provided the most complete exposition of the Populist case against the churches and their religion when he said that the ministers "honor and serve" the parasitic capitalistic classes first "and then Jehovah" and are "high priests of corruption." The nation's religion had become one "made up in mumbling prayers to God, asking Him to prolong our folly; to bless our lust for mammon and our efforts in teaching contented pagans the enervating vices and dubious philosophy of our vaunted culture and our watered and capitalized parody of civilization." This degenerate theology, he continued, "has formed a combine with mammon worship to drive Christianity from the churches, and in many cases the doors of so-called sanctuaries are already closed against the humble followers of the Son of God." It was only in the fields and forests, on the hills and highways, that God held "communion with His loyal children." Daniels concluded that our civilization "is a failure. . . . For us the Tablets of Stone are broken." The nation faced a choice: Either heed the Populists or "cling to these mocking idols till the woe and the prayers of the oppressed invoke the aid of an avenging power."[47]

Though not so comprehensive, the Populist arraignment of the church at the local level was just as unremitting. Alliance lecturers charged city ministers with "servility to the money power"; editors indicted churches for failing to demand social justice and declared that "the church is the subsidized agent of the rich"; and other Populists demanded mass ministerial resignations. Believing in the righteousness of their cause, Kansas Populists felt that clerical opposition to their Christ-like principles indicated more than temporal disagreement—it proved an apostasy "to the teaching of the Divine Master."[48]

A Populist official declared that ministers could not be trusted, for they had been corrupted by greed and incorporated into the "ruling class." Proclaiming that people who still worshiped in

churches were serving "strange gods," he equated the Kansas Populist leaders with the true gospel "ministers of the Lord." A Populist
judge castigated clergymen "who should be fighting His battles
against the hosts of Mammon" for throwing down "His standard"
and deserting to the enemy. Another Populist expressed his exasper-
ation at "the spectacle of the so-called minsters of God preaching
stereotyped sermons in the interest of the Republican party" in
three-fourths of the Kansas churches: In response to poverty, hun-
ger, or unemployment these clergymen always preached, "You must
be temperate." Was it any wonder that when a Populist lecturer assailed the church of God for being corrupted by wealth, he was interrupted by a shout, "Don't call it the church of God, it's the church
of the Devil"?[49]

Kansas Populism, then, involved a great deal more than economic
and political protest. A movement with religious and mystic leaders
and with followers drawn from an evangelical society expressed itself
religiously—a fact often noticed before. But this was a religious expression that rejected prevailing religious sentiments, for organized
religion had failed its responsibilities. Seeking to save, or to reinsti-
tute, Christian civilization, Populist leaders condemned the irrelevant religion of the day and formulated a Gospel of Populism to
change American society to such an extent that political, social, and
industrial relationships would be based on the fatherhood of God
and the brotherhood of man in the spirit, and according to the
teachings, of Jesus Christ.

The eventual failure of Populism resulted from more than the return of good times or "the blare of the bugle" of the Spanish-Ameri-
can War. Also important was the new attitude of the churches in
Kansas toward their responsibilities to the Kansas farmer; and as the
new attitude spread through the churches, new reports of religious
growth seemed to coincide with the decline of Populist zeal and support.[50] The failure of Populism perhaps resulted from discouragement as well; for as the Kansas Populists learned more of the world
beyond their farms and homes, the task they had set for themselves
loomed hopelessly large.

But failure was the element of tragedy in Kansas Populism from
the beginning. "The thousands who assembled under the school-
house lamps," William Allen White later wrote, "believed that when

their Legislature met and their Governor was elected, the millennium would come by proclamation." A sympathetic observer further explained the pathos of Populism: "They propose to do in a few months what God has failed to do in a good many thousand years."[51] And another Kansan provided the epitaph when he wrote that the Farmers' Alliance and the People's party were

> composed generally of honest men. Their original intentions were good. . . . Their conditions were not enviable, they desired to improve them; they aimed too high. They desired to make terrestrial conditions as celestial as circumstances would allow. This was an innocent, even laudable aspiration. Ought we to blame the farmer that his ideas of Heaven were crude? Surely Heaven without lawyers or bankers is not a violent conception. A celestial city composed entirely of farmers may seem to our prejudiced vision a rather dreary abode of the blessed, but the rustic eye views things from a rustic point of view.[52]

4

THE MOST PICTURESQUE DRAMA:
THE KANSAS SENATORIAL ELECTION
OF 1891

In the late nineteenth century, senatorial elections in Kansas were among the more sensational of the nation's political events. The state legislature rather than the general electorate named the U.S. senator, and this arrangement provided opportunities for both venal bargaining and intense melodrama. The senatorial election of Alexander Caldwell in 1871 resulted in congressional investigations and Caldwell's sudden resignation. The defeat of Sen. Samuel C. Pomeroy two years later amid mounting scandal and more investigations attracted such attention and so seemed to demonstrate the corrupt nature of American politics that Mark Twain incorporated it in *The Gilded Age*. John James Ingalls, Pomeroy's successor, entered the Senate under extraordinary circumstances, and his successful bid for reelection in 1879 was disgraced by charges of bribery and corruption and investigated by the U.S. Senate.[1] The most exciting senatorial election, however, occurred when Ingalls sought a fourth term in 1891.

Kansas was enveloped in a deep depression, with the economic distress exacerbated by the political indifference shown by Republican leaders to the state's problems. The 1889 Republican legislators had promised to enact a series of agrarian reform demands designed to alleviate the distress but had callously repudiated their pledges, leaving many farmers convinced that a new party was necessary if they were to have any control over their own political system. Building on the structure of the Farmers' Alliance, a militant agrarian organization, these dissidents created the People's party out of quarreling groups of Republicans, Democrats, Union Laborites, and Prohibitionists, united only by economic hardship and common opposition to continued Republican political hegemony. To mobilize their followers, these Populists seized upon the issue of the reelection of Ingalls, a cold, distant man, insensitive to the psychological if not the physical needs of his fellow Kansans, and a perfect symbol of all that they despised in Republicanism. The Republican party accepted the challenge, and Ingalls found himself the center of what he termed "the most vindictive and passionate campaign of the generation." The new party met with surprising success in the 1890 elections and captured a majority of the legislators, despite the fact that the state senators, all but one Republicans, were not up for election.[2]

National attention now focused on the imminent senatorial election. Reporters and correspondents of many of the country's leading newspapers and magazines crowded into Topeka to cover the senatorial election by the state legislators in January 1891. *Harper's Weekly* explained the remarkable "national attention and interest" attracted by the contest by pointing out those characteristics that made it "more than ordinarily noteworthy": First, Sen. John J. Ingalls was a major political and public figure who "occupies an extraordinary position as President *pro tempore* of the Senate"; second, "Kansas is the State in which the revolution wrought by the Farmers' Alliance is most conspicuous"; third, and "perhaps the most remarkable thing of all," there existed a possibility that the Populist legislators, "notwithstanding their clear majority," would be unable to elect a candidate and that Ingalls might triumph because of factionalism within the People's party.[3] One thing was certain: whoever emerged from the political struggle was assured of national prominence.

Ingalls and his Republican friends exhibited cautious optimism. During the regular campaign the senator had felt it "not improbable that my public career is drawing to its close," but soon after the November election he expressed confidence of his own reelection.[4] William Buchan, the chairman of the Republican state central committee, explained that although the Populist party had a majority of the incoming legislators, "eight out of every ten men elected to the legislature are [or were] Republicans, and there will be a division in the ranks and Mr. Ingalls will be reelected." Congressman Samuel R. Peters and former governor George T. Anthony also predicted that rivalry within the People's party would deliver Ingalls enough votes to win.[5]

Other leading politicians as confidently foresaw a sure defeat for Ingalls. Former governor George Glick assured an anxiously inquiring Grover Cleveland that "Ingalls is now eliminated from our politics." George Innes considered it "safe to bank on Ingalls' retirement," and Tom Fenlon, a Democratic leader of Leavenworth, declared, "I don't see how Ingalls can make it. The farmers have got it and will certainly elect their man." Populist leader William A. Peffer also expressed a judgment against Ingalls's chances but pointed out the weakness of the Populist position: "People's party members are all pledged *against* Ingalls, though not pledged *for* any other man."[6]

It was this lack of unanimity that the Republicans depended on, and Judge Peffer realized it. In fact, as the reform-minded editor of the influential *Kansas Farmer,* Peffer was the leading candidate among the Populists to succeed Ingalls and throughout the campaign had been the only candidate mentioned for the position. Many felt that the party had already implicitly nominated Peffer, first by its action in the state nominating convention when it declared him "the man above all others to fill that position" and then by designating him to face Ingalls in public debate. Republicans generally regarded Peffer as the Populist senatorial candidate and acted accordingly during the campaign.[7] But the expressed campaign preference for Judge Peffer was evidently not binding, and as the possibility of success became greater so did the number of his challengers. Most formidable of these appeared to be John Willits, the defeated Populist candidate for governor. Most Populists believed that Willits had been counted out of the gubernatorial contest, and such leaders as Stephen McLallin, the editor of the *Topeka Advocate,* and S. W. Chase, the People's party state chairman, argued that Willits deserved the senatorial recognition.[8] P. P. Elder, a successful candidate for the legislature, and Democratic gubernatorial candidate Charles Robinson also advanced their claims after the November election, and in the same month at least three others attracted some public support for the position: John H. Rice, a former Fort Scott editor and a vociferous campaigner; James H. Canfield, a professor at the University of Kansas, popular among genteel tariff reformers; and P. B. Maxson, an old-third-party and labor favorite from Emporia.

To ensure Populist solidarity and success, Peffer proposed a three-part plan. He advocated the instruction of Populist legislators by their constituents, the holding of a Populist caucus to prevent a division on the final vote, and the presence in Topeka of as many rank-and-file Populists as possible in order to bolster Populist confidence and to enforce obedience to the caucus decision. Members of all parties believed that Republican managers would bribe and otherwise pressure Populist legislators in order to gain support for Ingalls, and Peffer accordingly issued a warning to the Populists, many unfamiliar with the world of Topeka and its legislative politics, to be wary of strangers and to bring with them to Topeka several "strong men" selected by the party from their district. Republicans derided Peffer as an "old fogy" for this suggestion, but Populists readily assented to it.[9]

In fact, however, the feeling against Ingalls was so intense that Peffer's precautionary suggestions may not have been necessary. One Democrat observed that "it would not be healthy for an alliance man that will vote for Ingalls to face his constituents. They would mob him—the feeling against him among the farmers is bitter." A newspaper reported that the Populist legislator-elect from Montgomery County "has been notified that if he betrays his pledge and votes for Ingalls he had better abandon all idea of returning home." J. D. Hardy, the representative from Brown County, asked his constituents to hang him if he voted for Ingalls, and fiery Mary Elizabeth Lease expressed the wish that "if an alliance representative votes for Ingalls, I pray God I may be permitted to pull the other end of the rope which swings him into eternity."[10]

If Populist legislators could be depended upon not to vote for Ingalls, it was still necessary for them to agree upon one candidate of their own. Many suballiances in December 1890 requested a state delegate convention to meet and settle upon a candidate before the legislature convened, but the policy as evolved followed Peffer's original suggestion: instruction of legislators by local meetings and a demand for a party caucus.

Populist hopefuls spent the remainder of the time before the legislature convened in contending for position. Peffer had three important advantages: recognition as the party's original choice; control of the influential *Kansas Farmer;* and the support of the national Alliance. L. L. Polk of North Carolina, president of the National Farmers' Alliance and Industrial Union, had pledged his support to Peffer during the regular campaign and reaffirmed it in November in an attempt to center Alliance strength before other candidates appeared to create division. Polk's determination to use the influence of the national organization for Peffer stemmed from the former Confederate's appreciation of Peffer's strong support for him during the Populist campaign in Kansas when Republican editors had flogged him with the "bloody shirt"— a political appeal to the animosities and sectional prejudices stemming from the Civil War in an effort to keep dissident Republicans from deserting to the new party.[11] When the Farmers' Alliance elected Willits national lecturer of the order at its annual convention in Ocala, Florida, in early December, it was alleged that Polk had arranged the election "to get Willits out of the way of Judge Peffer for the United States senate."[12]

In response to Peffer's suggestion that the local Alliances and Populist groups instruct their representatives, the *Kansas Farmer* was deluged with endorsements of Peffer. Peffer avoided a declaration of candidacy and announced the *Farmer* open to all candidates, but for weeks the paper printed hundreds of recommendations for Peffer and none for anyone else. The extravagant praise clearly demonstrated Peffer's status among Populists, especially Alliance members, for no one doubted the authenticity of the endorsements. Sarcastic reference to the propriety of claiming impartiality while publishing such material, however, did appear. The *Topeka Capital* found amusing the *Farmer's* assertion that Peffer had neither announced his candidacy nor supported his claims to the office:

It would be interesting to know who it is then that is writing the able editorials in the *Farmer* [indirectly] supporting the Judge's candidacy. The distinction between Judge Peffer in his individual capacity and Judge Peffer in his capacity of editor of the *Farmer* seems to be insisted upon with a seriousness which is somewhat Pickwickian, in view of the fact that so long as the editor of the *Farmer* supports the Judge it makes no particular difference whether the Judge supports himself or not.[13]

Peffer responded to such gibes with the assertion that "resolutions favoring any other man for this position have not, as yet, been received at this office." In January the *Farmer* did begin to publish letters and resolutions supporting other candidates, and not infrequently Peffer added praise of his own for such possibilities as P. P. Elder.[14] In the meantime, Peffer did answer questions about himself and did refute campaign charges against him, but he did not editorially advocate his own election and maintained he was making no active canvass whatever and had not conferred with one legislator on the matter.[15]

The earlier acceptance of Peffer as the party's candidate gave him one of his strongest claims to the position, and many Populists believed the party honor-bound to elect him.[16] But this very prominence made Peffer the target of those who supported Ingalls and those who themselves sought the prize from the Populist legislators.

The Republican press again seized upon the bloody shirt to conceal narrow demands for Ingalls's reelection. The campaign charges against the People's party as an arm of the southern Democracy received impetus with the decision of the Ocala conference to postpone a national third-party movement, thereby apparently restricting the effects of political discontent to the Republican states of the Northwest while the Democratic party continued to profit from the unaffected South. Polk's support of Peffer, moreover, encouraged Republicans to allege that southerners actively manipulated the Kansas Alliance and to direct sectional prejudice against the *Farmer's* editor. The *Manhattan Nationalist* and other rabidly partisan Republican papers even began to charge that Peffer had assisted and defended the Confederacy in various ways during the 1860s. Peffer easily refuted these charges, however, as Congressmen E. N. Morrill and B. W. Perkins had both served with him in the Eighty-third Illinois Infantry, and other more responsible Republican papers denounced such accusations.[17] Indeed, some Republican newspapers, as opposition to Peffer developed within his own party, became frightened at the prospect of the People's party electing a "wild demagogue" and began to support Peffer as the best possible choice of the new party, though they continued to advocate the reelection of Ingalls.[18]

This latter development may have harmed Peffer among his fellow Populists. The disrepute in which Populists held such papers as the *Topeka Capital* because of scurrilous campaign accusations made many suspicious of a man who attracted support from such sources.[19] Already, many Populists objected to Peffer because of his history of Republicanism and his relatively recent conversion to independent political action. The Winfield *American Non-Conformist* believed that "to overthrow Ingalls and elect a nine-months old convert would sound to the world as a very mediocre type of reform." Other longtime third-party men expressed reservations about the permanency of Peffer's loyalty to Populist principles and feared that as senator he would act with Republicans, especially on tariff matters where his reputation as a confirmed protectionist hurt him.[20] These former Union Laborites demanded the selection of one of their own, as a reward for their persistence in the cause of reform, and generally favored either P. P. Elder or John Breidenthal.

Democrats within and without the People's party also feared a latent Republicanism in Peffer and opposed his election. Many Democrats believed that the defeat of Ingalls was vital; "The success of any man be he either Democrat or Alliance is to be eagerly sought for and *fought for*," wrote one, and though a Democratic replacement would be desirable, "we propose to beat him with *any sort of man if we must.*"[21] Other Democrats, however, insisted that if the Populists "want our support they must select a candidate that will at least be unobjectionable," and they warned that Democratic legislators would support neither Peffer nor Willits.[22] Democrats suggested the selection of either Charles Robinson or W. A. Harris. When Democratic and Union Laborite sentiments combined, as in the editorial policy of W. H. T. Wakefield's *Lawrence Jeffersonian,* Peffer was sharply proscribed. But, according to one observer, nearly all Populists of Republican antecedents suffered from "the suspicion that they have too much republican blood in their veins to be up to the wild-and-woolly standard of reform."[23]

One major objection specifically to Peffer involved his age and health. Already nearly sixty years old, he was frail and frequently ill. Indeed, a severe attack of bronchial asthma confined him to bed from December 12, 1890, until January 6, 1891, and two weeks later a sympathetic reporter excused the brevity of one of Peffer's speeches as resulting from "the judge's enfeebled physical condition as he had just risen from a sick bed." This illness also prevented his fulfilling his appointments in December in the special election in the Thirty-second senatorial district.[24] Opponents of Peffer exaggerated his illness, moreover, and brutally predicted his rapid demise if elected senator, adding that Republican Governor Lyman U. Humphrey could then appoint Ingalls to serve out the remainder of the six-year term, making the political reformation short-lived.[25]

Others saw in Peffer's precedence in the senatorial contest evidence that he and others in the party had joined in a ring to control the party and distribute offices to supporters. Mary Lease thought this to be the case but in her characteristic fashion believed that Willits, Peffer's major adversary for the Populist nomination, was a partner. When a scandal developed that implicated the new state president of the Farmers' Alliance in an attempt to gain the senate seat for Republican congressman E. J. Turner through bribery, the accused attempted to divert attention to this alleged ring. A special Alliance committee absolved the president, and few took the ring allegations seriously.[26]

Peffer responded in the *Kansas Farmer* to the charges against him and in the January 7, 1891, issue he openly began to seek the nomination. He reminded the *Non-Conformist* that he was a charter member of the People's party, as it was not merely the old Union Labor party but a new and distinct party made up of former Republicans, Democrats, and Prohibitionists as well as Union Laborites. Moreover, Peffer pointed out, he had supported the Alliance demands before either the *Non-Conformist* or the Farmers' Alliance had even been established in Kansas. "The plain truth," Peffer declared, was that while the third-party papers had encouraged the Union Labor and Greenback elements, the *Kansas Farmer* had delivered the bulk of the new party's voters through attracting converts from the major parties and thus had provided the actual victory. Peffer also countered the criticism of his tariff position by repeatedly explaining the peculiar nature of his protectionist stance (free trade for common necessities and high taxes on luxuries; protection of the poor, the laborer, and the consumer rather than the rich and the manufacturers). He insisted that his break from the GOP was permanent and asserted his support for a national third-party movement, vigorously denied any connection with rings or political combinations, and pointed out that he had not actively sought the nomination but that the people and the party had denoted him the rightful recipient in the state convention, in the campaign, and in local endorsements since.[27] Others deemphasized the issue of Peffer's age and health by noting that Elder was even older than Peffer and that although the Judge was "not a strong man physically," he had a mental and moral courage that fortified him. One reporter observed that Peffer's campaign in 1890 had been both more intense and protracted than any other Populist's and that the robust Willits had not begun until after his August nomination and had still broken down under the strain three times before the November election.[28]

Such explanations apparently satisfied the party's rank and file. Even while Peffer lay ill in Topeka, unable to fill his speaking appointments in the Thirty-second senatorial district, the Populist party of that district instructed its successful candidate to vote for Peffer. When Chase County farmers heard that their representative favored Judge Frank Doster, they called an emergency meeting of the county Alliance in which they unanimously declared Peffer their choice and instructed their representative to vote only for him. Other Alliances and local Populist clubs continued to endorse Peffer's election, and it seemed clear that he was the popular favorite.[29]

As the legislators began to arrive in Topeka in early January, however, it became evident that Peffer was not the first choice of a majority of Populist politicians. Though Willits's election as national lecturer of the Farmers' Alliance had injured his senatorial chances with some, others felt him to be the party's best candidate and pushed his claims as a compromise candidate if Peffer proved unable to increase his lead to a majority. Willits's supporters believed he could attract votes from the Union Laborite faction without alienating those former Republicans that composed Peffer's strength. Doster, one of the most brilliant of Kansas' public figures, also appealed to former Republicans among the Populists, but he did not have Peffer's personal popularity. Nearly every other figure of Kansas Populism appeared as a local or group favorite, including John Davis, Jerry Simpson, W. A. Harris, John Breidenthal, Harry Vrooman, John H. Rice, and P. B. Maxson.

The most important development was the candidacy of P. P. Elder. On January 3 the *Topeka Daily Capital* ranked the senatorial candidates in order of their estimated strength and placed Elder third behind Peffer and Willits. These three were easily the most important candidates; Doster in fourth place was far behind. A week later, the *Capital* reported that Peffer had lost ground and that Elder would probably win the nomination. On January 12 the Populist legislators held their first caucus and unanimously agreed to elect Elder speaker of the house. Elder's election inaugurated a senatorial boom for him, and a prominent Allianceman predicted that within a week Elder would be regarded as the strongest Populist candidate. The *Capital* explained Elder's ascendancy: While Peffer, Willits, and others were public candidates and thus generated opposition and defense, thereby creating dissension and animosity, Elder had remained quietly at home. Once in Topeka, Elder discovered "his party all torn up as between the Peffer and anti-Peffer factions," and his election as speaker gave him through the power of committee appointments the opportunity to unify the Populists behind him. The Union Labor and Democratic elements of the People's party swung to Elder, moreover, stigmatizing Peffer as "too recently a republican." "On the other hand," the paper added, as a public candidate at last Elder would henceforth be subjected to the same attacks that Peffer had endured.[30]

The debate over the Populist candidate obscured the fact that Ingalls had not conceded and, indeed, provided him with reason not to do so. The division within the People's party might prove so bitter, Republicans hoped, that the Populists would be unable to unite on a candidate, and with solid Republican support Ingalls might be able to win. The ease with which each side of any Alliance dispute, such as the Turner scandal, accused the other of being "Ingalls' fixers" delighted the Republicans, who confidently expected the People's party to break into its constituent parts. Ingalls himself was active in Topeka before the legislature convened and before leaving for Congress promised his supporters to return "if advised later that my presence will be of advantage." He cautiously appraised his chances: "Everything *depends*. If the Ghost Dance continues and the expectation of a political Messiah is not repressed, it goes one way. If the frenzy subsides, it goes the other. We cannot tell until the great medicine men have a palaver." In Washington, Ingalls expressed more confidence: "The indications are favorable, and with courage and vigilance success is apparently within reach."[31]

Ingalls depended upon more than courage and vigilance. Republican boss Cy Leland arrived in Topeka "to remain a few days in the interest of Senator Ingalls," as a newspaper delicately phrased it; legislators apparently felt pecuniary pressure; the Republicans increasingly emphasized the Ingalls specialty of bloody-shirt politics; and Ingalls himself in a Senate speech on January 14 capitulated to Alliance principles and advocated agrarian and debtor relief. He also repudiated an earlier statement that the purification of politics was an "iridescent dream," an assertion that had outraged the reformers.[32] Peffer denounced Ingalls's belated gesture to Kansas farmers, adding that it was "a pity that so great an effort should have been conceived in sin and brought forth in iniquity." The *Capital* and other Republican newspapers, however, expected that this speech would ensure the senator's reelection.[33]

The possibility that Ingalls might indeed achieve a victory through Populist dissension activated Populist preparations as the legislature convened. Alliances met and selected men to go to Topeka to watch and protect Populist legislators, "in accordance with Peffer's advice."[34] The record of previous senatorial elections in Kansas seemed to warrant all but the most extreme fears of the Populists, and these earlier elections had involved merely intraparty struggles and nothing so convulsive as the overthrow of the GOP. Not only Populists but Democrats and Republicans expected Ingalls to attempt to bribe legislators, and many were convinced that violent tactics including assassination had not been ruled out. Lease warned of spies and wanted a dozen bodyguards for every Populist legislator. Her wish was not completely granted but one reporter noticed that three bodyguards escorted every legislator to prevent Ingalls from practicing his feared "amoral tactics to secure his reelection."[35] In Topeka, the Populists avoided the major hotels, crowded together in cheap rooming houses, and absolutely refused to talk to anyone about anything. They held all their meetings secretly, behind locked and guarded doors, and in order to keep a united front decided to make no move on any question without caucusing first. All five Populist congressmen-elect arrived in Topeka vowing to use their influence to keep the Populist legislators in line.[36]

Ingalls and his supporters certainly had no intentions of obtaining his election through violent means, but apparently they did not completely rule out extralegal tactics. Republican senators suggested adjourning the Senate to prevent the possibility of holding a joint ballot with the house, thus giving Governor Humphrey the opportunity to appoint Ingalls to the Senate.[37] Frank McGrath, Alliance state president, and Jerry Simpson both reported that bribes were offered to Populist legislators, though these offers may have been without Ingalls's authorization.[38] Ingalls, however, did give $250 to John Livingston, president of the New York State Farmers' Alliance, to go to Topeka in an effort to influence Alliance legislators for his election.[39]

The legislature convened on Tuesday, January 13, 1891, in a week filled with electioneering. As Elder privately worked his political wiles, Peffer, Doster, and others addressed public meetings, each attempting to make clear his candidacy without announcing it. On Friday night the Populist legislators held their first caucus on the senatorial issue but failed to reach any agreement. Jerry Simpson explained that "the friends of the various candidates have injured them by pressing their claims. No one can tell now who will be agreed upon, and it seems to be anybody's fight."[40]

The same caucus debated the question of the Populist candidate for the state printer. Observers believed the vote on the state printer would indicate the result of the Senate race, and Republicans hoped for a Populist wrangle. The Friday night caucus, however, postponed action for the weekend after splitting over Edwin H. Snow, editor of the *Ottawa Journal and Triumph,* McLallin of the *Topeka Advocate,* and B. E. Kies of the *Kansas Commoner.* Both Elder and Snow lived in Franklin County, and Elder approached the editor and told him to withdraw from the contest for state printer lest his own senatorial chances be weakened. Snow rejected Elder's threats and on Monday received the caucus nomination from a coalition of his supporters, those who opposed Elder's senatorial candidacy, and others who objected to Elder's high-handed tactics. Snow's selection was a serious setback to Elder's senatorial ambitions, and the unanimity with which Populist legislators stood by the caucus choice in the official balloting on Tuesday discouraged those Republicans who had hoped for victory through Populist divisiveness.[41] Populists rejoiced that "if the vote for state printer is an index, the 'Iridescent Statesman' will be a political corpse next Tuesday."[42]

Faced with apparent defeat, Republicans made valiant efforts to triumph in the senatorial contest. The *Capital* disputed the reasoning that, having held together to elect Snow, the Populists would be able to close ranks behind one candidate to defeat Ingalls. The senatorial election involved other factors, the *Capital* declared, and each favored Ingalls: reputation, experience, image, tradition.[43] Ingalls himself did not rely upon the past. He left Washington and arrived in Kansas City's Union Station Friday night, January 23, where he spent nearly three hours in secret talks with William Buchan, his campaign manager. Both men refused comment and continued to Topeka, where they set up headquarters at the Copeland Hotel. Republican legislators had caucused Friday only to postpone action until Ingalls arrived. Ingalls conferred with politicians all day Saturday, January 24, and then attended the party caucus held that night in the senate chamber. He told the Republicans that he had a good chance of success but would withdraw if they thought another Republican would be able to attract greater support. Amid optimism, his listeners unanimously agreed to stand by the senator.[44]

In their final efforts, Ingalls and his Republican supporters relied upon their traditionally successful political weapon — waving the bloody shirt to stir up partisan and sectional prejudice and animosity. Republican newspapers hammered at the theme that the southern Confederacy directed the People's party, that unfrocked but unrepentant Confederate officers controlled the Farmer's Alliance, and that the People's party opposed the flag and old soldiers, needlessly pointing out that Ingalls was a national leader in keeping the traitorous southern Democrats under control. John Livingston arrived and on the basis of his position in the New York Alliance persuaded Annie Diggs to introduce him to a Populist audience, whereupon he "revealed" how the goals of the Confederacy were to be realized through the Alliance, declared he possessed letters from other Alliance leaders exposing their intentions to punish Union veterans, proclaimed that southern brigadiers dictated to Kansans, and announced his support for Ingalls.[45]

Republicans especially emphasized the old-soldier aspect of bloody-shirt politics. They distributed printed petitions to the Kansas posts of the Grand Army of the Republic with instructions to flood the legislature with these demands for the reelection of Ingalls.

In a few days hundreds of these pro-Ingalls petitions from Grand Army posts throughout the state descended upon the lawmaking body. The Republican-controlled senate printed them with pleasure in its *Journal,* but the Populist house usually refused to enter them upon the *House Journal* or else tabled them.[46] Veterans staged mass meetings in Topeka and elsewhere on the weekend before the election and in sanguinary and emotional language described how the South viewed Ingalls and old soldiers and how the irreconcilable traitors had welcomed the Alliance at Ocala as a friend of the Democracy. Three thousand Topeka veterans enthusiastically greeted Ingalls and resolved that "the election of any other person to fill his present position . . . will be regarded by us as a direct blow to the defenders of our country in the hour of her greatest need."[47]

Republicans hopefully anticipated that old soldiers among the Populists would vote for Ingalls regardless of the caucus decision. The *Capital* emphasized the increasing Democratic control of the Kansas People's party evident in the apparent displacement of Peffer and other former Republicans by "Confederates" in the senatorial contest. In the *Capital's* final plea for Ingalls, it waved the bloody shirt while arguing that if Ingalls were defeated, it would represent the triumph of sectional prejudice and demagoguery.[48]

In a last effort to divide the Populists, Republicans promoted a late senatorial boom for W. A. Harris, a former Democrat and Confederate officer and a leader of the Leavenworth County Farmers' Alliance. The Democrats had avoided any public statements of their intentions but had maneuvered to dictate the selection of the People's party. They preferred a straight Democrat, but, recognizing the Populists' ability to elect a candidate totally without Democratic help, determined to press for a Populist with Democratic tendencies. In conjunction with some Democratic-Populists, then, the straight Democrats argued for the selection of Harris. Ingalls's supporters quietly encouraged the Harris boom, expecting that combined with bloody-shirt passions a successful Harris nomination would split the People's party.[49]

Democratic influence upon the Populists was weak, however, and when Populists also perceived "Buchan's handiwork in the Harris candidacy," as one reporter described the Republican interest, the Harris boom faded rapidly.[50] In the last weekend before the senatorial election many other candidates appeared and vanished, leaving Peffer, Willits, and Elder still in the front. With Snow's election, for example, some Populists of Union Labor background swung to John Davis, but the legislators decided in a caucus not to consider any proposals for the five Populist congressmen-elect. Former governor John P. St. John appeared briefly as a dark-horse candidate when he made a sharp attack on Ingalls, but he was a Prohibitionist and not a Populist. Others suggested S. M. Scott, the Alliance state lecturer, as a possible compromise candidate.[51]

On Thursday, January 22, Elder caucused his own supporters, the first time a candidate assembled his followers, and they decided to push his candidacy in spite of Snow's election. Elder announced the following day that "the election of Snow will not hurt me in the least. The men who were in my caucus last night are among the strongest members of the House and prospects seemed to them more flattering than they had yet been."[52]

On Saturday the Populist legislators caucused as a group in the Stormont Building and required all those ever mentioned as possible senatorial candidates to speak briefly and to pledge their support for the eventual nominee. Caucus officers permitted no demonstrations and made no attempt to take a vote. The legislators ruled out any surprise candidate by agreeing to select their nominee from the men who spoke. Reporters believed that Breidenthal emerged from the Saturday caucus with increased support and that Willits reappeared as the most likely compromise candidate between the pro-and anti-Peffer forces. They also judged that Peffer retained first place because so many of the legislators felt themselves instructed or obligated to vote for him but expected that after the first ballot some of his followers would desert him.[53] Rumors abounded on Sunday as the Populists "observed the Sabbath by holding a caucus all day." Most rumors involved Elder, who watched his strength flow to Breidenthal, another former Union Laborite. One report held that if Elder failed to receive the caucus nomination, Ingalls would throw his support to Elder and thereby disrupt the People's party and make the new senator indebted to Republicans. Others claimed that Elder had declared his intention to break the caucus pledge if he were not selected.[54]

"It is not a mere figure of speech to say that the eyes of the nation are fixed today upon Topeka," reported the *Kansas City Star* on

Monday, January 26, 1891. "It has been for the past week the great news center of the country. It is thronged with newspaper correspondents from all the leading cities of the United States. . . . The [senatorial] contest is altogether the most notable which has ever occurred in a state whose history has been enriched by a variety of startling political episodes." The day passed tensely, the Republican senate reading into the record nearly 100 old soldiers' petitions for Ingalls's reelection and the Populist house observing a struggle between Elder and his opponents over control of the galleries and lobbies. Both the Populists and the Republicans had scheduled their decisive caucuses for Monday night, for the two houses of the legislature would vote separately Tuesday before Wednesday's official election for senator.

Republicans gathered in the senate chamber and amid confidence and harmony quickly pledged themselves unanimously for Ingalls.[55]

In a remarkably different atmosphere the Populists convened their caucus at 8 P.M. in the Trades Assembly Hall. Search parties first systematically cleared the hall and ousted the Trades Assembly itself. Populist marshals stationed guards at the entrance, placed "a cordon of stalwart farmers" on the stairs leading to the second-floor caucus room, and posted sentinels outside the windows of the building. An Associated Press reporter described other precautions taken on the Monday before the caucus:

> A system of the most rigorous espionage was established, and when a member went out he was accompanied by at least one of his brethren. These guards stood over the alliance men in the hotel corridors, accompanied them on their strolls about the streets, went to their meals with them and walked to the capitol with them this afternoon when they attended the meeting of the house, watching the proceedings from the gallery, buttonholed them after the session and stayed with them until the caucus hour arrived.[56]

The caucus balloting revealed both the variety of positions and personalities within the People's party and the dominant status of former Republicans and Peffer in particular. Seventeen aspirants

split the 93 caucus votes on the first ballot, with Peffer receiving
35 — as many as the total of the next four candidates: Willits, 12; Elder, 10; Breidenthal, 8; Doster, 5. Generally eliminating the candidate with the fewest votes on each preceding ballot, the caucus
struggled through over five hours of debate and voting before declaring Peffer the party's nominee for U.S. senator. Peffer led on every ballot, but the persistent strength of Willits and Elder required
eighteen ballots before he secured a majority. Finally, the caucus
sang "Hallelujah" and adjourned at 1:15 Tuesday morning.[57]

Despite a caucus pledge to secrecy, the news of Peffer's nomination
spread rapidly. The Republican legislators had awaited news of the
nominee with hope that the Populists would choose someone like
Harris and splinter the party. They had received reports that only
seventy legislators had attended the caucus and persuaded themselves that these would be unable to give a majority of their party's
total votes to one man. Buchan believed that the allegedly absent
Populist legislators would support Ingalls. Peffer's nomination made
it improbable that more than a few Populists would bolt the caucus
choice, and when word of the nomination reached him, Buchan
raged over the defeat of his plans and then conceded Peffer's election, adding "it is idle to hope longer." Ingalls received the news
calmly and appeared resigned to defeat.[58]

Elder learned of his caucus defeat at the National Hotel where he
waited in his room. While his son and his friends tried to calm him,
he raged in a profane tirade for several hours. Threatening to resign
his office and destroy his opponents, Elder acted, one friend reported, as though he had temporarily lost his sanity. He considered
that his long career in the reform movement entitled him to senatorial recognition and wept in the realization that at his age "it was my
last chance."[59]

Other Populists who had opposed Peffer conferred secretly in the
Copeland Hotel after the caucus adjourned (causing some Populists
to fear they were bargaining with Ingalls in his rooms). These were
largely old-third-party men who objected to Peffer's nomination in
the conviction that one of their own should have been recognized.
They reluctantly agreed, one wrote later, "that our proper course,
under the circumstances, was to stand by Peffer until he proved him-

self false to the principles of the party, a consummation we then expected."[60]

Still other Populists viewed Peffer's candidacy more hopefully.
Former Republicans such as Congressman-elect William Baker ad-
mired Peffer and expressed pleasure at his selection. Benjamin Clover declared, "Of course, the Judge will do; he is pretty close to the
old gang, but we are hoping that he will turn about-face now and
get a move on him in the other direction." Jerry Simpson approved
Peffer's past record and added that he was respectable—something
that the party needed to counteract its boisterous and bizarre public
image. John Davis regarded Peffer's nomination as a "very creditable
one. . . . Peffer seems to be the second choice of everyone, but he
will do to beat Ingalls with, and that, after all, is the main point."
McLallin, Lease, Diggs, and others also accepted the nomination
unenthusiastically but without protest.[61]

Only superficially had the contest within the People's party appeared as a struggle between moderate and radical factions. Only a
few among the former Republicans, like McLallin, genuinely viewed
the choice as an ideological decision, favoring the moderate wing of
the party. Nearly invariably, the reaction among Populists to Peffer's
selection was governed by their previous party affiliation. The opposition of the former Union Laborites arose from partisan prejudice
and pride at least as much as from any theoretical disagreements.
Indeed, Elder, the Union Labor candidate for governor in 1888 and
the current national chairman of the Union Labor party, ascribed
his rejection to the influence of the radicals, and others added that
between Willits and Peffer the radical Populists favored the latter.[62]
In many respects, too, former Republicans proved the most militant
in arguing for immediate implementation of sweeping reform proposals, in the time-honored fashion of converts, whereas most Union
Laborites exhibited a practical fatalism produced by a life of defeat
and a custom of compromise through fusion with the other political
minority, the Kansas Democracy. These critics simply wanted recognition through senatorial honors for their generation of reform agitation as they saw it come to fruition. Democrats and Democratic-
Populists also rejected a true ideological approach to the contest,
except insofar as such practical political issues as prohibition influenced their viewpoint. They were willing to accept Elder or another

"radical" candidate from the Union Labor faction of the party but were adamant against a "moderate" Republican like Peffer. Years of deliberately inflamed prejudices and exaggerated hostility separated Democrats and Republicans on principle, as well as on principles.

"Today at Topeka," the *Atchison Champion* announced on Tuesday, January 27, 1891, "will be enacted the last act in the most picturesque drama which has ever been performed on the Kansas political stage." A turnaway crowd packed the galleries of Representative Hall by early morning. The senate requested a joint session at noon for the senatorial ballot, but the house, fearing some deception, refused to consent and each chamber voted separately. The senate quickly balloted, giving Ingalls 35 of 40 votes. Peffer received two votes, one from Sen. Sydney C. Wheeler of Cloud County, elected by Populists in a special election and the only member not a holdover from the GOP's triumphant success in 1888, and the other from Republican senator L. P. King, who described himself as an Allianceman who believed that Peffer was a good Republican and a good old soldier, too. In the house Speaker Elder called for the vote promptly at noon. He allowed no nominating speeches, and only Republican cheers for Ingalls interrupted the roll call. The Populists were mute except to respond to their names. The ranks of the party held firm, resulting in a strict party vote, 96 Populists for Peffer, 23 Republicans for Ingalls, and 5 Democrats for Charles W. Blair of Leavenworth. When the clerk announced the final vote the Populists erupted in a paroxysm of shouts, songs, laughter, and tears. Representatives danced on their desks in their excitement over Ingalls's defeat.[63] Because each house of the legislature had not given Peffer a majority there remained the necessity of a ballot in joint session on Wednesday, but the demonstration of Populist solidarity made it only a formality, and all involved conceded Peffer's election.

Populists continued their celebrations throughout the day, culminating in Metropolitan Hall that night. The crowd enthusiastically sang "alliance hallelujah songs" and listened to speeches by Jerry Simpson, Mary Lease, Annie Diggs, and Sam Wood. Simpson congratulated the Populists for closing "their ears to the seducing offers of bribes" and standing together behind Peffer, whose election, Simpson declared, marked a "most important epoch in history." Wood offered his own resolution opposing the old-soldier resolutions for Ingalls with "the brilliant soldier record of Judge Peffer," and the meeting adopted it.[64]

Tuesday night Democratic legislators held the last of the senatorial caucuses. Displeased with Peffer's nomination, they had voted for Blair on the first legislative roll call. Some, however, felt that by voting for Peffer on the official ballot they might be able to exert more influence upon the course of the People's party. Others, like Sen. Edward Carroll, steadfastly opposed supporting Peffer, and the conference left Wednesday's votes up to the individual Democratic legislator.[65]

Expectation if not suspense brought another overflow crowd to Representative Hall on Wednesday. There had been rumors that the senate, in a final effort to prevent Peffer's election, would refuse to meet in joint session, but realizing that even such an audacious act would prove futile before Peffer's tremendous house majority, the senators assembled in the hall at noon. Peffer's family sat near the speaker's table while the judge remained in the sergeant-at-arms' room. Ingalls did not attend but stayed in his hotel room with a few friends. Again there were no nominating speeches and few explanations of votes, and the voting continued without interruptions or demonstrations. Three Democrats changed their votes from Blair to Peffer in the only variation from Tuesday's balloting, and Peffer was declared senator by a vote of 101 to 58 for Ingalls, 3 for Blair, and 3 scattered. The senate quickly moved that the joint session be dissolved and left the chamber before Peffer, who had emerged in tears, could speak.[66] He was "pale, nervous, and trembled like a leaf in the wind," declared one observer, and with "a ministerial swing of the arms, a sing-song voice, a constant looking up to Heaven, a reverential attitude, and the nervous walk of an exhorter," Peffer spoke briefly, thanking the legislators for their confidence and promising that he would work to establish the People's party through which a new society would be created.[67]

Alliancemen and reformers throughout the country joined Kansas Populists in celebrating Peffer's election. A Missouri Alliance characterized it as "the greatest victory of the times"; L. L. Polk regarded the defeat of Ingalls as "the greatest blow at sectionalism that has been struck for twenty-five years"; and the National Farmers' Alliance considered Peffer's election "the beacon light that

will lead to better times and happier conditions." The Missouri legislature telegraphed congratulations to its Kansas counterpart for
this step toward uniting the nation; the Knights of Labor rejoiced
over the first Knight senator; and a composed P. P. Elder told a great
Topeka rally that Peffer's election represented "the victory of the
people."[68]

Peffer's election also demonstrated several things about Kansas
politics. It revealed the continuing domination of the People's party
by former Republicans, the persistent factionalism of the party and
the distrust each faction had of the other, the lack of Democratic influence on Populist decisions but the repeated Democratic efforts to
control the party, and the Republicans' unbroken reliance upon traditional sectional and partisan prejudice in their effort to destroy
the People's party.

The day following the election the streets were deserted and the
hotel lobbies empty, as many Populists had returned home and a gi-
ant ratification meeting Wednesday night had completed the emotional exhaustion of those who remained. A *Kansas City Star* reporter found barely a quorum present when the house convened
before empty galleries, and he noted that "in accomplishing Senator
Ingalls's defeat the representatives of the People's Party had been
subjected to a strain which told in their faces. They had been edu-
cated to believe that murder would be resorted to, if necessary, to reelect Senator Ingalls, and the sentries on duty in a besieged garrison
never watched an enemy more closely."[69]

But the Populist legislators did their job well. Peffer's election not
only overthrew a national symbol of Republicanism and sectional
and partisan hatred, but it also provided a national leader for the
new forces of political reform. *Harper's Weekly* pointed out the impact of the contest: "The election of Mr. Peffer has been enthusiastically welcomed by Alliancemen in all parts of the country, and has
greatly encouraged them in their political action. It is one of the
greatest purely political victories they have won, and will doubtless
tend to strengthen the third-party movement in that body."[70] The intense national interest in the Kansas senatorial contest guaranteed
Peffer a vast audience and immense publicity to use to advocate his
plans for reform. The *Philadelphia Evening Bulletin* commented
after his election that "there has been no senatorial election this win-

ter which has attracted more attention from the country than the one which has just been decided in Kansas. . . . Whether Peffer is a cunning demagogue or whether he is an honest dreamer remains to be seen, but his election to the senate is one of the most curious results of the political upheaval of 1890."[71]

Whether demagogue or dreamer, Peffer had become the first national figure of Populism and, as he told one reporter, "I shall not be the last."[72]

5

PARTY OFFICIALS AND
PRACTICAL POLITICS

The essence of Populism was that it was a political movement, prompted by popular anger with politics as usual, the indifference of political institutions, the failure of political parties to represent the expressed interests of their constituents; the essence of the People's party, however, was that it was a political party, seeking electoral success within an established political system. The tension between these two positions, at first only latent in the revivalistic popular campaigns of 1890, dramatically emerged to shape the course of the Populist experience in the next few years. It first became evident in the 1892 election in Kansas but then also dominated developments on the national level leading to the 1896 election. The issue that most brought these differing perspectives into play was the question of fusion with another political party.

Viewing the mixed results of the 1890 state election, most party officials and political actives in the Kansas People's party inclined toward a policy of fusion with the Democrats in 1892. Concerned primarily with the immediate task of organizing an election victory, they argued for "using a little political sense this year" and announced that the antifusionists "ought to know that three state tickets insures the election of the entire Republican ticket." Some recommended placing Democrats directly on the Populist ticket; others such as Levi Dumbauld, chairman of the state central committee, merely favored the nomination of those Populists with Democratic backgrounds who would attract Democratic support. Most fusion-minded Populists, in fact, came from either the former Democrats or Union Laborites within the People's party. Both groups had traditionally regarded the Republican party as the enemy and had customarily fused against this common opponent in the past. Now they saw little reason to discontinue the procedure at a time when its success seemed assured.[1]

These party leaders frequently met privately with Democratic politicians in early 1892 in hopes of reaching an agreement on fusion. In January Populists of Democratic antecedents led by Van Prather met straight Democrats in Kansas City and arranged to publicize fusion sentiment through Populist papers to be subsidized by Democrats. In March Democratic former governor George Glick and several Populist committeemen met in Atchison to divide offices between the two parties in order to construct a joint ticket. In April the Second Congressional District committees of the two parties met in Fort Scott to choose a mutually acceptable candidate to place before their actual nominating conventions in the summer. Party leaders of a number of counties likewise held private sessions in the spring in an effort to design local fusion tickets.[2]

At no time, however, did the Democrats indicate their agreement with the Populists on principles. Democrats based fusion proposals only on calculations of political bargaining and practical politics and not on ideological grounds. Indeed, Kansas Democrats stood solidly behind the conservative Grover Cleveland in his quest for another presidential nomination. In March the Democratic state central committee voted overwhelmingly for both fusion with the Populists and the nomination of Cleveland. The Democratic state convention in April selected a Cleveland delegation to the national convention with instructions to vote as a unit for him. The Kansas Democracy, Glick assured Cleveland, was "unanimous for you."[3]

As fusion arrangements between the two parties became more likely, Populist senator W. A. Peffer repeatedly issued admonitions against the course. "Any bargain and sale of the offices which might be arranged by the Democrats and a few of the leaders of our party," he predicted in April, "would never be accepted by the thousands of alliancemen who went into the third party because they were done with the

Democratic and Republican parties for all time. They did not go into the People's party to assist by combination or coalition in the election of either Democrats or Republicans; they went into the new party as a matter of principle." A week later, after the Democratic House had voted down a silver bill, Peffer declared that Democratic duplicity as much as Republican injustice and corruption had caused the establishment of the People's party, and it was "now more apparent than ever that to fuse with either of the old parties simply because some politicians want office, would be to surrender principle for spoils and constitute a ridiculous blunder and one that would do great injury to the movement." Populism, he maintained, aimed "to benefit the whole people and not a few scheming . . . politicians who . . . spend their entire time in seeking to form combinations to get nominations and then devise ways and means to secure the office at the polls."[4]

The reaction of Populists to Peffer's pronouncements against fusion seemed to depend largely upon their attitude toward the movement in general. Those who viewed politics in broad, national terms and thus considered the national ramifications of Kansas action and who most strongly believed that the People's party would become a national force to remake society typically opposed any proposition to fuse with Democrats in Kansas. Congressman Benjamin Clover, for example, agreed with Peffer that Democratic dissemblance in Congress, "if there was no other reason, ought to prevent any combination between the Democrats and alliancemen in Kansas or any other state."[5] With the exception of Jerry Simpson, who had long cooperated in fusion campaigns with Democrats, other national figures among Kansas Populists also concurred with Peffer's antifusion views. Brought into prominence in 1890 by a mass movement that repudiated the old parties by its very existence, they saw no valid reason to retrogress. Furthermore, they were primarily responsible for launching the party into national politics at the 1891 Cincinnati Conference. Agrarian editors such as Stephen McLallin of the *Topeka Advocate,* who considered reform from a national perspective, or W. C. Routzong of the rural *Kincaid Kronicle,* who sought to preserve the ideological purity and idealistic fervor of the movement, provided effective support for the middle-of-the-road position.

Rather than indicating a conservative policy, the term "middle of the road" referred to those radical Populists who rejected fusion and its inevitable compromises of principles. Populism, these men and women logically argued, demanded national action to correct national abuses, and the party could not expect to create the necessary dissolution of the Solid South if it cooperated with the Democracy in Kansas. Moreover, Populism condemned both old parties, for they had combined, in the Populist viewpoint, to oppress the people through a confusion of real interests and plays on sectional, cultural, and partisan prejudice. The Populist intention, after all, was to destroy both old parties, which were corrupt in outlook and malevolent in operation. Cooperation with either would mean the betrayal of the promise of the people's movement; the adoption of the sordid practices of voter manipulation for offices and spoils that Populists believed they had abandoned with their former partisan allegiances; the admission that the motivating hope of a glorious political reformation in America was groundless, that the period of increasing acceptance of reform principles had ended, that the assistance of the unregenerate was necessary. The people's movement had developed as political rebellion against the cynical methods as much as against the callous objectives of the old parties, the mid-roaders remembered, and their political reformation could not with reason adopt the methods of the old parties without acknowledging failure of its objectives as well. "If it was merely to turn Republicans out of office, a fusion of the People's and Democratic parties would be both desirable and sensible," conceded mid-roader W. O. Champe:

> [But] the offices are only a means to an end. To turn Republicans out of office, and then admit others not friendly to the reform movement, would be a piece of egregious folly. If the Democratic party believed in People's Party principles, or did the Republican party, then the organization of the People's Party was folly to begin with, and to fuse with either party is virtually an admission that the People's Party is not needed, has no distinct principles, and would stamp it as being merely a political excrescence.[6]

Fusion Populists in Kansas, on the other hand, were usually politicians concerned with strictly local and state political matters. They had little regard for the wider consequences of their immediate actions, in respect to either national politics or party principles. They represented less the party's evangelistic, idealistic, and morally motivated wing, personified by Peffer, and more the pragmatic operators, long experienced in the hard politics of compromise and expediency. Indeed, while mid-roaders predominated within the Washington contingent and perhaps the rank and file of the People's party, it was party officials and activists on state and county committees who usually adopted the fusionist rationale, thus making the fusion position stronger in the actual party organization than in either the highest leadership or the general membership. To further consolidate their control over the party apparatus, fusionists attempted to isolate mid-roaders or undermine their influence. A mid-road member of the state central committee, for example, complained that the fusionist majority of the committee refused to notify mid-roaders of committee meetings.[7] Fusionists liked to consider themselves as realists and mid-roaders as "cranks," devoid of political sense and hopelessly utopian. Their arguments for fusion with the Democratic party never considered subjects of political or doctrinal consistency but merely emphasized the probable Republican plurality in a three-sided contest. Indeed, fusionists claimed that those who were most concerned with the preservation of distinctive Populist principles were Republicans seeking only to prevent the fusion of their two dissimilar opponents. Populist hostility to such a coalition was proof to the fusionists that the mid-roaders were working in the interest of the GOP, either as traitors or as dupes. This low allegation that antifusionists were crypto-Republicans proved perhaps the most effective weapon of these practical men.[8]

Mid-roaders objected to the fusionist appropriation and interpretation of the term "practical politics." A strict adherence to that conception of practical politics, after all, would have avoided the quixotic tactic of forming a third party in the first place. Antifusionists now argued that a truly practical policy, designed to achieve the complete objective, required total separation from the old parties: Without traditional sources of support such as the old parties boasted, Populism must necessarily emphasize its distinctiveness. Mid-roaders in particular rejected the fusionist contention that political common sense dictated cooperation with the Democrats. The party's primary problem since its inception, they pointed out, was to combat the idea that the People's party was "a Democratic aid society, or that it was in collusion with Democracy in any way." This fundamental necessity had forced them to establish a national third party and to attempt to destroy the Democratic South in an effort to maintain the allegiance of their adherents who had only with difficulty broken their powerful emotional ties to the GOP. "In separating from the Republican party, Kansas farmers have had no intention of aligning themselves with the enemy whom they so long opposed and despised," declared one newspaper, and the ardently antifusion *Kincaid Kronicle* added that such Republican-Populists "look upon the Democrat party as being even worse than the party they left. It is folly to expect these men to vote to increase the power of a party they consider the worst that ever existed."[9]

Despite such strong resistance to their proposed course, fusionists of both parties evolved a plan for collaboration in a series of meetings in late spring. Democrats would name candidates for a joint congressional ticket in two districts and receive two places on the state ticket, congressman-at-large and associate justice, in exchange for their endorsement of the remaining Populist candidates on congressional, state, and electoral tickets. Published reports generally accorded David Overmeyer and John Martin the Democratic spots on the state ticket, and although only the First and Second Congressional districts were to be given to Democratic candidates, the Democrats made it clear they would not support Benjamin Clover or John G. Otis, the Populist incumbents in the Third and Fourth who represented their party's agrarian origins in the Alliance and the Grange.[10] Jerry Simpson was more than acceptable, and in the two remaining districts, represented by John Davis and William Baker, the Democrats did not even have the balance-of-power strength necessary to make demands though they objected to both Populist congressmen.

The party managers had thus arranged for the disposition of Populist votes, but there remained doubt as to whether the rank and file would accede. Prather admitted that "the rub will be with the people's party in controlling the conventions." Glick expressed optimism but added, "Some crank though may spoil our plans." And another Democrat convinced himself that "such an arrangement, I am assured the People's Party generally desire, (there are a few cranks in every party who have no practical sense) but the sensible element is now in control."[11]

The various Populist nominating conventions soon revealed that those antifusion cranks were stronger than either Democrats or fusion Populists had hoped but also that in their inexperience and ignorance they were at the mercy of the fusionists, for whom politics was often a profession. The result was frequently the appearance of nonfusion coupled with the actuality of fusion. In May Populists began to hold county conventions and overwhelmingly instructed their delegates to the state convention to oppose fusion plans and candidates. Particularly averse to fusion propositions were the Populists of north-central and northwestern Kansas, where former Republicans greatly predominated in the party. There the Sixth Congressional District convention renominated Baker on June 2 with strong expressions of antifusion sentiment. Such an outcome was expected in that district, however, and the first test of the fusion scheme came in Holton the same day, when the First Congressional District convention met.[12]

The question of fusion immediately split the convention, with the mid-road faction led by former Republican Ezra Cary and the fusionists led by former Democrat J. W. Fitzgerald. Fitzgerald even declared that he would not accept the convention's decision unless he thought it would attract Democratic support. Toward that end, Leavenworth Democratic leader S. F. Neely, arriving directly from a conference in Kansas City between fusionist leaders of the two parties, intervened in the Populist convention to advocate the nomination of William A. Harris, promising that the Democrats would accept him as their own. But a division within the fusionist ranks among the supporters of Harris and Fitzgerald led to the surprise nomination of Fred J. Close, a stockholder with Peffer and McLallin on the antifusion *Advocate*. The swing to Close began when one Populist refused to "be a party to the Democratic scheme to nominate Colonel Harris" and added, "I have never been a Democrat and I pray to God I never will be a Democrat, and I don't propose to be led into the Democratic camp at this time."[13] The defeat of Harris disappointed fusionists of both parties and caused many to fear that no agreement at all would be reached. Democratic leader Charles

Robinson more calmly observed that elsewhere fusionists would act less arrogantly and stupidly and antifusionists would prove unable so easily to stampede conventions. Glick was also unperturbed, and he predicted that Populist party officials would honor the fusion plans by withdrawing their competing candidates. "This cannot be done in the convention," he conceded, "but it will be done by the committees later in the campaign."[14]

Before the state convention, the Populists held three more congressional nominating conventions. As expected, the Fifth District in north-central Kansas made no concessions to the Democrats and unanimously renominated mid-roader John Davis. Congressman Otis was not so fortunate. Democrats were stronger in his district and Populists weaker, and his harsh antifusion statements had alienated the Democracy. The district's Democratic convention met in late May, resolved in favor of fusion, and then adjourned until June 14 in Emporia, the scheduled time and place of the Populist convention, thereby pressuring the People's party to nominate a Populist other than Otis. Overmeyer joined Martin as the guiding spirits of the Democratic convention in this attempt to force fusion upon the Populists. The Democrats signaled that although Otis was unacceptable they would support Levi Dumbauld, a former Democrat and, as chairman of the Populist state central committee, a leading fusionist.[15]

Dumbauld had already initiated a campaign to succeed Otis but had only succeeded in angering many Populists who then called a meeting in Emporia to demand an explanation. Dumbauld confessed to his critics that the Populist state central committee had met with the Democrats in hopes of arranging fusion and had agreed, among other things, to replace Otis with Dumbauld and to nominate Overmeyer for congressman-at-large. The indignant Populists replied, one of them later wrote, "that the committee were either fools or traitors . . . , and that the people were able to make their own ticket without the help of the bosses, and further . . . that Otis had done his part by us and we would stand by him first, last, and all the time, and Overmeyer would have to bid good-by to the Democrats before we could support him."[16]

Though Populists were determined to reject Dumbauld and explicit Democratic dictation, many of their leaders remained ready to make some concession to attract Democratic support in the normally Republican Fourth District. The Populist convention consequently turned down both Otis and Dumbauld and selected E. V. Wharton, a Yates Center physician and a Democratic-Populist. The Democratic convention, which, as Otis later explained, had "hung around our convention all day, threatening to nominate a candidate twenty minutes after I was named," immediately applauded Wharton as "a good, sound Democrat," ratified the nomination, and "gleefully adjourned."[17]

Otis and the other mid-roaders bitterly condemned these proceedings. Otis warned that Populism was "jeopardized by this gang of unscrupulous office-hunting gluttons. Fusion means our ruin. It is only the office-seeker who wants fusion and if our people allow themselves to be used in this way they will be pulling chestnuts out of the fire for others," he continued. "These fusion candidates won't come as near being elected as the candidates who made a straight fight on the Alliance platform and depend fully on the Alliance for support." Otis even hinted that he might run for Congress as an independent, for he believed that had the people still controlled the People's party he would have been renominated. Farmers particularly objected to the displacement of the "Milkman" by the nomination of Wharton, "who never farmed a day in his life, and probably never did a day's physical labor," and many supported a plan to defeat the fusionist politicians of the district by having an independent convention nominate Otis. Otis remained unreconciled, proud that "I was too much a middle-of-the-road man for the Democracy," but he abandoned his plan of running independently.[18]

Others accepted the defeat of Otis more willingly. The Populist convention of the Seventh Congressional District, meeting in Wichita on June 14, cheered the news of Wharton's nomination. Former Democrats had more influence in the People's party of southwestern Kansas than generally elsewhere, and the district, represented by the agreeable Simpson, was strongly profusion. Straight Democrats had promised to endorse Simpson if Populists outside the district cooperated with Democratic plans and candidates, and the rejection of Otis seemed to ensure Simpson's dual nomination. Simpson had actively sought Democratic support, promised to encourage Populists to endorse Democratic candidates in other districts, and assured his

Democratic backers that if Grover Cleveland were elected they could control the district's patronage. Simpson easily won renomination at the Populist convention, and shortly thereafter the district's Democrats adopted him as their own candidate as well.[19]

The Populist state convention opened in Wichita on June 15, 1892, amid intense discussion over fusion. The very selection of Wichita by the Populist state central committee, some believed, involved a bid for Democratic support, as did the choice of John Breidenthal for convention chairman. A former Union Laborite, Breidenthal provoked some opposition because a caucus of party officials had determined his nomination. The issue of fusion entered into the consideration of candidates too, but as many fusionists had feared, the ungovernable convention apparently rejected their arrangements. The alleged fusionist candidate for governor, John Ives, had lost most of his backing because of his recent involvement as attorney general in reducing railroad taxation, and Lorenzo D. Lewelling, a Wichita produce dealer, received the nomination instead. Martin lost to Stephen H. Allen for associate justice, and W. A. Harris received the nomination for congressman-at-large instead of Overmeyer.[20]

The apparent defeat of the schemes for Democratic fusion encouraged the mid-roaders and misled historians. Others were not deceived. If the Populist delegates had rejected what would have been blatant political manipulation in the proposed nominations of Martin and Overmeyer, they had allowed themselves to be led under Breidenthal's skillful direction into an unwitting implicit endorsement of fusion. The Populists' policy of letting the office seek the man, combined with their relative lack of access to the news media, resulted in the nomination of a number of surreptitious fusion candidates. Allen was presented in the state convention as the mid-road alternative to Democrat Martin and nominated easily; ten days previously he had been the unsuccessful straight Democratic candidate for Second District congressman in opposition to a Democrat who favored fusion with the Populists. Harris, who filled the other position promised to the Democrats, had been a Democrat, was perhaps the leading fusionist among the Populists, was very popular in his heavily Democratic home county of Leavenworth, and opposed the more radical elements of Populism while accepting little more than free silver from its financial program. Following his nomination, moreover, Harris declared that he was still "a good Democrat." Populists with Democratic backgrounds received other spots on the ticket, including Prather for state auditor. Even Lewelling, though a former Republican, represented a bid for Democratic support. Relatively new to Kansas, he had never worked with the GOP; promoted by Simpson, he was chairman of the fusionist Sedgwick County People's party and certain to receive the critical backing of Wichita Democrats. In addressing the convention, moreover, Lewelling clearly indicated his desire to cooperate with "honorable allies."[21]

Generally, the Democratic press expressed pleasure with the Populist ticket. "An investigation of the political antecedents of the men who were nominated by the People's Party convention" convinced the *Leavenworth Evening Standard* that the Populists were actively "bidding for Democratic success." It especially applauded the nomination of Harris. The *Wichita Beacon*, although disappointed that no Democrat qua Democrat was on the slate, described six of the nine candidates as former Democrats and urged Democratic support of the ticket, especially of Lewelling. The *Garnett Journal* likewise declared the majority of the Populist nominees "good Democrats," rejoiced that the "cranky element" of the People's party "has been relegated to the rear," and advocated Democratic fusion. Most Democratic politicians agreed. Martin praised the Populist ticket, and Glick promised that the Democrats would fulfill their part of the fusion agreement.[22]

In their own state convention in July, Democrats divided into three groups, all for fusion but in varying degrees. One favored total fusion; one advocated fusion on the electoral ticket and state candidates who were formerly Democrats; and the third favored only electoral fusion. Harris, Allen, John Little, the Populist candidate for attorney general, and other leading fusion Populists were present, actively seeking Democratic endorsement and conferring with Martin, Glick, and Robinson. After a long debate, the convention declared for complete fusion and nominated the entire electoral and state ticket of the People's party. Democrats made no false statements of their motives for endorsing the Populist slate, and C. F. Diffenbach, the Democratic leader of Barton County, was remarkably candid: "The People's Party is fast becoming a part of the Democratic party and in two or three years we will have it all. Two years ago they would not have anything to do with us. Now they are glad to work with us, and the time is not very far ahead when the two parties will be one and the same, and it will be a Democratic party. That's why I favored the nomination of Jerry Simpson, and it is why I have favored fusion this year. It will eventually bring the new party into our camp."[23]

Elsewhere, Populists and Democrats attempted to complete fusion arrangements. In the Third District the issue was clear. Clover was unacceptable to the Democrats and the converse, and fusionists had agreed to replace him with a Democratic-Populist. At the convention only two candidates were presented: Clover and Thomas Jefferson Hudson, a lawyer and former Democrat. But Clover's feud with the popular Simpson, publicized marital troubles, and increasing passivity weakened his position, and the convention nominated Hudson with less contention than marked those struggles that were overt disputes over fusion. Hudson called himself a Populist in 1892, but Democratic papers still considered him a Democrat and praised him as the best candidate Populists had ever nominated except for Harris. Subsequently, Third District Democrats gratefully nominated Hudson.[24]

Politics in the Second District proved more difficult and illustrated the problems of the People's party. The district had been granted to a Democratic candidate by the fusion managers, and the Democrats were determined to defeat the Republican incumbent, Edward H. "Farmer" Funston. As early as March the district committees of the Democratic and People's parties had conferred about naming a joint candidate, and fusion leaders constantly thereafter tried to restrain antifusion activities. Mid-roaders were increasingly vocal, however, and complained that their party officials had not been authorized to consult the Democrats or to usurp the rights of a nominating convention.[25]

The Democrats forced the issue by rescheduling their convention to meet prior to the Populist convention and by nominating Horace L. Moore, a Lawrence banker. They then demanded Populist acceptance of the Democrat as the "only road to success" and denounced those who resisted as working in Funston's behalf. Populist indignation was intense. The *Kincaid Kronicle* censured the proposed "unholy alliance" and recited the past treachery of the old parties, specifically condemning their deceitful practice of making platforms to gain votes with no intention of fulfilling their promises: "It is said that Moore is in favor of the reforms demanded by the people. If that is correct why is he not in the people's party?" W. O. Champe, veteran editor of the Garnett *Kansas Agitator*, also implored Populists to keep in the middle of the road for the sake of principle and southern support. Southern Democrats believed, he wrote, that fusion in Kansas would destroy the People's party in the South, and Champe declared he had received letters from southern Populists urging Kansans not to fuse with the party that they were fighting to the death.[26]

The Populist congressional convention met in Garnett on June 22 amid a crowd of lobbying politicians. Moore and Robinson arrived from Lawrence to plead the Democratic cause, and they were supported by Populist state candidates Allen and Little, who hoped thereby to promote wider fusion in the pending Democratic state convention. John Willits, the Populist gubernatorial candidate in 1890 and a national official in the Farmers' Alliance, Champe, and other Populist mid-roaders of the district argued against Moore. "If we go into the business of helping to elect Democrats to office," Willits told his listeners, "we might as well quit and go back into the old parties." Many Populists agreed with their formidable leader. One mid-road delegate, for example, declared, "These fusion delegates . . . come here in the interest of the Democratic party and have no right here. I will not stand it, and am going home to vote the Republican ticket." Willits rallied the mid-roaders to reject the fusionist arguments, and S. S. King of Kansas City received the nomination.[27]

Democrats and fusion Populists complained fiercely. Robinson denounced Willits for preventing Populist endorsement of various Democratic candidates, especially Moore. Other Democrats, just returned from helping nominate Cleveland at their national convention, remained willing to fuse on the electoral ticket in his behalf but announced their new opposition to endorsing other Populist candidates. Populist fusion leaders Little, Allen, and J. E. Latimer continued to support Moore even though King had the Populist nomination, and they promised the Democrats to have King removed from the race. Latimer's *Herald* announced that Populists needed votes and should therefore accept Moore to gain Democratic backing elsewhere in the state. Latimer denounced those who opposed this course as not possessing "the least particle of political sense" and as working in the interest of the GOP. In advocating fusion, he asserted, he was working for principles.[28]

Other Populists rejected these fusionist rationales. The *Kansas Agitator* condemned Latimer for helping arrange and defend the fusion agreement between Populist and Democratic party committees. These actions by Populist leaders were not authorized by the rank and file, and "if anyone promised Moore an endorsement," added the *Kincaid Kronicle,* "they promised him something which was not theirs to give." The mid-roaders were especially harsh toward the fusionists who, "having failed to accomplish their nefarious designs," were "now trying to thwart the will of the people as expressed by their chosen delegates in convention assembled." Antifusionists ripped the reasoning of Latimer and his allies who argued for fusion as "anything to beat Funston." A banker who stood on a Democratic platform and supported Cleveland for president was no improvement over a Republican farmer, and his election would merely add to the Democratic majority in Congress that had already refused to aid the people. An honorable defeat would not injure Populism as much as such a victory. "To be consistent," one mid-roader charged, the fusionists who still intended to support Moore "should oppose Weaver because the Omaha convention did not endorse Cleveland."

Mid-road Populists were especially annoyed that the actions of the fusion leaders usurped the right of popularly chosen delegates. The fusionist attitude that votes were to be bartered by those who better understood the political situation ran counter to the original Populist demands that the people should participate directly in political decisions and that democracy should be effective within parties as much as within other elements of the social system. The dictatorial approach of the Democrats angered Populists as much as the arbitrary actions of their own leaders: "Who ever heard of the politicians of one party trying to control the nomination of another party as was done at Garnett?" Moore's appearance before the Populist convention and his request for the nomination, they maintained, made him honor-bound by the convention's decision. Having failed to secure the nomination, however, he now attempted to subvert that decision. Fortunately for their party, they rejoiced, it was one thing to sell the Populists of the Second District but quite another to deliver them. The unconditional Populist would resist illegitimate authority even when his leaders demanded obedience as necessary to the success of their schemes.[29]

Those who demanded fusion as "practical politics" further irritated the mid-roaders of the Second District. "If the convention had endorsed Col. Moore," Champe pointed out, "such action would have driven thousands of voters, formerly Republicans, back into the old party; and the failure to endorse him is being used to drive Democrats away from the Populists. It would seem that men of ordinary shrewdness could have foreseen this difficulty," he believed, "and have avoided it, by each party strictly minding its own affairs. The parties are certainly separate organizations, with principles and aims that widely differ; therefore, any attempt to fuse could only lead to a vast amount of friction, without advancing the cause of either party." Moreover, if the fusionists proved successful in removing King from the ticket, Champe predicted, Moore would not receive one-quarter of the district's Populist votes, for real Populists could not vote for a Democratic banker. Truly, he concluded, Funston could not have asked for a better situation than the expedient, practical, and sensible fusionists had created—a sharply divided and bickering, quarreling opposition.[30]

The fusion Populists did not renounce their schemes. Democrats assisted them by promising to endorse Populist nominees elsewhere in Kansas if King were withdrawn. And Moore pointed out that he could finance a campaign himself; the Populist party was nearly penniless. Both groups pressured the Populist District Central Committee to replace King with Moore. The new Populist state chairman, John Breidenthal, an able exponent of practical politics, also worked to remove King. Finally in July, the harried King grudgingly informed Breidenthal that he would withdraw if the party thought it best. Breidenthal immediately called a meeting of the Populist committee to accept King's offer. Although the Wyandotte County committeeman asserted that King's withdrawal would drive all former Republicans among his county's Populists back to their old party, the committee conferred with its Democratic counterpart and then substituted Moore for King on the Populist ticket. A Populist who had ably advocated his party's financial and social arguments in his book *Bondholders and Breadwinners* was thus replaced in a contest against a Republican farmer by a Democratic banker who insisted that the tariff was the real political issue.[31]

Disaffection among Populists was severe. The *Kincaid Kronicle* asserted that the committee had no authority to set aside the will of the people as expressed in their convention, and it refused to accept Moore as the party's nominee. Its editor arraigned the political managers of the People's party for being as arrogant and manipulative as any in the corrupt old parties and denounced the committee for actions traitorous to the people and the cause it claimed to represent. Others joined in the indictment of the machinations of Populist leaders. The *Agitator,* for example, declared the party bosses had usurped the rights of the people and subverted their wishes. Most dissidents eventually accepted Moore as the Populist candidate because they saw no alternative, but they continued to censure the politicians of their own party. The *Kronicle,* however, proved unable to reconcile its campaign for political reform with the chicanery involved in this arrangement. Another writer expressed the paper's position well: "The great reformation for the purification of politics has fallen into the control of tricksters. Principles have been traded for expedients. The high moral plane has been abandoned." A Coffey County paper agreed: "What started out as a great uprising of the people for reform, a crusade against the evils of which both old parties were alike guilty, thus turns out to be a stupendous and perfectly shameless traffic for offices." The *Kronicle* suspended publication and expired.[32]

The transformation of the People's party evident in the differences between 1890 and 1892 was obvious to many. In 1890 idealistic and utopian-minded reformers had led discontented farmers in a movement to purge a corrupt society and political system as much as to reform financial legislation. In 1892 these men such as Peffer, Clover, Willits, McLallin, and Otis were either more involved in national politics or shunted aside on the state level. Technicians replaced ideologues as a mass movement was rationalized into an organized political party. Efficiency, expediency, and opportunism were adopted by "practical-minded" bureaucrats such as Breidenthal as either methods or objectives in their quest for immediate, tangible gains rather than the proposed reformation of society. Perhaps this was an inevitable process, but it might be argued that a reform movement demanded a clear vision of its purpose more than it required an efficient management of its adherents. Enveloped in the problems of organization, coordination, and administration of a political campaign, the professional activists succumbed to the ultimate enticement—victory at the polls—and concerned themselves little with the principles and ideas that originally had impelled the movement. These too often were merely obstacles in the path of fashioning a coalition that might prove successful. The tension between these two attitudes surfaced when such mid-roaders as Champe spoke of the basic differences between *movement* and *party.* A. J. R. Smith, radical mid-road editor of the *Topeka Populist,* in fact, described the degeneration of Populism as a direct result of the transformation of the mass movement into a structured party, with its institutional imperatives diverting politicians from reform to deceitful manipulation.[33]

Although many Populists believed that their party officials subverted the ideals of Populism in their cynical disregard of the concept of popular control and in their arrogant defiance of the limits of their proper authority, more immediately disturbing was the obvious Democratization of the party, stemming in part from the undemocratization of the movement. In 1890 Populists had spurned Democratic advances, and fusion had occurred only on Democratic initiative and through Democratic endorsement of Populist candidates. In 1892 Populist leaders had actively sought out Democratic leaders, proposed and agreed to fusion, repudiated movement figures such as Otis and Clover and replaced them with Democrats or Democratic-Populists, and nominated others whose chief qualification was their ability to attract Democratic votes. The party of the people was now committed to support a middleman in farm produce against a farmer for governor and a banker against a farmer for Congress. It had refused congressional renominations to two former Republican farmers and named two former Democrats, one a lawyer and the other a physician. On the insistence of Democrats, it had removed from its ticket another Populist, duly nominated, and replaced him with a declared Democrat.

The *Mound City Progress* drew the obvious conclusion: "Alliancemen would not believe Republicans two years ago when they told them that they were only playing into the Democracy's hands, but now the evidence is too plain to longer doubt it." The fusion policy in Kansas and other western states, together with the increasingly obvious intention of southern farmers to remain with the Democratic party, convinced many that they had indeed been playing the fool's part, and they rebelled against the dictation of their leaders. In some instances this took an organized form. In the Fourth District, many former Republicans denounced the deals made by the fusionists and asserted that "they did not leave the Republican party to go body and soul over to the Democracy; that if it has to be one of the old parties they will return to the one they naturally belong to." Many of these urged Otis to run as an independent candidate after Wharton received the Populist nomination. In the Third District, angry Populists organized an Abraham Lincoln Republican party as a factional straddle between their former partisan loyalties and their disappointed reform hopes. Composed largely of Alliance farmers, these dissident Populists objected to the nomination of the Democratic-Populist lawyer Hudson but refused to rejoin the GOP to support his opponent, Lyman Humphrey, a banker. They proposed to nominate an Alliance farmer for Congress.[34]

Many individuals protested Democratic influence so strongly that they did not hesitate to return to full Republican fellowship. Frank McGrath, a former state president of the Farmers' Alliance, disavowed the People's party after Harris's nomination and urged Alliancemen to follow him back into the GOP:

> The evidences are numerous in the conventions held this year that the middlemen, jackleg lawyers, and town loafers are more influential in directing and controlling the people's party than farmers. The success of the Democratic party seems to have become necessary with many leading People's Party leaders and to secure the defeat of the Republican party these leaders in the

People's Party and the Democratic party are ready to lay aside
their principles and by fusion secure the offices.

This party emphasis upon politics rather than Populism drove many
others back to the GOP, including John H. Rice, one of those most
prominent in organizing the national People's party. Benjamin Mat-
chett, speaker pro tem of the 1891 legislature, also renounced the
People's party and campaigned actively for the Republicans. He objected specifically to Populist support of middlemen such as Lewelling in opposition to farmer candidates. The president of the Rawlins
County Alliance similarly based his decision to return to the GOP
upon the action of the Populist conventions in nominating not
farmers but men of those classes Alliancemen had condemned as
parasitical. He also vigorously decried the Populist "truckling" to
the Second District Democrats: "I was a Republican and from this
time on hope to be." Many other Populists, from such prominent
leaders as D. G. Ollinger, chairman of the 1890 Populist First District central committee, to the twelve delegates in the 1892 Marion
County Republican convention who had voted Populist in 1890, followed the path back to the GOP, complaining of Democratic influence and elite manipulation.[35]

Although the *Kincaid Kronicle* had discontinued rather than support a debased ticket, other Populist newspapers determined in their
disillusionment to support the GOP directly once again. One Marion paper declared that the Populist party organization itself had repudiated Populism through its manipulations and other tactics to
arrange fusion. Methods condemned in the old parties, the paper
continued, should not be adopted by the new one, and the Populist
ticket formed by such methods should receive the support of "no
man who is in the party for the honesty, principles, and purification
of politics and the betterment of mankind."[36]

As party managers repudiated Populist principles and disrupted
their rank and file in pursuit of practical politics in Kansas in 1892,
similar developments transformed the national movement as well.
There were some among the Populist national leadership, as in Kansas, who believed that the party could best succeed by suppressing

the comprehensive reform aspirations expressed in its early days of enthusiasm and optimism and by then cooperating with those willing to accept such limited objectives though hostile to the sense of the initial movement. Again as in Kansas, some of these accommodators were men of hoary reform credentials who thought they saw the main chance, but many others were recent converts to the People's party.

These developments began gradually in 1893 as party leaders such as national chairman Herman E. Taubeneck and James B. Weaver sought to take advantage of the growing depression and the silver issue to pursue a "practical" policy toward fusion that deemphasized the party's original principles and contravened the wishes of many of its members. Weaver's entire career as a third-party advocate had been based on belief in the value of fusion, and he now sought to cooperate with the silver movement. In 1894 Weaver directed Iowa Populists to fuse with Democrats, accepting for himself a fusionist nomination to Congress, on the basis of silver. He also worked with Nebraska's Silver Democratic leader, William Jennings Bryan, in an effort to promote a wider fusion between the two parties. Criticizing antifusion Populists for "making the mistake of their lives," Weaver urged holding "a sort of interstate consultation over the situation in Neb, Dak & Iowa" to devise a silver fusion to prevent Republican success. He arranged speaking engagements for Bryan in Iowa while he campaigned for the Democrat in Nebraska. Bryan himself actively promoted fusion in Nebraska and found eager associates in Populists William V. Allen, elected senator in 1893 with the help of Democratic votes, and William McKeighan, a former Democrat elected to Congress by fusion in 1890 and 1892 and running as a fusion candidate in 1894.[37]

Of course, many Populists opposed these plans. The *Topeka Advocate,* for example, repeatedly denounced Bryan as "an enemy to the People's Party and to all true financial reform" because of his silver monomania. If the Populists restricted their platform to silver in order to promote fusion, the *Advocate* believed, it "would be a backward step that would be absolutely fatal." Another Populist newspaper censured Weaver, Allen, and McKeighan for their "high-handed proceedings" in attempting to "force such schemes down the throats of square Populists."[38]

But the elections of 1894 convinced party leaders even more of the need for fusion regardless of such objections. Although the party attracted vastly more votes than in 1892, they were disappointed that not more was achieved. Despite substantial gains in the South, the region remained heavily Democratic; in the West the party lost congressmen and state officials. Particularly troubling was the loss of the silver states of Nevada, Colorado, and Idaho, all of which had voted Populist in 1892. The only substantial results in the form of elected officers came from North Carolina, where Marion Butler had fashioned a fusion that placed a Populist in the Senate and three Populists in the House. A policy of fusion beckoned thus more seductively, and silver seemed to be the logical basis for it.

To promote this policy, party leaders concluded to eliminate the radical objectives of the Omaha Platform that might make others reluctant to vote with the People's party and to undercut those impractical Populists committed to the party's creed. Weaver spoke out freely after the election urging Americans not to believe "the ill-considered utterances of . . . overzealous, radical and unbalanced men. . . . All reform movements attract to their ranks men of radical and extreme views." He then made clear his definition of radicalism by proposing a combination on the basis of silver. Privately, moreover, he prepared to meet with Bryan and Allen to "shape things properly."[39]

Herman E. Taubeneck, national chairman, was equally ready to check radicalism within the party. In mid-November he advanced his interpretation of the failure of Populism to sweep the nation in the past election and his determination for its future course: "I regret deeply that the people's party has been honeycombed and undermined by all sorts of schemes, fancies, and abstractions. But for this unfortunate condition," he declared, "the people's party would have largely triumphed at the late election, but by rainbow chasing and endless freaks and foibles, we drove thousands upon thousands who are with us heart and soul on the money issue, into the ranks of the opposition." So believing, Taubeneck suggested that the party limit its platform to the single issue of silver. "No socialism or anarchism," he added, sounding like an old party politician, "indeed no 'isms' of any nature or side issue, nothing but the fight for bimetallism against the single gold standard." Taubeneck then attended a conference of the American Bimetallic League to coordinate the activities of the silverites and Silver Populists in preparation for the 1896 election. At the conference Taubeneck denounced the "cranks, anarchists, and socialists" in the People's party and recommended purging them to create a "pure silver" party.[40]

Taubeneck next decided to hold a conference of Populist leaders in St. Louis so that the party could "make known the fact that it has outgrown many of the 'isms' that characterized its birth and early growth, and take a stand on the financial question that will make it worthy of the support of those who . . . have not cared to support the party on account of its wild theories." He hinted that the St. Louis meeting would entirely remove the subtreasury and related demands from the Populist platform, and he particularly urged "conservative" and "level-headed" Populists to attend this critical meeting in December.[41]

With the exception of Senator Peffer, most Populists in Washington agreed with the decision to curtail the Omaha Platform. Apart from Peffer, few original Populists remained in the nation's capital. Kansas had replaced men such as Otis and Clover with men such as Harris and Hudson; southerners sent political opportunists such as Butler rather than early, unswerving Populists such as Tom Watson. Those who did remain from the first Populist contingent, like Simpson and McKeighan, had always run on fusion tickets and were willing to grant concessions to the Silver Democrats in their states. Another new type of Populist was the far western Silver Populist such as Lafe Pence of Colorado or Sen. William Stewart of Nevada, who joined the People's party in the first place only because of its silver declaration. Thus, products of direct fusion or inspired by silver zeal, Populist congressmen supported Taubeneck's proposal. Pence agreed that "the time has come to drop all weak 'isms,'" and Allen expressed his hope that the conference would "abandon all questionable doctrines and non-essentials." Another Populist endorsed Taubeneck by declaring, "Leave the cranks at home. Leave the impracticables at home," he urged in reference to the St. Louis meeting. "We can never expect to gain success when platforms are extended to take in the pet hobby or conciliate every crank in the nation. If the late election has taught us anything it is to push less issues with increased vigor."[42]

But Populists outside of Washington condemned Taubeneck's scheme to purge the party of its distinctive character. The *Dallas*

Southern Mercury even demanded that the national chairman resign if he refused to stand upon the party's platform. The *Topeka Advocate* denounced the "determination on the part of a few men" to redirect the party and declared that "Taubeneck can go with a free silver party if he chooses, but he will find that he cannot carry the People's Party with him." Davis Waite, Colorado's former Populist governor, launched a campaign against the conference, asserting that only another regular national convention and not a group of self-appointed political managers had the authority to alter the party's platform. He received strong support from such mid-roaders as Ignatius Donnelly, Paul Van Dervoort, and George Washburn, who recognized that silver was too narrow a basis upon which to build the party and condemned the "self-constituted crowd" for its short-sighted arrogance.[43]

Such radical Populists went to St. Louis, determined to defend the entire Omaha Platform. The Silver Populists found, to their dismay, that they were in a minority. Weaver failed first to secure a secret meeting and second to grant Taubeneck the power to appoint the resolutions committee. The discussions revealed a strong distrust of the party leaders by many in attendance, culminating in a mid-road denunciation of a proposed national campaign committee as "a political monopoly, the worst of all monopolies, led by office-seeking men, who care more for politics than for principle." The conference rejected all attempts to shorten the Populist program and reaffirmed the party's adherence to the Omaha Platform.[44]

Although rebuffed, the conservative Populists refused to accept as binding the declarations of the St. Louis meeting and continued to advocate the overthrow of the original Populist principles. Taubeneck's mouthpiece, the *National Watchman,* expressed disappointment in the St. Louis meeting and reproached "the overzealous and the crank" for their alleged lack of common political sense. It urged all the party's conservative members to attend future conventions to prevent another such folly and promised to campaign for the one-plank platform anyway.[45]

Taubeneck himself defended his actions vigorously. In two letters to W. Scott Morgan, a mid-road Arkansas Populist editor, the national chairman provided a classic exposition of the attitudes of the expedient, practical politician. Responding to Morgan's questioning of the Silver Populist plans, Taubeneck first bluntly asserted that "the party will either adopt my policy or we will never succeed as a party." When Morgan complained of his dictatorial tone and obvious indifference to Populist principles, Taubeneck replied:

> The trouble, Mr. Morgan, is, that you are dealing with theories and abstract ideas which are as pliable as the paper upon which you write. I have to deal with men and conditions. That is the difference between you and I [*sic*]. Mine is a cold-blooded, practical politics, and yours is a dreamland, living on theories and abstract ideas. I have never made a single mistake, when I followed my own views. . . . I have made mistakes in the past, I admit, when I listened to the council [*sic*] of others.[46]

Weaver also was dissatisfied with the outcome of the St. Louis conference. He corresponded with Taubeneck about holding a private meeting of those Populists willing to limit the party's platform to one issue ("our wisest heads," wrote Weaver). Such a conference could then publish a declaration favoring that course without facing the possibility of being outvoted on the issue again. Accordingly, Weaver went to Washington in January with an address he had prepared for publication. This manifesto urged Populists to concentrate their energies on the financial question and cooperate with all who opposed the gold standard, regardless of their attitudes on other issues. With one exception, all the Washington Populists signed Weaver's address. Peffer objected that the address, especially after the St. Louis conference, would convince rank-and-file Populists that their party leaders were trying to dictate to them and manipulate their loyalties in an effort to arrange fusion. Spurning Weaver's entreaties, Peffer refused to sign, protesting that Weaver's actions would lead to the destruction of the People's party through entanglement with Democrats over an unimportant issue.[47]

In publishing the address, the *National Watchman* confirmed Peffer's suspicions of Weaver's intentions. Sanctimoniously declaring its ignorance of why Peffer had not signed the document ("but presume it was through accident"), the *Watchman* expressed pleasure that its editorial position in favor of a one-plank platform had been endorsed by party leaders. It expected that "some of our papers . . .

may raise objections to the proposed lines of this address," but it warned mid-road papers not "to antagonize the propositions laid down in this manifesto." Arguing for the repudiation of Omaha Populism, the *Watchman* declared, "Let us be conservative and consistent in order to secure the support of the business men, the professional men, and the well to do."[48]

The *Watchman's* prediction of editorial objections to the policy proposed by the party officials was quickly fulfilled. The radicals voiced their complaints in the annual meeting of the National Reform Press Association (NRPA), which began in Kansas City, February 22, 1895, just one week after the publication of Weaver's address. Accusing Taubeneck of dishonesty, the editors expressed their apprehension that the chairman and his associates planned to betray the People's party to the "Philistines." Morgan's reading from his correspondence with Taubeneck created an uproar. Taubeneck's bluntly stated intentions to abandon "the socialistic features" of the Omaha Platform and his arrogant assumption that those who disagreed with him had no recourse brought outraged cries for his resignation. The editors approved resolutions declaring that no authority existed to alter the Omaha Platform except another popularly elected national convention, and they appointed a committee to investigate Taubeneck's activities, determine the intentions of the party's leaders, and warn them against trying to make silver the dominant issue. "These editors," reported the *Kansas City Star*, "say that if the Populist Party abandons the Omaha platform now and makes free silver the only issue the party will be swallowed up by the Democratic party which is sure to declare for free silver in 1896."[49]

Publicly, Taubeneck tried to appease the NRPA committee. With the secretary of the national committee, J. H. Turner, he agreed to sign a statement acknowledging that only a national delegate convention could revise the party's platform, and he entertained the editors at national headquarters, insisting that the People's party was prospering under his able direction. "So far as there being any danger of its being absorbed by the Democratic party," the practical-minded chairman maintained, "that is all nonsense." The NRPA committee also met with the Populist congressmen who had signed

Weaver's address and secured their written pledge that they had no intentions of abandoning any of the Omaha Platform.[50]

Despite these promises, however, the party managers continued with their plans. Taubeneck began a correspondence campaign to undermine the Omaha Platform and in summer 1895 urged Populist state conventions to ignore all but the money question. Weaver even more actively promoted silver and fusion schemes, traveling across the Midwest and West meeting with Silver Democrats and trying to arrange fusions in the 1895 state elections. He also used his influence to oust a mid-road editor from the *Des Moines Farmers Tribune* and replace him with an editor sympathetic to the plans of party officials. Stewart, Turner, Butler, and Breidenthal were similarly active in trying to shape the party's future.[51]

As the Populists prepared for the election of 1896, the first matter they had to consider was the place and date of the national convention, a decision that held deep significance for the direction the party would take in the campaign. As was clear from past experiences in state politics, a Populist convention held before either the Democrats or Republicans met would encourage an independent ticket or cause any fusion to be on Populist conditions and candidates; a convention after those of the old parties would facilitate fusion on a silver candidate already selected or promote a silver-only campaign, as the party would be influenced by silver accessions from the old parties that rejected bimetallism. Mid-road Populists came out in October 1895 for an early convention, one noting that only that course would still the fears "that our party machinery is being manipulated in the interests of the enemy."[52]

Taubeneck and his allies in control of the party machinery, however, favored a late convention as a means of securing a fusion campaign. When William Jennings Bryan, speaking for the Silver Democrats, urged the Populist leaders to delay their convention in order to ensure a fusion silver campaign, Weaver expressed his pleasure that Bryan's suggestions were "exactly in accord with the plan which Mr. Taubeneck and myself have been working to for some months past." Their next step was to have the Populist National Committee adopt the plan at its meeting in St. Louis on January 17. "We have had quite enough middle of the road nonsense," Weaver wrote privately, "and some of us at least think it about time for the exhibition

of a little synthetic force." In St. Louis, the party leaders easily overcame their critics, one of whom vainly urged the Populists to "at
once assert their supremacy over their party machine."[53]

Taubeneck, Weaver, and Butler had full control of the national
committee. They had taken advantage of the poverty of most committee members and secured the proxies of those unable to attend,
giving them 51 of 87 total votes. The compliant committee then followed their script exactly. It scheduled the party's convention after
the dates already selected by the old parties and adopted an as-
tounding resolution for an allegedly independent political party
with distinct principles. It urged all those favoring financial reform,
"but who are not ready to become members of our organization," to
hold a separate convention at the same time and place that the Populists chose so that there could be a fusion on candidates. Taubeneck
even hoped that the conventions themselves would meet together to
name candidates on a single platform. As the Silver Populists thus
maneuvered their party into a rather subservient cooperation with
the nonpartisan silverites, the initiative the Populists had cherished
as the vanguard of reform in the early 1890s was completely gone.[54]

Dispirited Populists complained not only of the committee's decisions but also of the methods by which they had been made. Referring to the manipulation of proxies, one wrote, "the so-called practical politician is in control. And principles are to be simply a foot
ball to [be] tossed and kicked all about." The *Advocate* reproved
Taubeneck: "To be the successful head of a great party requires
more ability than is necessary to fix up telegrams appointing proxies
to suit the chairman, and more candor and truthfulness than has
been exhibited by the chairman for the past two years." The *Mercury* charged that the party's politicians had betrayed Populism
through their actions: "As a reform party, seeking to deal honestly
by the people and eradicate the abuses, corruption and rottenness
that festers in the government, a result of old party rule, the people's
party must pursue an open, honest course with the people, or it will
fail in accomplishing the reforms it champions."[55]

Brushing aside these complaints, party officials now worked to secure compliant delegations to the national convention in July. The
national committee established a news bureau to provide Populist
readers with a stream of propaganda advocating one-plank silver

Populism and fusion, supporting the decision for a late convention, and creating presidential booms for old-party silverites. In Texas in February, Taubeneck addressed the Populist state committee, which then resolved in favor of a union of all silver advocates and praised him for his efforts. With Stewart and Weaver he encouraged fusion in Oregon's early state election as another step toward an obedient delegation. Elsewhere, one state after another instructed its delegates for silver fusion until Taubeneck exulted that "everything now is facing in that direction." By early spring he estimated that 375 of the 400 delegates already chosen had been instructed for fusion "on a purely silver platform, in which other questions should be ignored." The Iowa Populist convention, under Weaver's and Taubeneck's personal management, was atypical only in its lack of pretense. After Taubeneck told the Iowans to "do nothing by word or action to offend the silver wings of the two older parties," they voted down a minority report that called for a reaffirmation of the Omaha Platform and instead enjoined their delegation to support silver fusion. In Kansas, Breidenthal, Harris, and Simpson joined Taubeneck in directing the state convention to resolve for silver fusion and to instruct the party's delegates accordingly. Stewart was particularly pleased that the state's fusionist delegation to the national convention "will be headed by John W. Breidenthal, whose principle in politics is to get there if possible." There would be no need to stampede the Populist National Convention for silver and fusion; it was already so instructed.[56]

But such a course, far from being practical politics, was suicidal. As the wily Kansas Democrat John Martin pointed out in March, "If the Democrats nominate the right kind of man on a proper platform, the free silver Pops and free silver Republicans will vote with us. Those parties are not being conducted on logical plans and by proper action the Democrats will gain the support of thousands of the members of those parties."[57] By June Martin's observation was confirmed. When the Republican convention nominated William McKinley on a sound-money platform, the Silver Republicans led by Sen. Henry Teller of Colorado bolted the party and publicly urged all silver advocates to unite behind Teller as a joint presidential candidate.[58] Although they had long anticipated McKinley's nomination, the gold platform, and the Silver Republican bolt, the Populist leaders suddenly recognized the barren nature of the policies they had pursued. If the Democrats declared for silver, as now seemed likely, the People's party would be destroyed. In the Far West, most Populists had never been more than silverites, and under Stewart's leadership they would vote with either major party that advocated silver. In the Midwest and Plains, the Populists by 1896 depended upon former Democrats for their strength and were accustomed to fusion campaigns with the Democrats under the leadership of Weaver, Allen, and Breidenthal; these Populists too would prefer a Silver Democrat candidate to a Populist program and nominee. Even in the South, a Silver Democratic ticket would weaken Populism severely, for though Populists and Democrats were bitterly divided, the silver education of recent years would convince many Populists that their former party had returned to proper Democracy and so should they; moreover, the leading southern Populist, Butler, was completely committed to a silver campaign, and much of the alleged Populist strength in the South was anticipatory only, dependent upon a Democratic rejection of silver that now seemed improbable.

The Populist party leadership seized upon Teller's projected candidacy as the only opportunity to redeem at least partially its position and retain some influence in the prospective silver union. Taubeneck and members of the Populist national committee issued their own address urging Populists and all other silver groups to nominate Teller. Speaking of the impending Democratic convention, Taubeneck declared that the Democrats "must take Teller." Such a position was politically unrealistic. The Silver Democrats were the masters of the situation and would not waste their efforts of the past few years by nominating a Republican. This desperate maneuver of the Populist leaders only revealed more clearly how their own earlier actions had trapped them. Deception had become self-deception. Teller himself never believed in the delusion to which the Silver Populists clung and soon declared that the Silver Republicans would support a Silver Democrat nominee. His announcement sent the short-sighted Populist politicians reeling again, for they finally recognized that their lavish praise of Teller would simply backfire if he supported a Democrat.[59]

Shortly thereafter the Democratic convention nominated William Jennings Bryan on a silver platform, throwing the People's party into

further turmoil. As Henry Demarest Lloyd lamented in attacking
the "practical politicians" who had brought the party to this crisis,
the Populists had

> only the Hobson's choice of sinking ourselves out of sight and
> resurrection in the Democracy; or, of beginning, de novo,
> within a few weeks of election, the task of making an issue and
> finding followers. The masses have been taught by us that "sil-
> ver" is *the issue,* and they will of course have the common sense
> to give their votes to the most powerful of the parties promising
> it. . . . If we fuse, we are sunk; if we don't fuse all the silver
> men will leave us for the more powerful Democrats. And this is
> what Glaubenichts Taubeneck calls politics! Curious that the
> new party, the Reform party, the People's Party should be more
> boss-ridden, ring-ruled, gang-gangrened than the two old par-
> ties of monopoly . . . tricked out of its very life and soul by a
> permanent National Chairman—something no other party
> has![60]

Weaver, Breidenthal, Allen, and other Populist leaders promptly
advocated the Populist nomination of Bryan. Stewart declared that
western Populists supported Bryan so completely that "any attempt
to run an opposition candidate by the Populists will be a failure and
will destroy the Populist Party." Insisting that Populists approve
Bryan, Stewart added that "the attitude of the Southern delegates
will have no effect at all." Simpson proved just as imperious. "So far
as Kansas is concerned," he remarked, "it matters not what this convention does. We will endorse Bryan and vote for silver." Most party
officials also announced immediately for Bryan's endorsement—J.
H. Turner, the secretary of the national committee even intimating
that there was no further need of the People's party at all and that
Populists should join the Democracy—but Taubeneck reacted to
Bryan's Democratic nomination with dismay. Upon the eve of the
Populist convention he rejected the idea of Bryan's possible Populist
nomination as representing "the surrender and destruction of the
People's Party organization."[61]

Taubeneck's reactions suggest that unlike Weaver and Stewart,
who saw personal power and free silver as the only ultimate objec-

tives, he had sincerely believed that his schemes would deliver the nation's silver voters to the People's party. If so, however, it reveals at the same time that his vaunted "practical politics" were even more absurdly obtuse than the mid-roaders had earlier thought. In any event, the western Populists doubted Taubeneck's sincerity, perhaps because they had worked closely with him before. They asserted that with his Teller manifesto he had tried to force upon the party a man who agreed with Populists only on silver but that he now opposed a man who agreed with them on many issues in addition to silver. Kansans particularly denounced Taubeneck because, they argued, he had formulated their state platform so that Democrats would accept his Populism; now the Democrats had adopted a stronger platform and fusion should be no less desirable. When the Populist National Convention opened, Taubeneck reversed himself again and demanded the endorsement of Bryan.[62] His political and, presumably, mental acrobatics so wearied all Populists by the end of the convention that he was not reelected national chairman and thereafter dropped out of Populist sight. Only the natural results of his misguided policies remained to torment the People's party.

With Allen chairing the convention and Weaver the resolutions committee, the Populists nominated the Democratic Bryan for their party's highest honor. In an attempt to preserve the party's identity they narrowly rejected his Democratic vice-presidential running mate for a separate Populist candidate. The effort was futile, and the party stumbled toward oblivion. The Populists had failed in their attempt to ensure popular control even over their own politicians. Those who dominated the 1896 convention — Allen, Butler, Harris, Stewart, and others — were all officeholders explicitly forbidden from participating in the party's deliberations by the Omaha Ordinance for the Purification of Politics, adopted at the 1892 convention as fundamental party law. At the 1896 convention the Populists agreed to subordinate party to principle, but they had already subordinated principle to politics. Populists had failed to heed Ignatius Donnelly's earlier warning: "Let us subordinate everything to the success of the cause; but do not let us subordinate the cause to success."[63]

Moreover, subordination failed to bring that seductive and delusive success, for the Bryan fusion campaign failed to carry the election. And compounding the original disaster it had inflicted upon Populism, the party organization surrendered during the campaign much of the party's independence that its existence was designed to preserve. The national committee worked closely with the Democratic committee, sought and received Democratic funds, failed to coordinate Populist state campaigns, urged Populist candidates to withdraw in favor of Democratic nominees, and accepted electors pledged against their own vice-presidential nominee. Watching these maneuvers, one Illinois Populist concluded that "the party organization [was] a disgrace to populism."[64]

Indeed, the significance of original Populism, after all, was that it developed outside the political system. Yet in the transformation of Populism from a mass movement into the People's party, much of its democratic and directly responsive nature was lost. Populism became incorporated within the same system and the People's party became subject to the same influences that guided the other parties. The history of the People's party became one of a continuing struggle against the subversive tendencies of politics, undermining the original goals of Populism and substituting those of the old parties. The People's party, if originally for different reasons, became primarily concerned with winning office and gradually accepted institutional objectives. Under the direction of professional politicians such as Taubeneck and Breidenthal, Populist politics too became more of a struggle for office and power than for reform. The party became increasingly oligarchic and more easily dominated by its officials, and it became more and more difficult for the rank and file to influence policy. As early as 1892 the party leadership rigged conventions, lied to its rank-and-file members, and overturned duly nominated candidates in the search for office.

In 1897 Davis Waite looked back at the Populist failure already evident and blamed the party organization. There had been no means to hold the party to principle, he lamented. It had adopted the same caucus system and the same party committees, used the "rotten delegates" and the "bossism" of the old parties. An "inside ring" had usurped the right and circumvented the action of the rank and file, Waite asserted. "A few leading officials of the People's party by as bald trickery in the way of bossism, bogus proxies, and paper delegates as ever distinguished 'Tammany Hall,' assumed supreme control of the party and exercised that control without consulting the popular will and without appeal."[65]

Percy Daniels, a Populist pamphleteer, similarly recounted the tragedy of the People's party. Populism had repudiated "the methods of the old party machines" and denied "the celebrated theory of Mr. Ingalls that intrigue and corruption are essential to political success." But the party leaders set aside the original purpose of the movement, disobeyed the wishes of the rank and file, and adopted as legitimate tactics and appropriate goals what had been condemned.[66]

Those in control of the party machinery justified their manipulations in the name of "practical politics." Such machinations, however antithetical to the original professions of the movement, were necessary, argued Taubeneck, Weaver, and Breidenthal, if the party were to secure election. Those who disagreed with such a policy were "impractical visionaries" and hopelessly utopian. It was not practical politics that the country needed, however; it had that in the Democratic and Republican parties. America needed realistic politics, a policy of ignoring facile prejudices, investigating the realities of problems, and formulating relevant programs without resorting to traditional and outmoded dogma. There were those who demanded just such a necessary radical reappraisal of American society, but they were precisely those damned as impractical visionaries.

Gradually the Populist politicians succumbed to the same temptations affecting the old party leaders; too often converts to an elitist ideology, they proved as cynical as any of their opponents and certainly no more open and honest. (Peffer marveled at "how filthy the corruption of 'practical politics' among Reformers" became.)[67] Ultimately, with less experience in dissembling, they lost to past masters. As much as the irrelevant tariff had served the old parties, the practical Populists used the issue of free silver as a political panacea. Essentially a minor reform, clearly of limited effectiveness, free silver nevertheless promised an electorate to the People's party because as a panacea it was attractive to those who shrank from the requirements of realistic politics. Populist party leaders seized upon the issue to the exclusion of a consideration of vital problems and realistic reform proposals that the People's party had been created to advance. Fusion, too, was a practical political maneuver in a political system that rewarded only one winner; but too often it required the betrayal of the promises of Populism, and it gradually changed the composition, ideals, and objectives of the People's party. Silver and fusion, the tangible death instruments of Populism, did not dominate the People's party until its leaders subordinated the early demands of the movement in a practical grasp for power.

Observing the fiasco of the 1896 campaign, one Populist wrote his party's national chairman that he was renouncing all allegiance to the party, and he provided a poignant final assessment of the Populist experience: "I shall remain a Populist, but do not recognize the so-called People's Party as a political organization animated and directed by the spirit of true populism."[68]

6

TO DISFRANCHISE THE PEOPLE: THE IOWA BALLOT LAW AND ELECTION OF 1897

The great political realignment of the 1890s has attracted considerable attention from historians, but they have shown much less interest in the legal parameters of the political system — ballot and election laws and other structural features — within which the exciting contests took place. The only election law to receive significant notice established the Australian ballot system, providing for state-regulated ballots and secret voting. Generally regarded as a reform, the Australian ballot has been seen as ending the worst abuses of partisanship and corruption in voting, for which the Gilded Age had a well-deserved reputation, while having secondary effects upon party regularity and straight-ticket voting.[1]

But if the conduct of elections lost much of its earlier unsavory aspects, the electoral process was not purged of a partisan character altogether. Indeed, structural reform itself resulted from the interaction of politics and law. The enactment of secret ballot laws opened the whole range of political activity to state control, for by providing official ballots at public expense in place of party ballots privately distributed, the Australian system gave the state the authority and responsibility for regulating nominations, campaign procedures, and other party activities. Those who controlled the state thus gained the power to structure the system in their own behalf, to frustrate or weaken their opponents, in a manner that would have astounded their predecessors and that was not only effective but by definition legal. This development was all the more attractive to those partisans disturbed by the political volatility of the 1890s.

Perhaps the most widespread attempt to use election machinery for partisan purposes involved the so-called antifusion law. After the election of 1896, when the possibility of defeat through a fusion of their opponents had thoroughly alarmed Republicans, it was enacted by virtually all midwestern legislatures, safely if perhaps temporarily controlled by Republicans. The goal of antifusion legislation was to guarantee the perpetuation of that control by disrupting and antagonizing their opponents. The effects of such activity can be seen readily in Iowa, which held an election immediately after passing its antifusion law in 1897 and attracted national attention.

Fusion politics, or the cooperation of two or more parties on a joint set of candidates, had been common in Iowa since the 1870s. Although Iowa traditionally was a Republican state, fusion had permitted Democrats, Grangers, Anti-Monopolists, Greenbackers, and Populists to secure election and sometimes to influence legislation.[2] The dramatic 1896 election seemed again to threaten Republican power. Many Iowans had strong silver sentiments, and some observers expected that the state might support William Jennings Bryan. Leading Republicans downplayed the national party's gold stance in order to retain the allegiance of the rank and file. Republican apprehension peaked when Democrats, Populists, and Silverites fused. Fusion meant not merely that the three parties named the same ticket but that the ticket would be listed under each of the fusing parties' symbols on Iowa's official party-column ballot. It would not be necessary for an ardent Populist or a bolting Republican to have to cast his vote as a loyal Democrat to bring about bimetallism. And a private poll found 30,000 Republican bolters in Iowa, enough to alarm Mark Hanna and perhaps to carry the state for Bryan. Republican state chairman H. G. McMillan regarded prospects as "threatening." Entire townships formerly "strongly Republican" were deserting the party "en masse," he complained.[3]

An elaborate campaign enabled the Republicans to turn the tide, and the November results gave them a solid victory. While Republicans crowed "this is a state without a blight of Populism. It is a businessman's state," fusionists claimed bitterly that the Republican vote had been artificially inflated. Bryanites charged that electoral abuses were widespread despite "this being the first presidential election under the secret ballot system." Some charges were undoubtedly the product of wishful thinking, as when the *Des Moines Farmers Tribune* asserted that "the only way the Hannacrats could carry this election was by fraud, intimidation, coercion, bribery, false promises, illegal voting, and ballot box stuffing." On the other hand, specific instances of electoral chicanery were revealed, as in Wayne County where election judges refused to add the Populist vote to the Democratic vote, thereby crediting the county to McKinley rather than to Bryan.[4]

Not surprisingly, Democrats wanted to remedy flaws in the voting system, but Republicans also advocated, vaguely, changes in election law. One Republican editor noted that the adoption of the Australian ballot had produced "numerous complications in the election laws," adding that "it has been possible to greatly vary the details so that there is a wide difference in the results obtained." Some Republicans believed that the methods of marking ballots under the election law needed revision; others concluded that "defects" in the process of acquiring places on the ballot had to be corrected. What prompted these latter observations was the fusionist nature of the 1896 campaign against the GOP and the attempts of various factions of each party to control the official party designations on the ballot.[5]

Moreover, the fusionists seemed determined to continue their collaboration. Populists and Silver Republicans, reflecting the strong partisan prejudices of the time, were reluctant to merge into the Democratic party and wanted to maintain their separate organizations, but they recognized that only in fusion was there hope of success. Populists, moreover, believed that their principles had gained wider circulation and acceptance in the Bryan campaign "than could have been secured for them by and through a middle of the road course for years to come." In December, representatives of the three parties met in Des Moines and agreed that in the future the parties would hold simultaneous conventions and nominate common candidates to appear on each ticket on the official ballot.[6]

The Republicans also believed that the Populists had gained the most from the 1896 fusion arrangements. Again like the Populists, moreover, Republicans failed to recognize the permanence of the

1896 political realignment and believed the struggle would continue, perhaps with time as the ally of their opponents. The Republican *Sioux City Journal* expressed these fears early in 1897. Worrying over "increasing radical aggression," the *Journal* saw "a disposition to consolidate the radicals, to organize and fuse and propagandize." The recent silver conference was an alarming case in point. The *Journal* had hoped that the Democrats would accept their 1896 defeat, repudiate the Populists, and welcome back the Gold Democrats. Republicans, the paper admitted, "are profoundly interested in having the Democratic party the organ of conservative rather than of radical and revolutionary purposes." But the announced fusion plans convinced the *Journal* that the Populists had captured the Democratic party and thereby created "a grave menace." The GOP had to obstruct the radicals and ensure conservatism.[7]

One Republican reaction to that perceived menace appeared promptly. The Iowa legislature was scheduled to convene in special session in January to codify the state's laws. Although the session would consider a number of important matters, the *Chicago Tribune* called attention to one in particular: "The Iowa legislature will have the distinction of being the first law-making body in this country to put the Australian ballot system in codified form. . . . The adjustment of this law, as made in Iowa by a commission of able lawyers, will be of more general interest than any other part of the new code."[8]

Senate Republicans moved quickly and imaginatively in "doctoring the ballot," as one Democrat described the process. Most important, the Elections Committee sought to end traditional fusion arrangements by prohibiting the printing of any candidate's name more than once on the official ballot and by requiring the candidate of two or more parties to be listed within the column of the party first filing nomination papers. Such provisions would of course introduce divisive competition between groups that hoped to cooperate and force some partisans to transgress their own strong party allegiance to vote as members of a different party. The regulations would also render the second party ineligible for the partisan benefits of straight-ticket voting, for any fusionist wanting to support all his party's candidates would have to indicate them individually and in more than one column rather than simply marking the party circle heading his ticket.[9]

This last was more involved than immediately apparent. Iowa had allowed voters to mark the party circle and still vote for a candidate of another party for any specific office by also marking the individual box corresponding to that candidate's name. This rule obviously left an opening for fusion even under the new restrictions. Accordingly the Republicans next proposed to permit use of the circle only when a full straight ticket was voted; if the voter wanted to scratch even a single candidate or vote for anyone in another column, then he would have to mark separately each desired candidate and avoid the party circle. Though Republicans defended this change as a reform to simplify the voting process, one senator pointedly observed that whereas the old procedure encouraged independent voting the effect of the revision would be that, having "become accustomed to marking according to the present law, . . thousands and thousands of men will be disfranchised this year." Not surprisingly, perhaps, did some Republicans regard the ballot-marking provisions as "the real question" in the whole election law tangle.[10]

The same fear of independent voting led Republicans to reject a proposal to eliminate the party circle altogether. The Des Moines *Iowa State Register*, the state's leading Republican newspaper, denounced political independence and praised the retention of the party circle, which permitted even "voters who cannot read to vote their full party ticket." On the other hand, the *Register* added disdainfully, "voters who desire to vote a mixed ticket should be wise enough to know how to mark their ballots." One senator emphasized this discriminatory differential by observing that "a man can do two days' work on election day in addition to voting a straight ticket, but if he wants to vote a scratch ticket it requires the entire day in addition to two weeks' preparation before hand."[11]

Several more proposals completed the Republicans' "tinkering up the Australian ballot." The first required county auditors to print party names on the ballot in the order established by the secretary of state. The rationale was that this would lead to a uniform ballot since auditors had arranged the tickets according to their own preferences, but it also centralized power in Republican state officials and limited the discretionary power of local, potentially non-Republican officials. "This is of course to give the republicans the first place on the ballot," noted one editor, "which would be quite an advantage in a close election." The Elections Committee then eliminated the requirement that sample ballots be published in newspapers prior to the election, thereby making it difficult for those who would have to contend with the ballot revisions to anticipate their predicament. A final change of electoral rules required an earlier closing of the polls, which Democrats regarded as an "inconvenience" in the manufacturing towns along the Mississippi River, traditional Democratic strongholds.[12]

A dramatic public debate developed over these revisions, focusing particularly on the antifusion provision. The Republicans offered numerous rationalizations for their proposals. Some argued in terms of equity, claiming that a candidate nominated by more than one party gained an unfair advantage by having his name listed in each party's column on the ballot. A more reasonable if still disingenuous argument held that the voter should know which party and platform a candidate supported: "The amendment does not say two parties shall not nominate the same man for the same office but it does say he shall sail under his true political principles." Others maintained that the elections bill involved merely procedural reforms, designed only to "prevent the ballot from becoming more unwieldy" and "expensive." Throughout, however, the Republicans' partisan motivation was transparent and repeatedly, if inadvertently, confessed.[13]

Opposition arguments were wide-ranging. Some Populists conceded that the antifusion proposal technically "does not deprive any man of voting," but together with other reforms it "deprives a candidate from receiving votes from those who may be afraid to scratch their ticket for fear of losing their entire vote and in a degree it prevents massing of different party votes." The Populist legislative reporter for the *Farmers Tribune* regarded the proposals as merely another way to continue the Republicans' 1896 obstruction of a fair ballot and an honest count in their efforts "to hold sway in this state at all hazards." Others argued that the Republicans were motivated by fear of popular reaction against several "boodle" scandals being reluctantly exposed by the same legislature: "They know the people of Iowa are getting mad and they must by some means be kept apart or the golden calf will be swept from its pedestal. . . . To do this they pass this unrighteous law which is intended to stifle the voters and either prevent [their] voting or divide them up into different parties, though they may agree in sentiment." Several dissident Republican senators insisted their colleagues *were* motivated by partisan considerations in seeking "the disfranchisement and circumscribing of the powers of the individual voter." One argued that the antifusion provision was un-Republican since it was comparable to the discriminatory ballot restrictions being enacted in the South by Democrats.[14]

The chairman of the Elections Committee moved to close debate, saying the discussion had assumed "too wide a range entirely." The senate then passed the elections bill by 31 to 17, with ten Republicans joining the Democrats in opposition. One reporter recorded the struggle: "There was a scene in the senate chamber this morning the like of which has not occurred in the memory of the oldest member of that usually dignified body over the final passage of the long elections bill. The senate spent eight days in amending the elections law and getting the bill in shape and then on its passage encountered the fiercest fight of years."[15]

The crux of the matter, of course, was that despite the great debates no one was certain of the bill's political effects. Most Republicans believed it would fragment their opposition and guarantee an easier victory than they might otherwise achieve. Others feared that the obvious partisanship of the bill would provoke a popular backlash and guarantee instead an even more effective coalition against the GOP. A few Republicans simply opposed it on principle. The *Indianola Record,* for example, condemned Republican legislators for using the power of the state for private purposes: "A small bunch of men, supposed to be seeking the welfare of all the citizens of the state, suddenly transform themselves into a Republican partizan caucus and pass a law that is supposed to perpetuate or render more certain its continuation in power. . . . If we must bolster up our party with legislative enactments, it is not worth preserving." Populists and Democrats overwhelmingly protested the proposed electoral changes, but some Democrats recognized that the antifusion clause was primarily directed at the minor parties, which would have to be absorbed into the major parties to retain any influence. In this respect Democrats might even welcome the bill. But it did interfere with their immediate fusion plans, and the Democratic members of the house promptly caucused to organize their opposition to the elections bill.[16]

The points made in the senate debate and public discussion were repeated in the house when the elections bill was reported. One Populist expressed no surprise when the bill bogged down: "The more the people think of that proposition the more they wonder, if the legislature passes it, why it did not go on a little further and say there shall be but one ticket allowed on the ballot, and that must be the republican ticket." House Republicans did move closer to outlawing their opposition by adopting an amendment requiring candidates to decline nominations from parties other than the one they would be listed under on the ballot, a step Democrats and Populists regarded as another "hard thrust" against their possible cooperation. But the Republicans, as before, insisted that the bill would merely "diminish the power of trafficking party bosses" and not interfere with the franchise. A Democratic representative easily countered by noting that the Republicans had coupled the antifusion provisions with the retention of the party circle, and "if, as has been said by the chairman of the elections committee, in opposition to doing away with the circle, that it would deprive hundreds of the right to vote in his county only, I wish to ask how many thousands will be deprived of that right if they are deprived of the right to use the circle?" Tiring of embarrassing questions, the Republican majority passed the bill on March 25.[17]

The *Farmers Tribune* immediately posed the question: Now what should the silver forces do? Their early plans to continue the form of the 1896 fusion had reflected their belief that "neither the populists or democrats are ready to surrender their name and identity to assume that of the other nor a new one." Many Populists now believed that the latter alternative was the only solution—the abandonment of all former organizations and the creation of a new party, thereby avoiding both the disagreeable aspect of fusion and the new law. But the party leaders determined on the other course of action under the law. Meeting repeatedly in Des Moines during the spring to discuss the effect of the ballot regulations on their fusion plans, the fusionist leaders became convinced that the Republican legislation was born of desperation and presented them with a winning issue should they be able to minimize partisanship and cooperate despite the law. When the spring elections revealed a swing away from the Republicans, James B. Weaver, Iowa's leading fusionist and the former Populist presidential candidate, could not restrain his optimism: "Their attempt to disfranchise the people through antifusion legislation . . . will physic the doctor instead of the patient."[18]

To complete their preparations, the state committees of the Democrats, Populists, and Silver Republicans met again in Des Moines on May 12. They decided to hold their three state conventions on June 23 and nominate a joint ticket. They agreed to give each party equal representation in writing the platform and to divide the ticket by allowing the Democrats to choose the candidates for governor and supreme court justice, the Populists for attorney general and railroad commissioner, and the Silver Republicans for state superintendent. For the interim, a joint committee was formed to petition the legislature to repeal the hated antifusion law. The only controversy at the meeting involved the party name to head the joint ticket under the new law. Finally the party leaders tentatively adopted "Democratic" in the belief that if the Democrats dropped their name, even to accept a compromise name, the Gold Democrats would run a ticket as the regular Democratic nominees and thereby still further disrupt the voting.[19]

The validity of that fear was demonstrated shortly thereafter when the Gold Democrats called a convention for July 7 to consider nominating a separate ticket, depending on the action of the regular state convention in June. Still, for many Populists that was not reason enough to surrender their party's name and accept Democratic tutelage. The circumstances surrounding the decision further angered such Populists, for they resembled past leadership attempts to manipulate party members without regard to their wishes or to open procedures. That Weaver had been a major mover in the Des Moines conference, without being an official party committeeman, particularly irritated A. W. C. Weeks of the *Winterset Review*. Denouncing the action as unauthorized since there had been neither an official call for the conference nor a quorum of the committee, Weeks urged Populists to repudiate these party bosses. If Populists voted under the Democratic heading, Weeks warned, "we could not certify that we had cast any votes this year, and the only way we could get on [the ballot] next year would be by petition."[20]

The *Atlantic Bimetallist,* another Populist paper, similarly condemned the arrangements made by the state committees, maintaining that they involved the practical destruction of the People's party. A motivating fear was that the Democrats, after absorbing the Populists and other reform groups through the operation of the antifusion law, might become "once more a reliable tool in the service of Wall Street and the trusts." Like the *Winterset Review,* the *Bimetallist* was willing to have all reform parties temporarily organize in an "honorable and just" union, under a single and appropriate name, such as "Independent" or "Reform," in order to "win a victory for the people" and repeal "the UnAmerican and fiendish measure passed by the Republican legislature," but it rejected the proposed arrangements as disruptive and dangerous.[21]

The official call for the Populist state convention confirmed such fears. Assailing "the extraordinary and unwarranted legislation enacted by the party in power to keep the people from uniting to punish them for their perfidy," the proclamation announced that the convention would have to devise some new means of political cooperation. The allocation of convention delegates was not based on the 1895 state election, when Populists ran their own ticket, but on the 1896 fusion vote. The effect of this decision, as Weeks noted, was to give "all advantage to the Democratic counties and just about eliminate Populists from the convention." This conclusion was reinforced by the provision for 1,215 delegates, three times as many as ever before in an Iowa Populist convention. Heavily Democratic Dubuque County was thus allocated 33 delegates, though it had cast but 185 Populist votes in 1895, while Madison County, with 780 Populist votes in 1895, received but 12 delegates. To Weeks and others, the intentions of the state committee were obvious: "to pack the convention with Democratic delegates to overawe and outvote the Populists in the interests of fusion and a Democratic ticket."[22]

Final preparations for the convention were not reassuring. The party leadership scheduled the local delegate-selection caucuses to enable Democrats to attend the Populists' as well as their own. In Plymouth County the Populist convention was transformed into a mass meeting to choose delegates, opening up the process and positions to Democrats. Other counties selected the same delegates to represent them in each of the three state conventions, guaranteeing joint action and the submergence of policy disagreements.[23]

Indeed, when the Populist state convention opened, the temporary chairman, selected by the state committee, was a Silver Republican, who, after attacking the Republicans for limiting the political rights of their opponents, called for a reform coalition and a campaign based on opposition to the antifusion law. Although willing to accept such proposals, Weeks wanted them under different auspices, and he moved to change the basis of representation to the 1895 Populist vote in order to prevent Democrats from controlling the convention. But the delegates tabled this motion, chose Weaver as permanent chairman, and authorized a committee to confer with similar groups from the Democratic and Silver Republican conventions meeting simultaneously elsewhere in Des Moines. While these committees decided the basis of cooperation, Weaver addressed the Populist convention on the subject of the antifusion law, which he described as "an attempt to disband a party . . . by legislation." The disfranchising effect of the ballot law convinced Weaver that the Republicans intended "to overthrow free government." So persuaded, the convention accepted the report of the conference committee to nominate a combination ticket with the Democrats and Silver Republicans and to name it "Democratic." Weeks's counterproposal to nominate the ticket under the Populist heading was rejected by a three-to-one margin. Weeks and twenty-eight other delegates then withdrew, charging that through the actions of the state committee the convention had been captured by "the opponents of Populism."[24]

The remaining Populists tried to overcome that apprehension by instructing party officials to attempt first to place the ticket on the ballot under the Populist name. A failure in this effort, the delegates declared, would reflect not their wishes but "republican legislation that interferes with the right of the free ballot." In the official platform, the Populists denounced the antifusion law as "the most infamous measure ever enacted by a partisan legislature, and one to legislate the dominant party into power in Iowa by disarming and disfranchising the sovereign electors in whose hands there rests the sovereignty of our institutions and the rights and liberties of the people." The Democrats in their platform similarly attacked the

antifusion law as "the last refuge of the enemy of popular government." Sharing these attitudes and a belief in free silver, each party
nominated its allotted candidates and forwarded their names to the
other conventions for endorsement.[25]

These developments did not resolve the political confusion. Attempting to frighten Democrats away from fusion, Republicans had
earlier maintained that Populists had captured the Democracy; now
they began to insist that the Democrats had "swallowed the little in-
fant of Populism" in an effort to frighten Populists away from an obviously disagreeable arrangement. Without mentioning the antifusion law, the *Iowa State Register* declared that Populist managers
had sold out their partisans by agreeing to designate them as Democrats on the official ballot. It wishfully predicted that the mid-roaders would gain support, for "the name of their party, together with
its achievements, are dear to [Populists] and they will hardly give
them up without a struggle."[26]

Fusionist Populists, of course, sought to counter these efforts. The
Farmers Tribune urged all to deemphasize the partisan features of
the joint campaign, especially asking Democrats to refrain from
claiming that Populists and Silver Republicans were becoming Democrats by voting the Democratic ticket. It was a movement outside
normal party lines, the paper insisted; the Democratic name was
used "merely from necessity." The *Tribune* also attempted to attract
the bolters back to the fusion campaign, justified as the only practical course under the legal circumstances. Temporary compromise
might lead to victory and the repeal of the antifusion law, but a separate campaign would only help plutocracy. The editor believed
that the fusion ticket had been properly chosen and therefore the
mid-roaders would be unable legally to nominate another ticket,
but, ruefully, he admitted, "Of course the state election board and
the courts are under control of the republicans and may not decide
according to law and justice, for a party that will go to the extremes
to which that element has already gone in order to retain an undue
advantage will do anything."[27]

The first disruption to the plans of the "triple alliance," however,
came from within the Democratic party. Though fusionists had insisted from the enactment of the antifusion law that the Gold Democrats would rejoin the regular Democrats, they had necessarily based

their campaign on silver. Some Gold Democrats reluctantly accepted the state ticket as the only practical means to defeat the Republicans and thereby secure a number of achievements, including repeal of the antifusion law. Other conservative Democrats reacted differently. The *Davenport Democrat* asserted that "a vote for the fusion ticket is a vote for populism carried to its extreme." And the *Burlington Gazette,* another gold organ, expressed its support for a traditional Democratic ticket but its opposition to the "hybrids" on the fusion ticket. Similar sentiment was voiced during the Democratic convention itself when the platform, to promote the coalescence of the triple alliance, avoided many hoary Democratic concerns. This prompted some delegates to shout, "What about the liquor question?" and even "Is this a Democratic convention?" Thus, efforts to attract Populists and Silver Republicans into a unified coalition under the Democratic name antagonized other potential allies.[28]

When the Gold Democrats gathered in July, then, they nominated a full ticket to appear separately on the ballot. Though they attacked the Republicans for tariff legislation, they reserved much of their hostility for silver and the fusion ballot arrangements. Spokesmen predicted 40,000 votes for the ticket, but the limited attendance and uncontested nominations suggested a more restricted base of support.[29]

Trying to cut their losses, fusion leaders claimed that the action of the Gold Democrats eliminated any reason for mid-road Populists to fear Democratic dominance and run their own ticket. Such appeals apparently did lessen the widespread disaffection among Populists in the aftermath of the joint state conventions, but others remained adamant. Particularly galling for these was the unusual nature of the Populist convention that had accepted the Democratic name. Among the "Populist" delegates to that convention Weeks discovered a Democrat from Dubuque with thirty-two proxies — all from other Democrats. Indeed, another Populist estimated that three-fourths of the delegates in the Populist convention under Weaver's rules had been Democrats. Directly and indirectly, Republicans encouraged such discontent. The *Iowa State Register,* for instance, broke its silence on the antifusion law to explain that the law did *not* prevent Populists from putting their own ticket into the field. Democratic officials complained that Republicans aided the mid-roaders, but Weeks insisted that he was receiving support from the Populist rank and file, one of whom proclaimed that those Populists who wanted to become Democrats should do so but not "tear the house down from over the heads of those who wished to stay."[30]

As such attitudes crystallized, the mid-roaders organized formally, elected Weeks state chairman, and issued a call for a nominating convention to meet in Des Moines August 19. The basis of representation was the 1895 Populist vote, but the arrangements obviously would be difficult: "Where the county machinery of the party is in the hands of loyal [i.e., mid-road] People's party men the county conventions should be called by the regular chairman," Weeks announced; "otherwise it is recommended that the straight People's party men assemble in mass convention" to choose delegates to the state gathering. Privately, Weeks urged mid-roaders to "get *double* delegations from all counties you can. A *crowd* is what we need. D——n how they get there so they are true blue."[31]

Unexpected support came in late July when Weeks orchestrated the simultaneous resignations of five of the eleven Populist state committeemen and their acceptance of similar positions on the mid-road committee even as regular Populist state chairman James Bellangee frantically sought to retain their support. The excited Weeks described the conversion as "the most stupendous blow ever struck in Iowa politics and . . . unparalleled in the Nation." None of the committeemen had been among the original bolters at the state convention, but each now reacted to what one called "the management of that convention." Except for the old Greenbacker, Calamity Weller, who affirmed his opposition to all fusion as self-destructive, the committeemen expressed a willingness for a union of forces, on terms of "strict equality" or resulting in "mutual good"—as they regarded past fusions. "But to have the People's party picked up bodily and dumped into the Democratic cauldron was too much to be endured." The campaign arrangements under the antifusion law would help only the Democrats, they contended, while destroying the People's party.[32]

Some fusionists charged that mid-road activity would merely help the Republicans and that Weeks, at least, was under Republican pay. Bellangee was less sure that Republican money lay behind the

bolt. "Disappointed ambition, personal animosity, and party prejudice are as common as avarice," he noted, "and are often much
more controlling." Bellangee feared the effects of partisan prejudice
most and speculated that the mid-roaders would not poll a large
vote except where past Democratic hostility would "require much
sacrifice of personal feeling" to vote under the Democratic heading.[33]

Still others sought a way to reconcile such feelings with the ballot
requirements that seemed to provoke them. One Populist suggested
labeling "the county tickets peoples party, so that we can hold our
identity on the county ticket and the democrats on the state ticket."
Otherwise, the Democratic heading would produce many "stay-at-
home votes, as it wipes us out so that in the future we will have to get
on the ballot by petition." Others worried about the "confusion consequent upon having to vote in more than one column" and the corresponding inability to use the party circle under this expedient.
One silverite warned against the suggestion as leading toward defeat, for the new election laws were designed to confuse and mislead
those who hoped to follow precisely such tactics, and "I would hate
to lose my vote on account of republican shrewdness and trickery."[34]

Nevertheless, ballot design became a major issue in local Populist
conventions in late summer. In some counties, when the fusionists
controlled the party machinery and arranged for fusion slates, mid-
roaders called separate conventions to nominate independent tickets. In other counties, the insurgents dominated the conventions,
spurned Democratic fusion propositions, and named straight local
tickets and delegates to the mid-road state meeting.[35]

In most counties, however, the regular Populists overcame the
mid-roaders, and the state convention attracted no more than 100
delegates from fifty counties. The mid-roaders refused to listen to a
conciliatory speech by Chairman Bellangee of the regular Populist
state committee and nominated a separate ticket. The high point of
the convention was a forceful address by the national mid-road
leader, former senator W. A. Peffer of Kansas. He stressed the basic
radical insistence that the Democratic party was ultimately as much
an enemy to Populism as was the Republican party and that manipulative schemes of party officials pursuant to fusion constituted the
very denial of Populism. Abe Steinberger, another Kansas mid-

roader in attendance, was even more explicit, telling a Republican journalist, "We feel that we have made a good riddance in being enabled, by your election laws, to hand the Weaver crowd of reform party wreckers over to the Democrats."[36]

Republicans reacted with pleasure. Their plans had been realized. They had supported the antifusion law in the belief that it would either prevent fusion or, if fusion occurred, split off mid-road Populists and traditional Democrats, for the former would not vote under the Democratic label and the latter would not accept the necessary recognition of Populists on a Democratic ticket. The fragmentation of the potential opposition coalition was completed in August when the Socialist Labor party organized and, appealing for support from disgruntled Populists, nominated a ticket to be placed on the ballot by petition. Finally, despite their support for silver, Iowa's Prohibitionists also nominated a separate ticket rather than vote in the Democratic column.[37]

Republicans firmed up their own ranks by nominating a new slate of candidates untouched by the Republican scandals. The hostility toward those scandals, of course, was not simply fueled by moral outrage or taxpayer anger. Rather, it also expressed itself in the same form that characterized much of the outburst against the ballot law: the use of state power for partisan objectives. When, for example, the *Farmers Tribune* revealed that Republican party workers were on the state payroll, it had headlined its account, "How to Run a Campaign at State Expense."[38]

The ballot law, then, seemed all of a piece with Republican actions to many Iowans. One Democrat, for instance, attacked the law for interfering in the nominating process and denying full opportunity to the state's voters to express themselves. "The essence of the right of suffrage," he maintained, "is to exercise the right without the dictation of state authority." A Republican countered triumphantly that, from suffrage and ballots to election booths and marking regulations, "the whole thing is strictly under 'the dictation of state authority.'" That, of course, was precisely the trouble, said another Democrat. "Those clothed with authority were always reaching out beyond their authority for the purpose of aggrandizing themselves and oppressing those who it is their privilege to govern." Controlling the state, the Republicans next moved to use that authority to complete their campaign arrangements, ensnarling their opponents in procedural restraints.[39]

Through tangled maneuvers, the legislature had provided for the new code to go into effect October 1 so that the antifusion law would be operative for the November election. The combination of the extensive electoral changes and what the *Dubuque Herald* termed the legislature's "action not allowing the laws to be made public until October 1" particularly alarmed the Democrats. The *Herald* urged them to observe the old requirements as well as what they understood to be the new regulations. Indeed, because nomination papers had to be filed thirty to sixty days before the election many of the campaign procedures were undertaken in comparative legal uncertainty. Following the convention's instructions to attempt to file under the Populist name but preserve fusion, the triple alliance leaders agreed that on September 3, the first official day for filing nominations, Democratic state chairman Charles Walsh would submit both sets of papers, Democratic first so that it would have precedence should the antifusion law take effect. Then, to prevent mid-road interference, on the night of September 2 they secured an injunction from Silver Republican judge W. A. Spurrier restraining Secretary of State George Dobson from recording nomination papers under the names People's party or Populist party. Meanwhile, A. W. C. Weeks, fearing just such a development, arrived in Des Moines and went to the home of Dobson's deputy, routing him out of bed to accept the mid-road Populist nomination papers. Thus in the morning when Walsh presented both Democratic and (fusion) Populist papers, the latter were rejected because a set of Populist papers had already been recorded. The sheriff arrived with the injunction minutes too late. Furious, Walsh threatened further legal action, sputtering, "I prefer to file my papers in the office of the secretary of state instead of the china closet of Mr. Smith's boarding place."[40]

Republicans had a field day with these developments, assailing the Democrats for attempting to "disfranchise" an entire party by an injunction keeping it off the ballot—"a serious inroad," one ironically noted, "on the right of men to vote their own convictions." The mid-roaders objected in similar fashion and with less hypocrisy: "With what grace," Weeks asked of the Democrats, "can they howl at a republican legislature passing the antifusion law, when they don't intend to let a Populist vote any ticket at all?" It was, he concluded, the "same old Democratic game of hollering 'Frod! Frod!' while at the same time trying to cheat and degrade the voter and prevent his coming to the ballot box and voting as he pleases." Another mid-roader also was uncertain which of the major parties was more outrageous: "The two old parties have issued their mandate against a free ballot. The Republicans by act of legislation, and the Democrats by injunction."[41]

After lamely attempting to defend their injunction, the fusionists dropped it to pursue another strategy. On September 7, Populist officials filed with the state election board a formal complaint against the mid-road ticket being placed on the ballot under the Populist name. The election-board hearing between the regular and mid-road factions began September 16 and dragged on until "it threatened to occupy the remainder of the natural lives of the members of the board." Bellangee argued that the fusion slate, not the mid-road one, should be listed under the Populist name for only it met the legal requirements of being nominated and certified by the regular convention and its officers. The only legal way for the mid-road ticket to appear on the ballot, Bellangee contended, was by petition — and that under a name other than People's party. The mid-roaders countered that the basis of representation at the regular Populist convention had allowed, as Bellangee allegedly had anticipated, Democrats, not Populists, to control the proceedings and that the regulars did not intend to use the Populist name themselves.[42]

The fusionists were confident of their legal position but doubtful that the all-Republican election board would uphold it. And, indeed, on September 21 the board ruled that the mid-roaders could be designated on the ballot as the People's party ticket. The decision was based on the antifusion law, not operative for another ten days. The board, however, adopted the mid-road argument and held that Bellangee knew that the law would control the election and that the regular Populist nominees, already filed under the Democratic heading, could not be listed again. Having not intended to use the Populist name, therefore, the regulars had no claim to it and could not prevent its use by another Populist faction. Fusionists of all parties denounced the board's reasoning and insisted that the regulars had not abandoned their name but were prevented from using it by

Republican legislation. But the *Farmers Tribune* was not surprised by the board's decision: "Is it not simply a completion of the infamy commenced by the republican legislature?"[43]

Bellangee's attorney next filed suit in Polk County (Des Moines) District Court to overturn the decision of the election board. On October 16 Judge Spurrier ruled that the board had acted illegally by exercising judicial functions. He ordered the mid-road ticket stricken from the ballot for it had not been nominated by a party that polled the legal minimum of the vote in 1896 nor was it accompanied by the requisite petition signatures. Secretary of State Dobson, however, had already transmitted the official ballot, including the mid-road ticket, to the county auditors. He had been under no injunction and had merely acted despite the pending suit, thereby making the whole election of doubtful legality.[44]

Weeks responded by securing a writ from the state supreme court to stop the proceedings of the Polk County District Court. In a hearing on October 23 Weeks contended that the election board was the final authority and that the district court did not have the right of review. On October 27, scarcely a week before the election, the supreme court rejected that contention and dismissed Weeks's writ, returning the case to Judge Spurrier. Spurrier promptly issued bench warrants for the election board members for certifying the mid-road slate as the Populist ticket. The Republican officials insisted that they had acted properly in order that the election take place as scheduled. By now it was too late anyway. The county auditors were printing the ballots pursuant to the secretary of state's instructions, and even Democrats declared it "a physical impossibility to change the ballot between this time and election day." No matter what the court decided, it would have no effect on the official ballot used.[45]

Faced with that reality and the prospect of the secretary of state, attorney general, and state auditor being thrown in jail, the supreme court issued an order staying any further proceedings in Spurrier's court. Thus the mid-roaders would appear under "People's party" on the ballot without the courts determining their right to the name. Informally, Spurrier declared that the election would be illegal, based on a ballot "conceived by republicans, carried out by republicans, and supported by a republican . . . supreme court." From his perspective, Weeks was even sharper: "Talk about election frauds, shooting negroes, and ballot box stuffing in the south will you. There never was a more desperate game anywhere attempted against freemen than that in the district court of Polk county by this creature Bellangee."[46]

As the election approached, Republicans observed with pleasure the quarreling within the ranks of their opponents. "I must admit," noted one, "that it hardly seems necessary for Republicans to work very hard in Iowa this fall—everything seems to be going that way." Even a special trip into the state by William Jennings Bryan, and his denunciation of the antifusion law and his insistence upon the continued relevance of the 1896 issues, did not mobilize the reformers.[47]

The Republicans easily swept the election. Confused or discouraged, many voters never went to the polls, and voting turnout dropped from the peak of the previous year. Others who tried to vote found the task too difficult, for large numbers of ballots were disallowed. The *Cedar Rapids Gazette* estimated that an average of 200 voters per county had their ballots disqualified through the operation of the new marking requirements. Almost certainly, given the circumstances, they were opponents of the GOP. The mid-road Populists failed to poll the necessary percentage of the vote to guarantee Populist representation on future ballots, their legal demise symbolizing the end of Republican uncertainty until the 1930s.[48]

Thus, Iowa's Republicans had been able to use the legal power of the state to advance their own partisan purposes and to protect their own political position. Though issues were undoubtedly important and the electorate traditionally Republican, a subtle change in the structural parameters of the electoral system had shaped both the campaign and its outcome. Instead of merely establishing the procedures for expressing political preferences, the ballot law had limited the opportunity for political expression. By exploiting partisan prejudices, the antifusion law had splintered the opposition into groups that quarreled more with each other than with Republicans. And by minimizing the practical value of some votes, by restricting effective political participation, and by weakening the real influence of third parties, the ballot law had indeed done much to "disfranchise the people."

7

REGULATING DEMOCRACY:
ELECTION LAWS AND DAKOTA
POLITICS, 1889–1902

In recent years, legal historians have widened their frames of reference to investigate new areas, particularly the interplay of law and
society, in order to understand, as James Willard Hurst has put it,
"how law has really worked in social experience."[1] But while research in legal history, by expanding its focus beyond the earlier emphasis on courts and the judicial process to include legislative, administrative, and other legal agencies, has illuminated topics as
diverse as economic development, technology, and the environment,
other relevant subjects have been neglected. Surprisingly, one of
these is the political arena and the relation between election law, itself a product of politics in America, and the rough-and-tumble
world of parties and politicians.[2] Historians may describe and analyze elections in terms of the political issues or constituencies involved, but the contests themselves took place within and were
shaped by the parameters of election laws regulating parties, nominations, ballots, and voting. Although historians ignore or take for
granted many of these now standard electoral parameters, they were
often matters of major concern at the time of their adoption and
during the political campaigns that followed. For, as Austin Ranney
has observed, "decisions on rules are never politically neutral. . . .
In politics as in all other forms of human conflict, the rules make a
difference in determining who wins and who loses."[3] However equitable procedures might seem, they are rarely impartial in their effects within a specific political context. An examination of the early

156

development of election laws in two states, North Dakota and South Dakota, reveals the partisan motivation and consequences of election laws and emphasizes the role of ballots, courts, and election officials in political history.

The basic and most important election law established the Australian ballot system. Before its adoption, citizens voted openly, using separate party ballots—strips of paper printed and distributed by the party itself and listing the names of its candidates. At times, moreover, each party printed its ballots on distinctively colored paper so that the voter's choice of party was readily apparent. Under these circumstances, there was considerable opportunity for fraudulent voting and intimidation. Eventually laws required all ballots to be printed on white paper of uniform size. Even so, according to one observer of elections in Dakota Territory, "bribery was then open at the polls, and ballot-box stuffing was often resorted to."[4]

It was to prevent such abuses that both North and South Dakota adopted the Australian ballot system in 1891.[5] In addition to providing secrecy for the voter, this system mandated that ballots be printed at public expense, that they be distributed by public officials, and that they contain the names of all candidates. One Dakota correspondent for the *New York Times* explained that "the Australian ballot law will restrain corrupt or fraudulent voting" by depriving "the purchaser of a vote of the satisfaction of knowing whether he will get what he pays for or not."[6] But in enacting the Australian system for such purposes, lawmakers necessarily had to consider other subjects, such as the structure of the ballot, the question of who could be listed on the ballot, and the rules for registering nominees, printing ballots, and so forth—all of which heretofore had been left up to the parties. In establishing these procedures, politicians responded to political conditions and manipulated the rules to achieve partisan ends.

There were two general types of ballots. One, initially adopted by both North and South Dakota, was the office-group ballot, which listed candidates in blocs according to the office sought and required the voter to sort through the various candidates to find his choice. Though partisan affiliations were indicated, the "pure" office-group ballot minimized partisanship by depriving the voter of an opportunity to cast a straight ticket with a single mark. The second general format was the party-column ballot. This grouped candidates by parties in parallel columns. Most states added to this ballot a provision for voting a straight ticket with a single mark, usually in a "party circle" at the head of the party column. The political effect of using this ballot was to promote straight-party voting. Although both Dakotas established the office-group ballot, North Dakota provided a circle for straight-ticket voting, and many South Dakota politicians favored switching to the party-column format in their state to facilitate partisan voting.[7]

Regardless of ballot format, most states required newspapers to print voting instructions and sample ballots before election day to acquaint voters with the task before them. Additionally, in North Dakota many candidates had printed in newspapers, as paid political advertisements, that portion of the ballot which contained their names, coupled with an explanation of how to vote for them. Some observers argued that practical demonstrations of voting would be more helpful than merely providing printed instructions, and in both Dakotas political parties soon organized campaign schools to teach their followers how to mark their ballots, while party headquarters distributed sample ballots for practice voting. Even so, voting errors were common in the first election under the Australian system. Ballots were frequently incompletely or imperfectly marked or even deposited entirely blank, reflecting voter continuity from the past when party ballots required no marking. Listing a series of such errors, the *Mandan Times* announced that "a large majority of the people are ready to admit that the Australian voting law is a nuisance."[8]

There were other difficulties arising from the new system. Necessarily, the ballot law had to establish rules for the size, number, and placement of voting booths and the amount of time a voter was to be permitted within one. In some areas, according to one observer, "many voters through ignorance or timidity would not venture into the booths under the new law."[9] There were other problems as well. South Dakota, for instance, established so many specifications for printing ballots that in 1892 only one printing firm in the state was qualified to do the work, and that company stalled for better terms, leading state officials to fear that no ballots at all would be available on election day. North Dakota legislators also devoted considerable effort to such details only to realize on the eve of the 1892 campaign that they had made no arrangements for choosing presidential electors or for canvassing election returns. The governor had to call a special session of the legislature to remedy the problem.[10]

The new laws led to one of the most anomalous situations in the history of the electoral college. In North Dakota Democrats and Populists nominated a joint electoral ticket in the 1892 election, and their three candidates for elector, on the face of the returns, narrowly defeated the Republican nominees. But the new state board of canvassers, controlled by Republicans, rejected some of the returns and declared one Republican elected by eight votes. Democratic state chairman Daniel Mara brought suit against the board and secured a court ruling that the board had to accept all returns as submitted. While Democrats and Populists celebrated the court's order, giving them the full electoral vote, Republican governor Andrew Burke ignored the decision and issued a certificate of election to the Republican candidate, declaring that the time permitted under the election law to contest the voting results had expired even as the court ruled. In the end, then, North Dakota cast one vote for each of three different presidential candidates: Democrat Grover Cleveland, Populist James B. Weaver, and Republican Benjamin Harrison.[11]

Other provisions of the new ballot laws had consequences just as serious and more enduring. Election legislation had to detail the procedures by which candidates could gain a place on the ballot. Generally, the law provided that a political party securing a certain percentage of the total vote in the preceding election could have its nominees listed on the official ballot. North Dakota's 1891 law, for example, authorized printing the names of, and limiting straight-ticket voting privileges to, those parties that had received at least 5 percent of the total vote in the preceding election. This rule bestowed benefits on the major parties that were not immediately available to the frequent but evanescent third parties of the period. In 1892 the Republican *North Dakota Capital* enjoyed the irony that reformers "now find that the Australian system of voting which they asked for . . . is something of an obstruction to the launching of the new people's party, as it is not entitled to a place in the heading of the ticket."[12] The implications of legally subordinating the Populists to the old parties were not only politically but also ideologically significant. Indeed, the California Supreme Court in 1892 invalidated that state's identical ballot provision for voting a straight party ticket with the statement that "it is an attempt to discriminate against classes of voters, and its effect . . . would be to subject such classes to the alternative of partial disfranchisement or to the casting of their votes upon more burdensome conditions than others no better entitled . . . to the free and untrammeled exercise of the right of suffrage."[13]

A second method by which candidates could secure a place on the ballot was by petition of interested citizens. Although some states made this process difficult by demanding large numbers of signatures, South Dakota's ballot law initially made the appearance of new candidates extremely easy by requiring the signatures of only twenty voters to nominate a candidate. According to the *Sioux Falls Argus-Leader,* this led to placing numerous candidates "in the field not with the idea of winning but solely to kill off some others."[14] This practice undermined partisan regularity and gave rise to demands to increase the number of required petitioners in order to limit voters' options and to protect the regular parties.[15]

However candidates qualified for the ballot, they still had to follow detailed regulations for filing their official nomination papers. Generally, state candidates were required to file their certificates of nomination with the secretary of state and local candidates with their county auditors. Even years after the passage of the law, candidates failed to file their certificates or did so with the wrong office or after the specified deadline and were accordingly disqualified from the election. The 1891 South Dakota ballot law required nomination papers to be certified thirty days before election and to state the candidate's name, occupation, home and business addresses, and the office sought. In some cases, still more information was required. These regulations often proved burdensome to parties lacking professional officials or regular legal counsel. This was demonstrated in 1892 when the Prohibition party failed to adhere strictly to these regulations, filing its certificates late and omitting some of the required information. Republican state officials refused to place the Prohibition party on the ballot, a decision sustained by the state supreme court after the Prohibitionists filed suit to compel acceptance of their nominations. Observers recognized that this disqualification benefited the GOP. As the *Brookings County Press* put it: "There are 3,000 or 4,000 Prohibitionists who will [now] have to vote the Republican ticket, and as the Republican majority would have been rather small these votes will be hailed with delight."[16]

Republican realization that election laws could provide partisan advantages soon produced an important and enduring innovation in ballot legislation, the so-called antifusion law. This legislation was fraught with serious implications for a democratic polity. The law became so widely adopted in other states — and so useful politically to the dominant party — that its provisions came to be seen as logically necessary and unexceptionable. But in the 1890s, the law was a source of great controversy and its implementation fundamentally changed the existing political process.

Fusion was the term applied to the common nineteenth-century practice by which two or more political parties attempted to combine the votes of their followers by naming the same candidates to their tickets. Fusion typically involved a third party cooperating with the weaker of the two major parties, in opposition to the stronger major party, in the hope of sharing political influence that would otherwise be denied to both when acting separately. In an electorate of multiple parties, fusion helped to prevent plurality rule, promoted majority rule, and protected the minority's access to power.

In the Dakotas during the 1890s, fusion usually involved the Democratic party and the radical Populist or People's party. The Populists first appeared in South Dakota in the 1890 election when they captured nearly one-third of the vote and displaced the Democrats as the chief opposition party. So many Republicans joined the People's party that the GOP lost its majority status and retained political control of the state by only a plurality. It seemed clear that if the Populists and Democrats could fuse in 1892, victory would be theirs, a conclusion that seemed confirmed when legislators of the two parties cooperated in 1891 to replace Republican senator Gideon Moody with Populist James Kyle. One alarmed Republican wrote privately after Kyle's election: "I predict that the parties who elected him will dominate state politics for the next five years."[17] Conversely, as another Republican put it, "No fusion means Republican victory."[18]

Party managers made their plans accordingly. The fusionist plans, however, were complicated by the intensity of partisan identification, which prompted many Democrats to insist on their own ticket, their own candidates, and their own principles. Partisanship also caused former Republicans now in the Populist ranks to oppose any cooperation with their traditional Democratic adversaries. As one Populist editor maintained, "We did not leave the corrupt Republican party to hobnob with the rotten Democratic party."[19] Thus even though partial fusions were arranged in many counties on local races, Populists rejected state-wide fusion in South Dakota at their 1892 state convention. Delegates to the Democratic state convention also spurned a fusion proposal to endorse the Populist nominees and instead nominated a straight ticket of their own. However, the convention did authorize the Democratic state committee to remove candidates from the ticket if such action would promote the party's interests: an implicit offer of partial fusion. Democratic officials promptly maneuvered toward fusion. Their plan called for each party to withdraw two of its four candidates for presidential elector and fuse on the other party's remaining two. The Democratic National Committee endorsed this plan, hoping to gain six electoral votes. As a Brookings editor explained, "The republicans would lose four votes they count on while the democrats would gain two they never expected to get."[20] Unofficial committees representing the two parties tentatively accepted this plan in September.

Many South Dakota Republicans concurred with the warning issued by Minnesota senator William Washburn to South Dakota senator Richard F. Pettigrew: "I don't see how you're going to save yourselves," he said, "if the Democratic fusion scheme is carried out."[21] Indeed, Pettigrew, the Republican state boss, was greatly distressed at the prospect of a Populist-Democratic fusion. Because of their minority status and consequent vulnerability to fusion, South Dakota Republicans devoted their political efforts, according to one political correspondent, "almost exclusively to the business of preventing a fusion."[22] To their relief, the tentative fusion agreement collapsed in October when Populist state chairman A. L. Peterman refused to convene his state committee to ratify the plan. By late October, with the expiration of the time during which tickets could be amended, the possibility of fusion had ended, and Republicans felt confident of success.[23]

The possibility of arranging fusion by revising party tickets already filed was called the Minnesota Plan. In that state, Democratic officials had pursued the tactic by withdrawing four of their nine candidates for elector and endorsing four Populist nominees. If the Democrats would not directly benefit from this maneuver, at least it promised to injure their major national opponent, and the Democratic National Committee had endorsed the plan. Because of the similarity of their political situations, South Dakotans closely followed developments in Minnesota.[24]

In preparing the official ballot under the state's Australian ballot law, Minnesota's Republican election officials ingeniously countered this fusion scheme. Though designating the four endorsed electors as both Populists and Democrats, the election officials refused to group them with the five remaining Democratic electors, scattering them instead among the other Populist candidates. Democratic leaders, fearful that their partisans would not support the fusion candidates if required to vote with a different party, charged that the Republican ballot design was constructed to "render it more difficult for the voter to cast his vote according to his preference."[25] However, they failed to secure a court order compelling the fusion electors to be listed with the Democrats as well as with the Populists. The election results confirmed Democratic fears, for the fusion candidates ran far behind the combined totals of straight Populist and Democratic candidates, allowing the minority Republicans to win by a plurality.[26]

This legal disruption of fusion was instructional to South Dakota Republicans, for they too polled a minority of votes and carried the election only because their opponents had failed to fuse for their own internal, and perhaps temporary, reasons. Other neighboring states also seemed to offer lessons. In North Dakota, Democrats and Populists had fused on a state ticket and easily prevailed over the GOP. The Republicans' only victor was their congressional candidate, who was elected by a minority vote when his Populist and Democratic opponents failed to fuse.[27] To the south, in Nebraska, Republicans triumphed on the state and electoral tickets in the absence of fusion but lost a number of legislative elections to fusion opponents. Several of the defeated Republicans filed suit to secure election certificates anyway on the grounds that the ballots were deceptive in listing fusion candidates twice, once as Democrats and once as Populists, thereby attracting votes from Democrats who would not have voted Populist and from Populists who would not have voted Democratic. Nebraska's ballot law, however, did not explicitly forbid printing nominees' names twice, and the state supreme court rejected the argument as an effort to use the law for partisan purposes and allowed the election results to stand.[28]

South Dakota Republicans already had learned of the political uses of a ballot law, for in the recent campaign the disqualification of the Prohibitionist party had apparently contributed substantially to the narrow Republican margin of victory. After the election Republicans suggested that the 1893 legislature revise the ballot law to promote other political goals. Many favored making independent nominations more difficult and facilitating straight-ticket voting. The major objective, however, was to use the Australian ballot for partisan ends and to prevent fusion by legislative enactment. Led by state senator Robert Dollard, who, as attorney general, had figured in the decision to keep the Prohibitionists off the ballot, the Republican majority revised the election law to provide that "the name of no candidate shall appear more than once on the ballot for the same office." This simple provision came to be known as the antifusion law. Related revisions also framed to obstruct fusion included prohibiting the withdrawal of nominees shortly before elections — thus blocking the Minnesota Plan; treating fused parties as one party in the appointment of election judges; and replacing the office-group with the party-column format, accompanied by a party circle for straight-ticket voting.[29]

This change in ballot format made more effective the ban against double-listing candidates' names. The party-column format meant that a nominee could be designated with but one party affiliation and the second party to nominate a candidate would appear on the ballot as having no nominee for that office at all. Those wishing to fuse would thus be deprived of the symbolic comfort of voting for their own party and be forced to vote as members of another party. The ultimate consequence of fusion for the second party, moreover, would be the sacrifice of its legal identity and existence, for by not having candidates on the ballot it would be unable to poll the minimum percentage of the vote required for legal recognition as a political party and a position on the ballot in subsequent elections. When fusion did not encompass complete tickets, fusionists would also be denied the very real benefit of the party circle — becoming subject, in the words of the California court, "to the alternative of partial disfranchisement or to the casting of their votes upon more burdensome conditions than others"— and instead be required to mark each individual name. This requirement was certain to complicate voting and cause the invalidation of ballots through improper marking.[30]

The political significance of these new ballot regulations in South Dakota became evident in the 1893 and 1894 elections. Populists and Democrats tried in several ways to evade the anticipated effects of the law but met with little success. On the local level, they attempted to cooperate in order to gain control of the next legislature and repeal the antifusion law, although they recognized that their cooperation would necessarily disrupt party organization by sacrificing the legal identity of the second party nominating a candidate. Indeed, in some areas the parties competed to schedule their conventions first, each hoping to arrange fusion on its own terms at the fatal expense of the other. In other instances, politicians attempting to promote local fusion accepted both nominations and then withdrew from one after the legal deadline for nominating anyone else. These efforts frequently produced bitterness and competition among groups trying to cooperate.[31] On the state level, Populists and Democrats felt compelled to nominate separate tickets to maintain their parties' legal existence, even though acknowledging that this would lead to Republican victory. Populists did hope, however, that Democrats would endorse their congressional nominees and thereby end what one Populist termed the Republicans' success "in preventing a united front against them."[32] But the Democratic state convention rejected all fusion proposals. The delegates believed, according to one reporter, that under the ballot law any cooperation would involve "not fusion but absorption" and that the party organization required a separate ticket that admittedly would "stand no chance to win."[33]

The *Sioux Falls Argus-Leader,* South Dakota's leading Democratic newspaper, demonstrated the difficulties of conducting a campaign constrained by the ballot law, partisan loyalties, and political necessities. Advocating faithful support of a Democratic state ticket that it conceded would be easily defeated, the newspaper also urged its Democratic readers to support a local fusion ticket that would appear on the ballot under the Populist heading but that the *Argus-Leader* referred to as simply "the County Ticket." The paper printed not only the Democratic platform at the head of its columns but also the Populist platform, which it carefully abridged to exclude the national demands that would surely antagonize the more conservative Democrats. But even with a common enemy and only local issues involved, fusion leaders predicted that at least 20 percent of the Democrats would refuse to vote in the Populist column, a falloff that in a close election could result in defeat.[34]

Republicans also anticipated that fusion candidates, as the *Brookings County Press* reported, would "lose many . . . votes by having their names printed only once on the official ballot instead of once under each party name," but of course they welcomed the "serious complications" the ballot law imposed on their opponents.[35] Moreover, the Republican-dominated judiciary in South Dakota obstructed those who did not vote the single-party straight ticket. Rejecting the argument that "the intention of the voter" should determine the counting of his ballot, state supreme court justice Dighton Corson disallowed numerous ballots that told of painful efforts to construct a personally satisfactory ticket. Corson announced disdainfully that "if the elector does not take interest enough in his vote to follow these simple and easily understood rules, he can complain of no one if his vote is not counted."[36] The courts even invalidated ballots on which the voter had written, in his own party column, the name of a candidate of another party. The courts held that the 1893 law prohibited the second appearance of a candidate's name, even if added by an individual voter attempting to create a political coalition while voting as a member of his own party. It is little wonder that after the Republicans swept the elections the demoralized Democratic state chairman E. M. O'Brien surveyed the results and concluded, "Under the present system of voting as arranged by the Republican party fusion results in confusion to Democracy."[37]

Democratic difficulties under the election law dramatically increased in 1896 when both the Democratic and Populist national conventions nominated William Jennings Bryan for the presidency, a move that necessarily imposed a fusion policy on the state parties. Numerically weaker, the Democrats in South Dakota recognized that under the ballot law they would have to sacrifice their party's organization to secure the state's electoral votes for their party's nominee. Accordingly, the Democratic state committee canceled the party's convention and adopted the ticket nominated by the Populists.[38]

Many Democrats, however, reacted angrily to this decision to drop their party from the ballot. The editor of the *Kimball Graphic* deplored the "killing of his party's organization."[39] Conservative Democrats, who might have loyally voted for Bryan as the party's nominee despite their hostility to his ideas, complained of being disfranchised by the surrender to Populism required by the ballot law. Some decided to vote Republican or not at all rather than vote as Populists. At the county level, in fact, Democratic opposition to voting under the Populist name, even among silver advocates, was so strong that in many instances a compromise name of Free Silver had to be given the local fusion ticket. But this ran afoul of the party-column and party-circle provisions of the 1893 ballot law, for, with the fusion state ticket printed under the Populist heading, the Free Silver local ticket had to be placed in a separate column. If the silver voter marked both party circles, reasoned one paper, "there would be no conflict in the names voted for, as the corresponding spaces in the different columns are left blank." But the courts held that crosses in the party circle of two or more columns neutralized each other, so the effect would be to leave the ballot as though no party circle had been marked, thereby eliminating the fusionist's vote altogether unless he also had voted separately for each individual office. This inability to effectively cast a straight-ticket fusion ballot, the *Sioux City Journal* concluded, would "result in the loss of numerous votes."[40]

Under these circumstances, the fusionists were able to eke out only a narrow victory in South Dakota. Moreover, although the famous campaign had been debated in the most enthusiastic language, the actual outcome was shaped not merely by ballot regulations but by election procedures generally. Members of all parties charged their opponents with illegal voting, bribery, colonization of voters from outside the state, and illegal acts by election judges and poll-watchers. A widespread demand developed in the aftermath of the election for revision of the state's election laws to prevent such occurrences in the future.[41]

The fusionists, in fact, planned radical changes in South Dakota's election laws now that they controlled the legislature. They were determined to punish bribery at elections, to enact a registration law, to make politicians report election expenses, and to require that ballots be counted according to the voter's intention regardless of compliance with the marking regulations. Fusionist legislators also intended to abolish the antifusion provisions, not only the prohibition against double-listing candidates' names but the party circle as well, for it encouraged straight-ticket voting to the detriment of fashioning a ticket out of candidates in separate columns. A legislative correspondent for the *Chicago Tribune* reported from Pierre that the Populist goal was to eliminate the Republican "technicalities" enacted in 1893 that had "so wrapped the ballot . . . that to deviate from a straight ticket the voter is very likely to transgress so that his ballot will be worthless."[42] Similarly, Populist governor Andrew E. Lee recommended that "the old safeguards which have been one by one repealed since the passage of the original law be reinstated," that the party-circle provision be rescinded, and that all parties be represented among the election judges.[43] The house Elections Committee drafted a bill embodying these provisions, and by strict party votes the Populists forced it through the legislature over Republican opposition.[44]

Another section of the Populist election reform law prohibited voters from receiving assistance in marking their ballot except in cases of physical disability. Republicans maintained that the political effect of this clause was to disfranchise several thousand German, Russian, and Scandinavian immigrants who were unable to read English. Populists countered that their intention was merely to prevent ballot fraud, for they believed that local Republican election judges disregarded these voters' wishes and marked their ballots Republican. The new law seemed to support the Populist rebuttal by also providing for the distribution of sample ballots in several different languages so that foreign-language voters would be able to prepare their ballots to reflect their own wishes, not those of the election judge.[45]

To cap their electoral reform, the Populists also passed two measures authorizing amendments to the state constitution, subject to voter approval in the 1898 elections. The first of these established woman suffrage, a Populist objective intended to democratize the political process. The second amendment, also viewed as a step toward greater popular democracy, provided for the nation's first initiative and referendum system, a famous construct that in practice was less important in defining the political process than the simple ballot laws the Populists were fighting.[46]

Ironically, at the very time that South Dakota Populists repealed their state's antifusion law, neighboring states under Republican control were copying those provisions into their own election codes. North Dakota, Iowa, and Wyoming passed laws in 1897 to prohibit candidates' names from appearing on the ballot more than once. North Dakota also revived a procedure for voting a straight ticket with a single mark, thereby benefiting the Republicans while further obstructing fusionists. If they attempted to fuse despite the new law, they would have to vote in different columns and would thereby be denied the advantage of the party circle.[47]

North Dakota's opposition political parties now went through the same convolutions that South Dakota's had suffered earlier. The state committees of the Democratic and Populist parties met to decide upon a course of action under the restrictive new election laws. With daring and imagination, they sought to circumvent the partisan law and create a new form of fusion. Their plan was to evade the divisive implications of the party-column ballot and to gain access to the party circle by finding a party name acceptable to both Democrats and Populists. In 1898, the state conventions of the two parties decided to drop their separate names and adopt that of Independent Democrat for the ballot; they then nominated a common ticket to appear under that heading. But equally imaginative Republican officials used the ballot law to frustrate this new style of fusion. Secretary of State Fred Falley ruled that the candidates of the new Independent-Democratic party would not be permitted on the ballot, for such a party had not attracted the required 5 percent of the vote at the preceding election — when, of course, it had not existed. And since the old Independent (Populist) and Democratic parties had formed a new party, Falley ruled, the two former parties had ceased to exist and also could not have a ballot position, leaving only Republican candidates on the ballot.[48]

Although the North Dakota Supreme Court partially invalidated this ruling, lower courts accepted such reasoning in other electoral disputes. In one county the district court forced the fusion nominees to be listed on the ballot simply as Democrats, producing a Populist fall-off and contributing to what the *Bismarck Tribune* called "a complete revolution" in local politics as the entire Republican ticket won for the first time in the county's history.[49] In other counties, the courts issued restraining orders keeping fusion candidates off the ballot altogether because of legal technicalities occasioned by the difficulties the two parties encountered in holding a common nominating convention. Subsequent fusionist attempts to secure a place on the ballot by petition failed either because of insufficient signatures or because the deadline set for filing petitions had already passed. The Republican secretary of state disqualified one petition effort by ruling that the fusion candidate, having tried to gain a ballot position through a convention nomination, had forfeited his right to a nomination by petition. Even some Republicans denounced this "forcing [fusionists] off the printed ticket" as "disgraceful" and "manifest scoundrelism," but the result remained that, in some localities, no Independent-Democratic candidates were on the ballot.[50]

The battered and demoralized North Dakota fusionists were not only crushed in the election but subsequently suffered the defection of Populists who announced that rather than be subsumed in an organization under the Democratic name they would return to the GOP. Democrats also abandoned the coalition, complaining that the response to the antifusion law had eliminated their traditional party. By shattering the opposition, North Dakota's ballot laws helped set the stage for twentieth-century Republican hegemony in the state.[51] The 1901 legislature strengthened the restraints by providing that no party could be represented by more than one list of nominees on the ballot. This prevented the recognition of minority or bolting factions, such as the mid-road Populists who had been on the ballot in 1900, and still further restricted the democratic electoral spontaneity that had been possible before the Australian ballot law. The 1901 law also ensured that any factionalism within the GOP itself would not lead to the party's defeat.[52] Finally, in a related development, Republican domination was enhanced in 1907 by North Dakota's adoption of the direct primary, which, however much it widened popular participation in the nominating process, effectively stripped other parties of their remaining role of controlling the political opposition. By regularizing intraparty competition

within the GOP, the primary minimized the possibility of a realignment of parties that would topple the Republicans from power.[53]

Republicans soon turned electoral legislation against their opponents in South Dakota, too, and Populist success in reforming that
state's election laws in 1897 proved as short-lived as Populist success
in the wider political arena. Though the traditional form of fusion
was revived in 1898 when Populists, Democrats, and Silver Republicans met in three simultaneous conventions and nominated a joint
ticket to appear on the ballot in each of three party columns, the
GOP nonetheless carried the legislature and all state offices except
that of governor, which Andrew Lee narrowly retained. Both Lee
and his Republican opponent Kirk Phillips ran well ahead of their
tickets, reflecting voter roll-off and the absence of a party circle on
the new ballot. Republicans, however, were more concerned with
other aspects of the 1897 ballot law. They charged that Lee owed his
victory to the legislation, which, according to the *Brookings County
Press,* was "never designed for anything except to promote fusion."[54]
The *Press* even claimed that Populists voted for Lee on each of the
three tickets listing his name and that partisan election judges
counted each mark as a separate vote for Lee. The newspaper insisted that a fair count would find Phillips the winner. Others maintained that ballots with multiple marks should not be counted even
once for Lee because such marks, however much they might suggest
the intention of the voter, might also constitute what the *Valley
Springs Vidette* called distinguishing signs revealing a voter's attempt to sell his vote and "let the purchaser know, by his markings
on the ballot, that he had performed his part of the bargain."[55] If
those ballots were thrown out altogether, the election of Phillips
would be easily secured. Some Republicans, in attacking the Populist emphasis on the intention of the voter when counting ballots,
even argued that "instead of officially interpreting the mind of ignorant voters it would be . . . more in the interest of good government
if a strict educational qualification was required."[56]

The Republican claims of fraudulent voting were apparently un-
founded, and the official canvass of returns certified Lee's victory.
Soon thereafter Phillips dropped his plans to contest the outcome,
citing imperfect procedures for such action. The new Republican
legislature, however, moved quickly in 1899 to advance the party's

position in future elections. First, the legislature resurrected the 1893 law by again prohibiting multiple listing of candidates and by restoring the party circle. In another attempt to prevent fusion, Republican legislators enacted a "pure caucus bill," forbidding voters from attending the caucus or convention of more than one party, thereby inhibiting the necessary consultation between parties contemplating fusion. To minimize the adoption of what one Republican termed "undesirable constitutional amendments," a reference to the recent voter approval of the initiative and referendum, they passed an act requiring separate ballots for constitutional amendments from those for the election of public officials.[57] To satisfy other Republican grievances from the 1898 election, the legislature also passed an act establishing procedures for contesting election results, a registration law to prevent the importation of illegal voters into the state, and a bill enabling voters who did not read English to obtain assistance from election judges in marking their ballots.[58]

Governor Lee tried to defend the Populist position on election law. He vetoed the bill for voter assistance, maintaining that it would increase ballot fraud and that existing law provided sufficient protection for the voting rights of illiterates. He vetoed the antifusion bill, describing it as an attempt to "disfranchise political parties" and frustrate majority rule. Lee also vetoed the caucus bill, which, he said, should have been titled "a bill to destroy political independence." Republicans had described the measure as reform legislation, designed to prevent fraudulent voting at primaries, but Lee argued that it was an attempt to "prevent men by force of law and under penalty from changing their political allegiance."[59] Lee's vetoes did not surprise Republicans, for they admitted that their election legislation was designed to destroy the means by which their opponents had been elected.[60]

Lee's vetoes only postponed the final Republican triumph. After the GOP swept South Dakota's elections in 1900, the 1901 legislature reenacted the antifusion law, demonstrating again the Republicans' conviction of the efficacy of such ballot regulations in protecting their hegemony. Several Democrats also voted for the bill this time, perhaps anticipating that their party would benefit by attracting Populists whose own party would be eliminated through the operation of the law.[61]

The new ballot legislation dominated the next election campaign. The 1902 Populist platform did not focus on the party's original issues of money, land, and transportation but on the election laws that threatened the party's ability to present a reform alternative on such policy issues. Meeting in Huron, the Populists adopted a platform that assailed the state supreme court for a decision emasculating the initiative and referendum, condemned one Republican election law for its undemocratic motive and effects, and denounced the ballot law as a partisan attempt to violate "the right of every citizen to cast his vote as his conscience dictates." The Populist convention then considered its options under that law and reluctantly dissolved into the Democratic state convention, meeting simultaneously in Huron. The joint convention named a ticket to appear on the ballot under the Democratic heading and issued a final blast at the legislature for "confining the number of parties represented on the ballot."[62]

Without admitting their own legal complicity, Republicans welcomed what they termed this Populist "suicide." One Sioux Falls editor pointed out that the Huron arrangements differed from previous fusions in that the delegates "extinguished the populist name and . . . agreed to leave the name 'democratic' as the sole appellation of the fusion idea." He concluded that "South Dakota gave birth to the populist party in 1890. It now sees its final extinguishment."[63]

Thus, although the People's Party had clearly declined from its peak influence, its actual demise was not mandated by the electorate but was legally imposed by the state. While Populists did not have to accept the Democratic name, it was their only practical course if they wanted any political influence. Fusion had provided for minority participation in politics and had been the primary avenue of success for third parties. Under the new legal conditions, a separate party would represent only a symbolic gesture. Those willing to accept that type of limited political participation turned to the new Socialist party, which polled 3.5 percent of the 1902 vote. Some Populists returned to the GOP rather than vote under the Democratic name, as Republicans had predicted. Other Populists, especially former Democrats, did move into the Democratic party, but large numbers simply dropped out of politics altogether. Unwilling either to vote as a member of the "corrupt" old parties or to cast a futile vote for a symbolic third party, they were citizens legislated out of the effective electorate.[64]

Their party's ascendancy assured, Republicans henceforth fought among themselves, safe in the realization that they operated in a closed system, and one faction made South Dakota a leading state in Progressivism. But Progressive reform often differed markedly from the reform impulses of the 1890s and took place within a truncated electorate. Indeed, the regulation of elections had established the legal parameters within which other subjects would be considered. Further electoral "reform" legislation, such as the introduction of the direct primary, merely fastened Republican control more tightly upon the state. In any event, in legislating the end to disruptive fusion, Republicans had demonstrated an early instance of the now familiar Progressive use of state power to promote self-serving conditions of order.

The 1901 Republican legislature demonstrated that practice in another instance as well. Spurred on by Gov. Charles Herreid, who as Republican state chairman in 1898 had been especially interested in the operation of election laws, the legislature passed a law requiring county commissioners to be elected on a county rather than on a district basis. Fusionists opposed the measure as partisan legislation designed to use the larger electorate to overcome local pockets of resistance to Republican domination. Indeed, the law represented the rural analogue to the simultaneous "reform" in Progressive municipal government so well described by Samuel P. Hays: the shift from ward to city-wide elections in order to limit "the expression of grassroots impulses and their involvement in the political process."[65] The South Dakota legislature, moreover, went beyond this practical restriction of political representation by also requiring that local elections coincide with general elections, the larger turnouts of which could be expected to overwhelm dissidents even on issues of intense interest to certain communities. Not surprisingly, the Populists, in their final platform, denounced this law as "denying the minority in each county from any representation whatever."[66]

Finally, completing the structure for political stability, South Dakota's Republican-controlled supreme court in 1901 sanctioned an extraordinary legal restriction on the rights and freedom of the individual voter. Building on Judge Corson's earlier rulings, the court prohibited write-in votes on the grounds that writing the candidate's name constituted placing a "distinguishing mark" on the ballot. One judge dissented by raising the larger issue of voters' rights against this procedural concern. Denying Corson's contention that prohibiting write-in votes did not violate constitutional rights, Judge Howard Fuller argued that it was "neither plausible nor reasonable to say that the right of suffrage can be freely, equally, and independently exercised under a statute which merely gives to qualified electors an option to vote for persons whose names are printed on the official ballot, or not to vote at all." The majority opinion meant that "the sovereignty of the nation no longer resides in the people" and that "there is nothing left worthy of the name of the right of suffrage."[67]

But Fuller stood alone in his concern for the undemocratic consequences of ballot legislation. Indeed, Republican judges in North Dakota had already dealt with the issue, holding that a consequence of denying citizens their suffrage could not serve as an argument against election legislation. Ruling that "the very franchise is subject to legislative control," they found perfectly acceptable "many regulative provisions in election statutes" that "deprive voters of their privilege."[68]

Thus, in scarcely a decade from the original enactment of the Australian ballot system, the political arena in the Dakotas had been significantly altered through the adoption of legal procedures regulating parties, ballots, nominations, and voting. The open and democratic, if sometimes disorderly, polity of earlier years had given way to one in which, by law, it was more difficult to organize new parties, to secure representation, to act with spontaneity or without special counsel, to cooperate politically with other citizens, to vote independently, or to express political dissatisfaction other than by dropping out. Now public officials talked casually of disfranchisement and, as one observer said, "idly trifled with . . . serious matters" reaching to the heart of the democratic process. Considering the political effects of such regulations, together with their partisan and ideological origins, one might wonder whether, as one judge wrote, "the boasted free ballot becomes a delusion."[69]

8

IDEOLOGY AND BEHAVIOR: LEGISLATIVE POLITICS AND WESTERN POPULISM

Populism has always been a controversial subject among American historians. The once standard interpretation of the movement portrayed Populists as reform-minded small farmers who reacted to harsh economic and political conditions by demanding a program of positive government action that responded rationally to their own needs in the 1890s and presaged the concerns of twentieth-century liberalism. Beginning in the 1950s, a series of scholars assaulted that image by describing Populists as parochial reactionaries who were responding irrationally to the present and seeking to revive a mythic past. This hysterical interpretation provoked another generation of historians to publish a number of careful monographs, often based on quantitative evidence and analysis, that refuted most of the disparaging and unsubstantiated claims made by the revisionists and pushed beyond the old debate to consider such larger questions as the determinants of mass political behavior and the processes of social change. But there has been one intriguing recent attempt, imaginatively using new sources of evidence, to revive the negative interpretation of the movement fashionable in the 1950s. In 1973 and 1976 Prof. Karel Bicha published articles that became the basis of his subsequent book, *Western Populism: Studies in an Ambivalent Conservatism.*[1]

In these works, Bicha maintained that western Populists were essentially conservative, primarily committed to a free-market economy, limited government, and state sovereignty, and that their laissez-faire views prevented them from effectively promoting the reforms they expressed in their platforms. The most important, and innovative, part of his work, first reported in the 1976 article, involved an examination of Populist legislative behavior in seven western states.[2] Here is a major achievement to all apparent purposes. With few exceptions, earlier Populist scholars focused on the electoral process to the neglect of legislative analysis.[3] Even some historians who have been less than persuaded by Bicha's general thesis have recognized his work on legislative activity as useful. One scholar, for instance, welcomed Bicha's "lists of bills and acts, the indications of which parties supported them, and much of the discussion of legislative . . . performance" as a valuable resource for other "students of Populism."[4] It is this acceptance of the accuracy and utility of Bicha's work on legislative behavior, as much as its role in reopening the debate on the ideological character of Populism, that requires it to be carefully evaluated.

Claiming to have examined more than 20,000 legislative bills introduced in seven western states from 1891 to 1897, Bicha found "only a small proportion" that possessed "reform" characteristics, and he published an extensive table described as "a substantially comprehensive compendium of reform legislation considered in the legislatures." For the reform bills he recorded both their sponsorship, by party affiliation, and their disposition, as "defeated in house of origin," "enacted into law," and so forth. He also indicated when Populist-sponsored bills failed in "a Populist or fusionist controlled House."[5] Bicha concluded that "Populist legislators, with the sole exception of railroad matters, were *not demonstrably* more likely to introduce major reform proposals than members of the other parties, and in some instances they were even less likely to do so."[6] As another indication of their basic conservatism, Populist legislators, again excepting railroad measures, "were not more inclined to support reform proposals in the plains states than were members of the established parties." Bicha also argued that "little Populist-sponsored legislation, except for railroad bills, triggered markedly partisan responses. Populist bills which passed one or both houses of a legislature were ordinarily approved overwhelmingly and did not seem to activate ideological sensitivities." The basis for division between Populists and Republicans, he concluded, was rhetorical rather than substantive or ideological. Indeed, Bicha even asserted that the scope of Populist reform interests was more limited than that of non-Populists, another sign of Populist conservatism.[7]

But a systematic reexamination of the original data and a careful reconstruction of Bicha's methods reveal strikingly different results. First of course there is the definitional question of what constituted "reform" legislation, a problem that Bicha properly and explicitly considered and that he conceded led to some "arbitrary inclusions and some equally arbitrary exclusions." His inclusions were logical enough: railroad regulation, land reform, labor legislation, tax reform, and so forth. But he excluded the regulation of insurance and telephone companies, municipal charter reform, and woman suffrage on the grounds that "Populists never attempted to make these issues Populist issues in a partisan sense."[8] A survey of Populist state platforms, however, reveals that these were in fact partisan issues, and their exclusion from analysis limits the apparent areas of Populist-Republican controversy and decreases the chances that Populists would appear as reformist.

On the question of woman suffrage, for instance, western Populists repeatedly expressed themselves. The Populist state conventions of Idaho, Kansas, North Dakota, Oregon, South Dakota, and Washington adopted platforms favoring woman suffrage while "the cowardly Republicans" (as one Kansan declared) avoided the issue.[9] In the state legislatures, moreover, Populists demonstrated again that this was indeed a partisan reform issue. In the 1892 Kansas House of Representatives, Populists introduced at least two bills to establish woman suffrage and overwhelmingly supported the issue when it came to a vote (56 to 17 and 65 to 18); Republicans, on the other hand, were even more united in opposing the question (3 to 16 and 3 to 12) as were the Democrats (1 to 6 and 1 to 4). Unable to defeat woman suffrage in the Populist-controlled house, the Republicans simply indefinitely postponed it in the senate, which they safely controlled.[10] Woman suffrage also failed in the South Dakota legislature, and again it was through the actions of the Republicans, the majority of whom opposed it, for the Populists supported the bill by a five-to-one margin. In Washington, Republicans were more sympathetic but still demonstrated a significantly weaker commitment relative to the solid Populist support.[11] In North Dakota, the Republican-dominated legislature defeated woman suffrage in both 1893 and 1895. The remarkable 1893 legislative struggle sharply revealed the depth of partisan differences on this issue. After Populists skillfully maneuvered a woman-suffrage bill through both houses, Republicans lashed back by recalling the bill and voting to expunge all record of it from the *House Journal*. The Populist legislators attempted to spirit the bill off to the governor anyway but were physically restrained.[12] Given the intransigence of such opposition, it should not be surprising that, in still another legislature, the Populists even tried to secure partial woman suffrage surreptitiously with an innocuously titled bill, "An act to confer the right of suffrage on certain persons herein named"—phrasing typically applied to routine bills restoring political rights to former Confederates or rehabilitated criminals. In this case, however, those named were all women.[13] Thus, woman suffrage was indeed a partisan issue, as the Populist editor of the *Norton Liberator* recognized when he declared, "The cause of woman has been solely championed by Populism."[14]

Similarly, Populists made reform issues of the subjects of insurance and communication regulation and changes in municipal government, adopting such demands in a number of state platforms. The Washington State Populist platform of 1896, for example, demanded regulation of telephone and telegraph rates. The Kansas Populists in 1892 insisted with respect to telephones and telegraphs that "public needs should be supplied by public agencies" and in 1896 pledged themselves to secure reductions in telegraph charges. And both Kansas and Nebraska Populists declared in favor of insurance regulation and reform.[15] Populist bills reforming municipal charters frequently represented efforts to translate their larger political principles into areas where their limited power applied. The 1895 Kansas Senate, for instance, sought to expand political democracy by making urban officials elected rather than appointed. Populists supported the bill by 16 to 3 while a majority of Republicans opposed it. Even more striking was a Populist "pet measure" to provide for municipal ownership of gas, water, and electric plants. The Populists unanimously supported the bill and overcame fierce Republican opposition and delaying tactics.[16] Obviously, excluding such issues as these biases the sample of legislation in the direction of deemphasizing the reform interests and support of Populists and their ideological disagreement with Republicans.

But even within the restricted sphere that Bicha did consider, there are serious problems. First, in identifying reform measures, Bicha apparently evaluated merely the titles of bills, not their substance, thereby ignoring legislative practice and political reality. On the one hand, many bills had titles that were not at all indicative of their content or were so vague as to be meaningless in determining their objective. There were, for instance, dozens of bills introduced in nearly every legislature with the simple title, "A bill relative to taxation." Such bills could provide for either taxation reform, a regressive taxation feature, or a minor clarifying revision in existing tax law. There is no way that these bills can be properly considered and interpreted with this approach. On the other hand, many bills had titles that were explicit in their announced intentions, but the actual provisions of the legislation were quite different. Calling such measures "buncombe" bills, one newspaper declared that "the old habit of introducing bills and then accusing the opposition of killing them off, has been growing, for there are bills pending in both branches that are no credit to any man or any party; yet, judging by the title they appear to be good and necessary measures." Finally, there were those bills that provided for substantive change, and their titles were explicit indications of that, but they were never intended for passage, certainly not by the legislator who introduced the measure. This was a favorite Republican tactic, designed to embarrass Populists, as in the 1895 Kansas legislature when Republican senator Lucien Baker, with "a twinkle in his eye," introduced a railroad regulation bill so strict as to be crippling. An approving Republican newspaper regarded it as a "dandy . . . takeoff" on Populist reform proposals, while Republican legislators viewed it as an attempt to "burlesque" the Populists.[17] It may be doubted that Senator Baker succeeded with the Populists, but this tactic may at times have misled Bicha.

Bicha then compounded the problems inherent in this approach by partially excluding similar bills from his "substantially comprehensive compendium of reform legislation" when "sponsored by members of the same party."[18] In one instance, comparing the number of reform bills "less duplication" to the uncorrected total number of bills introduced, this practice misrepresented reform activity in general, creating an image of indifference to reform.[19] But in particular this practice minimizes the appearance of Populist reform activity because Populists introduced more reform bills. In the 1891 Nebraska House, for instance, Populists introduced eight (of nine total) bills dealing with interest rates but receive credit for only one. Moreover, the only bill regulating interest rates that reached the voting stage was one of those omitted. Populists again demonstrated their reform commitment by supporting that measure by 38 to 4, though some Populists complained that the bill did not go far enough and reflected too much concern for the "poor banker" and the "curbstone broker." The other parties voted against this reform bill, Republicans by 3 to 16 and Democrats by 6 to 9.[20]

Finally, Bicha exercised an extraordinary selectivity in the bills he did consider so that even were one to accept his parameters one could not accept his conclusions. For the same 1891 Nebraska legislature, for example, Bicha maintained that only non-Populists introduced bills for labor and electoral reforms, overlooking seventeen such Populist bills, including one that became the state's first secret-ballot law. In other issue areas the 1891 Nebraska pattern is similar. Bicha did not report a Populist bill to prohibit combinations. He did indicate that a Populist measure to regulate stockyards failed to pass the Populist house; but he did not note that the bill was indefinitely postponed, as the *House Journal* explained, "for the reason that the House [had already] passed a bill of the same nature."[21] He even attributed a Populist antitrust bill to a Republican with the same last name.[22] Bicha also ignored several reform proposals advanced by Democrats and Republicans, but given the Populists' greater reform activity their legislative record suffered most from such imperfect reporting.

Indeed, most of Bicha's omissions and misstatements have the effect of supporting his thesis of Populist conservatism or unexceptionality. Writing of the 1897 South Dakota legislature, for example, he coupled a sentence referring to the passage of a ballot law with a statement that such laws "passed almost without dissent," suggesting that Populists and members of the major parties differed little in their attitudes. In reality, the ballot law was passed by a strict party vote, all Populists in favor and all Republicans opposed.[23] In discussing the 1891 Kansas legislature Bicha maintained that "*every* successful measure . . . originated in the Republican Senate and with Republican sponsorship. Every unsuccessful reform bill . . . derived from the Alliance-Populist House."[24] However, the actual situation was not that Republicans initiated reform while Populists proved unable to pass reform legislation but that the conservative senate, controlled by the Republicans by a thirty-eight-to-two margin, stifled bills from the Populist house so that reform necessarily was limited to what the Republican senate would allow in the first place. The Populists recognized this legislative reality in their 1892 state platform by carefully spelling out reforms they had passed in the house that the Republicans had not accepted in the senate: a weekly wage bill, an Australian ballot, a bill to elect railroad commissioners, a bill restricting Pinkertons, a bill to abolish labor blacklisting, a maximum freight-rate bill.[25] Rather than legislative activity indicating the lack of ideological differences between Populists and Republicans, then, it confirmed the expectations of the conservative Republican in 1890 who consoled himself by noting that "while the People's Party controls the house by a very large majority, the Senate is still Republican by 38 to 2, and a governor's veto also stands in the way of radical legislation of which businessmen and capitalists might have stood in dread."[26]

Ultimately, these errors of omission and commission render useless any conclusions that might have been drawn from the data compiled by Bicha. But even had he more carefully and accurately recorded his data, he still would have been unable to demonstrate what he sought to prove, for it is his research design and methodology that are fatally flawed. The subject of legislative behavior must be approached from the other end of the process—the voting on, not the introduction of, bills. And it should be handled in a systematic fashion to produce comprehensible and comparable results. To say that a reform measure was not passed by a Populist-dominated house does not identify its opponents or its friends in any useful manner, nor does it permit generalized conclusions about "the" Populists or "the" Republicans or their attitudes and behavior. Various forms of roll-call analysis have been developed precisely for such purposes. Roll calls represent what Allan G. Bogue has called "comparable expressions of opinion from almost all the members of a legislative chamber." Systematic analysis of such data can disclose the issues of most concern to the legislators themselves and the relative significance of those issues. It can also determine the questions that divide or unite legislators and suggest the ideological character of the resultant groups. The following analysis focuses on the 1895 and 1897 Kansas senates as case studies of Populist legislative behavior. These sessions were deliberately chosen in order to bias the case in favor of Bicha's position, for they represented to him the most obvious failure of Populist reform pretensions. To disprove Bicha's contentions with respect to these sessions, then, would make unnecessary any larger corrective effort. But this analysis can also allow the historian to advance beyond the usual debate over whether Populism was conservative or radical and achieve greater insight into the movement and its opponents.[27]

The members of the 1895 Kansas Senate had been elected in 1892, had weathered the 1893 legislative war, and in 1895 were balanced by a largely Republican house elected in the GOP's 1894 sweep. There were twenty-three Populists, fifteen Republicans, and two Democrats in the senate chamber. Excluding roll calls for minor procedural matters, local or minor bills reflecting neither controversy nor disagreement, perfunctory votes of confidence and appreciation, appointment of clerks, and bills passed unanimously, there were forty-two roll calls having discernible reform content and provoking at least some opposition.[28] The simple calculation of agreement scores of all individual legislators with the reform position for those forty-two votes provides an easy and clear indication of who supported reform bills and who did not. On a scale of 0 (representing complete opposition to all divisive reform) to 100 (representing complete support for all reform), the average Populist legislator scored 88 and the average Republican only 48. Moreover, only one Republican was as reformist as the least-reformist Populist. Significantly, if bills relating to reform issues such as woman suffrage are excluded and consideration is limited only to those bills that meet Bicha's definitions of reform, the difference between the parties remains virtually unchanged, though tending toward the Populists being even more, and the Republicans being even less, reformist. For those thirty-five roll calls in this category, the average Populist reform score is 89 and the Republican score drops to 43.[29] Though Republicans constituted only 36 percent of the total legislators from the two parties, they provided 74 percent of the total opposition to reform.

Despite some Republican support for many reform topics, there were numerous party splits over issues, as indicated by the index of disagreement for the two parties over questions of bond issues (100), electoral reform (95), free silver (91), railroad regulation (89, 86), banking regulation (85), civil service (78), public salaries (73, 70, 57), land legislation (71, 62), labor legislation (60, 50), taxation (60, 57), and interest regulation (56). These subjects demonstrate that Populists confronted Republicans on a much wider range of issues than Bicha suggested.[30]

Moreover, the Populist proposals hardly represented a belief in "a governmental apparatus of minimal scope and authority" and a commitment to laissez faire that Bicha maintained characterized Populists. The *Topeka State Journal* was not the only observer that found in Populist proposals dealing with subjects from freight rates to school books "a notable tendency toward measures which will transfer matters which have hitherto been under individual or corporate control to the care of the state." Indeed, one Populist spoke of the necessity "for the regulation of everything and everybody," and others agreed with Sen. H. S. Landis when he identified himself as "a state socialist." One Republican senator complained of rampant socialism among his Populist colleagues, maintaining that they not only advocated on the senate floor the nationalization of industries but also introduced "many bills" in this direction under "thin disguises."[31]

Nor is it true that Populists were not interested in issues of "economic welfare."[32] A dramatic indication of that came in the debates over destitute people suffering from drought and depression in western Kansas. Republicans even sought to reject offers of assistance from other states, arguing that they were "tired of having everybody on earth feel sorry for Kansas" and that "if there were people in Kansas who failed to make enough to eat it was because they were too shiftless and lazy to make a living." Populist senators, on the other hand, attacked the Republicans for "false pride," insisted on the necessity of helping the destitute, and voted down the Republican proposal. Moreover, the Populists were prepared to use state funds to aid the distressed, amending a House bill furnishing seed grain to farmers to provide money for necessities so that the destitute could survive to use the seed grain in the spring. For the urban distressed, the Populists also supported (by a vote of 20 to 1) a bill establishing free employment offices to assist the jobless while a majority of Republicans opposed the measure.[33]

The 1897 Kansas Senate produced similar results. Among the bills Populists introduced were many that showed a social sensitivity that seems quite modern and that contradict the assertion that Populists wanted to decrease the government's role in social services. Indeed, it was the Republicans who introduced and supported legislation to restrict the government's role by limiting tax levels, and it was the Populists who voted that bill down by 21 to 1. Though there are arguments to support Bicha's claim that Populism does not resemble modern liberalism, they are not of the order he suggested. Populists introduced bills to establish and maintain kindergartens, which even a hostile observer termed "an advanced measure"; to levy county (rather than district) taxes to support common schools, thereby helping equalize educational opportunities; to create the office of public defender to defend indigents and all persons charged with insanity; to reform penal administration and establish such concepts as indeterminate sentencing and conditional pardons; and to reform the state's charitable institutions, a bill praised by the Associated Charities of New York as an "advanced step" that set "the pace for other states to follow." In not unrelated matters, Populists voted down a harsh bill for capital punishment backed by a majority of Republicans and Democrats; and in the house, a Populist introduced a bill making it a felony for any employer "to make improper advances to any woman working under his charge."[34]

In the reform areas more usually associated with Populism, senators demonstrated great ingenuity in fashioning legislation to implement their national demands at the state level. To counteract the credit shortage and reduce the power of moneylenders, one Populist introduced a bill to put the state "into the money lending business" by lending the principal of the state permanent school fund to individual citizens at low rates and on landed collateral. Another Populist sought to promote monetary inflation and unemployment relief by proposing Coxeyite legislation to authorize townships and cities to employ the jobless and pay them with county-issued notes to be redeemed by the state. Republicans termed this "a rather remarkable and unusually interesting measure," and its Populist sponsor described it as a test case for the great Populist question of authority over the control and issuance of money. Populists also enacted laws reflecting Debsian concerns, providing for jury trials and the restriction of judicial authority in contempt-of-court cases and authorizing municipal ownership of gas, water, and electric plants.[35]

Roll-call analysis of the larger list of reform issues in the 1897 legislature confirms the findings for the 1895 body. Agreement scores with the reform position on eighty-one roll-call votes involving reform issues that provoked conflict averaged 83 for Populist senators and only 31 for Republicans. Republicans constituted only 28 percent of all senators but provided 58 percent of all votes in opposition to reform measures. Populists, on the other hand, constituted 68 percent of all senators but provided only 36 percent of all opposition to reform. Again, the range of issues on which there was significant interparty disagreement was broad. Of the eighty-one roll calls, forty-nine witnessed a majority of Populists opposing a majority of Republicans and over such issues as labor legislation (disagreement scores of 100, 83, 82, 81, 60), monetary issues (100, 100), electoral legislation (100), taxation (100, 100, 92, 76), corporate and banking regulation (100, 82, 66), railroad regulation (94, 68, 64), stockyard regulation (92, 79), municipal ownership (89), mortgage and interest questions (86, 76, 71, 70, 67), and pollution (70, 65).[36]

Again, as with the 1895 senate session, indices of cohesion and disagreement reveal that no other determinant—sectional, occupational, educational, or otherwise—seriously rivaled party in explaining voting differentials among senators. More sophisticated roll-call analysis, including the use of Guttman scales and cluster blocs, produces the same invariable conclusion: Populists consistently supported reform bills over a wide variety of issues, and Republicans consistently voted against many of the same bills.[37] The assertions that legislation did not provoke "markedly partisan responses" among legislators and that Populists were no more reformist than Republicans are wholly untenable.[38]

Bicha, however, did point to a major problem, one made even more interesting by the correct data presented here. The Populists did not succeed in enacting a large body of significant reform legislation. This is not a new finding, of course. All other observers, regardless of their interpretation of Populism, have noted this, and the Populists themselves bewailed this result.[39] But rather than treating Populists as monolithic, it is more productive to adopt an analytical approach that recognizes the diversity of the Populists and the complexity of their political context. Applied to this issue of legislative failure, such analytical sensitivity provides still further light on political behavior in the 1890s.

First, of course, there is the nature of legislative activity itself. In 1895 the anti-Populist *Topeka Daily Capital* noted, "In fifty days a legislature, composed in the main of raw material, may be expected to revolutionize society and reform every wrong. . . . It may be expected to enact scores of brilliant bills calculated to make life happier and prosperity more general. It may be expected to correct every abuse brought to its attention. . . . But if such wonders are expected, disappointments will be perennial and bitter." At another time the newspaper developed its underlying point: "The platform promises of all the parties find expression in the bills introduced upon a wide range of issues. The ground sought to be covered is so large and the work to perfect really good legislation so great that three-fourths of our good intentions fall through for lack of time and attention and strength divided among the many bills. This is the history of all legislatures we have seen come and go for more than thirty years in Kansas, and what is true of one state is true of other localities."[40] These factors were aggravated during the Populist years by the large number of inexperienced legislators in each session, particularly among the Populists, who necessarily had to spend considerable time learning legislative procedures. Nor were legislatures as controlled by the majority party as might be expected. Committee chairmanships frequently went to Republicans, and in some instances a majority of committee members were Republicans despite the Populists' overall greater numbers. The relative laxness of legislative procedures not only prevented forcing through a program but also led to gross miscarriages of legislative justice. Twice in 1897, for example, Populists found that the bill signed into law by the governor was *not* the bill they had passed, that the bills had been tampered with by their opponents. In one instance, a major banking-regulation bill, Populists discovered that a section that had been vigorously opposed by the state's bankers and by Republican legislators had been crossed out before the bill was printed. The Populist bank commissioner concluded that "some one opposed to the section borrowed the bill 'to look at it' and then proceeded to do a little legislation on his own responsibility."[41] Obviously, the informal procedures that permitted these activities did not facilitate legislative accomplishments, certainly not by reformers.

There were, moreover, other ways to prevent reform legislation besides surreptitious expurgation. The fact that with one exception the Republicans always controlled one house of the legislature made it easier to block the enactment of reform legislation. In addition to their obstructionist performance in the 1891 senate, the Republicans controlling the 1895 house adopted the simple practice of killing nearly everything the Populist senate passed. This knee-jerk policy alarmed even anti-Populist observers, including a Republican editor who complained, "The house of representatives contains a number of simpletons who think everything that comes from the Senate is Populist. They would even kill a quiet, inoffensive and necessary appropriation bill for that reason."[42] On reform matters, the 1895 house Republicans were at least as insistent, as indicated by the following partial list of legislation passed by the Populist senate and lost in the Republican house: insurance regulation (eleven bills), regulation of interest rates and related reform of laws dealing with usury and contracts (six bills), railroad regulation (four bills), electoral reform (two bills), telegraph- and express-company regulation (two bills), regulation of banks and building and loan associations (two bills), stockyard regulation, antibribery legislation, antioption legislation, grain warehouse regulation, and legislation to protect unions in their use of labels, to protect workers in their claim for wages, to exempt from garnishment the earnings of workingmen, and to establish free employment bureaus. When confronted with a similar cataloging of Republican failures to enact reform measures from the Populist senate, one Republican legislator "said he was making no pretensions because he did not come here as a reformer."[43]

In the 1897 legislature, however, Populists did control both houses, and reform failures must be explained in other ways. But it should be emphasized at the outset that the "failure" of the 1897 Kansas legislature was a relative one. That legislature passed laws providing for railroad regulation, ballot reform, stockyard regulation, the creation of a state grain-inspection department, banking regulation, a school-textbook commission, taxation of deficiency judgments, regulation of life insurance companies, municipal ownership, antitrust legislation, conservation, and a series of labor protections from anti-Pinkerton and antiscrip provisions to antiblacklisting, protection of unions, and improved health and safety conditions for miners. This is only a partial list of legislative accomplishments (all overlooked by Bicha), but as one Populist admitted later, "a part of the program failed, and unfortunately the failure was in some of the things nearest to the Populistic heart."[44]

Historians have speculated that lack of unity, "negligible discipline," and "inept legislative management" hampered Populist legislators. And yet cohesion indices and party-support scores reveal that Populist senators demonstrated as much solidarity and unity in voting behavior over the full range of legislative issues as did their opponents.[45] Clearly, another factor was responsible. Roll-call analysis again provides the key. On the fifteen roll calls in which reform legislation was defeated, the Republicans and Democrats voted virtually unanimously in opposition to the proposed measures, casting only 7 reform votes out of a possible 195. A small but decisive group of Populists were nearly as uniformly opposed to the particular reforms under consideration. When voting with the solid bloc of Republicans and Democrats this Populist minority made up a majority of the senate. This small group of Populists consisted largely of merchants and lawyers affiliated with the party.[46] The average reform score for these roll calls of the merchant and lawyer Populists was but 34, less than half the reform position of 70 of the far more numerous farmer legislators, the stereotypical Populists.

Thus the typical or representative Republican opposed reform measures, and the typical or representative Populist supported reform. Judging from contemporary reactions to the 1897 legislature, both Populists and Republicans recognized this reality. And when the votes of a relatively few relatively conservative Populists enabled the intransigent Republicans and Democrats to defeat reform legislation, most Populists were outraged. As the Garnett *Kansas Agita-*

tor phrased it, a few so-called Populists worked with the enemies of the people to defeat good legislation; the *Topeka Advocate* termed the Populist opponents of campaign pledges "traitors"; and the *Norton Liberator* listed the "conservatives" by name as "the Judases of Populism." At least three of those Populist senators, wholesale butter merchant L. D. Lewelling, creamery merchant George Hanna, and grain and cattle shipper Frank Field, were summoned to appear before their respective county committees to explain their legislative votes, and the local Populists demanded that Senator Hanna, at least, resign.[47]

Thus, from a careful examination of Populist legislative behavior, it is obvious that Populists were in fact more likely to introduce reform legislation, much more likely to support it with their votes, had wide-ranging interests and concerns for social change, were imaginative in trying to fashion legislation to deal with problems, and were demonstrably committed to an active government. It is also clear that when individual Populists deviated in any way from these positions they went decidedly against not only the party's principles and platforms but against the majority of their fellow Populists.

9

POPULISTS IN POWER:
PUBLIC POLICY AND
LEGISLATIVE BEHAVIOR

The great historiographical debate over Populism, begun in the 1950s, shows little sign of ending now, three decades later. For a generation historians had generally accepted the picture drawn by John D. Hicks in his 1931 classic, *The Populist Revolt*. The Populists, Hicks maintained, had been earnest farmers responding politically to agricultural difficulties and political indifference by agitating for political and economic reforms. Then in the 1950s a number of scholars, reacting to the tensions of their own times and reflecting different interests, depicted Populists variously as reactionary, nativistic, anti-Semitic, and irrational. This picture, so absurdly overdrawn and poorly substantiated, was in turn countered by a long list of studies that effectively destroyed all the claims of the revisionists. This scholarly debate, however, leaves the student of Populism little more knowledgeable about the subject than at the beginning. As James Turner has observed, "Reactionary Populists chased socialist Populists through the learned journals in a quarrel that generated more heat than light."[1]

Two basic problems underlie this impasse. The first is methodological, for too often the historian's position depends on the particular Populists studied — Tom Watson or Jerry Simpson, Texans or Nebraskans — and a blindness to the necessity and the difficulty of determining whether the choice was representative. The second problem evident in Populist historiography is its data base, as scholars continue to comb the same newspapers and manuscript collections, in the belief that (as one maintained) "we have no other sources."[2]

To resolve this impasse, new approaches and the use of new sources of data seem necessary. Several recent studies have employed quantitative analysis of the statistics of popular voting behavior to describe the constituencies of the Populists and other parties, thereby advancing our knowledge of the mass electorate. But there has been considerably less effort to exploit the data provided by legislative journals, what Allan G. Bogue has called "the largest body of opinion data, systematically collected and organized, that American society has preserved." Historians have traditionally ignored this information, perhaps because the labor involved is so great and their usual methodological tools have been so limited. And yet systematic analysis of the voting data derived from legislative roll calls can reveal the issues of most interest to the legislators themselves and the relative importance of those issues. It can identify the questions that divide or unite legislators and suggest the ideological parameters of the resultant groups. And by examining the often mundane world of policymaking, roll-call analysis provides a practical perspective on the concerns of the Populists not available through either the traditional analysis of campaign speeches or the quantitative investigation of mass politics. Finally, roll-call analysis allows historians, in considering these matters, to push beyond the now rather stale question of whether Populism was reactionary or radical and reach a deeper understanding of the movement.[3]

The 1897 Kansas Senate serves as a case study of the value of roll-call analysis. Much was expected of this legislature, which had skilled Populist leadership and a clear Populist majority, the only time Populists controlled both houses in this key state. After the disappointments of the 1893 legislative war and the 1894 election defeat, party leaders had used the silver issue as the catalyst to unite different groups into a successful coalition in 1896. To attract votes from Democrats and Silver Republicans, they had also traded off nominations for other offices in exchange for fusion support of legislative candidates and had nominated to the senate such popular figures as former congressman William A. Harris and former governor Lorenzo D. Lewelling to ensure that support. Such maneuvering helped place twenty-seven Populists in the senate chamber alongside eleven Republicans and two Democrats.

Operating under intense public scrutiny in this crucial session, nearly all senators actively engaged in legislative business and introduced hundreds of bills reflecting a variety of concerns. Of these, 241 bills were brought to a vote. Excluding roll calls for procedural or personnel matters, local or minor bills provoking neither controversy nor disagreement, perfunctory votes of appreciation, apportionment proposals, repetitive motions, and bills passed unanimously, there were ninety-two substantive roll calls provoking at least some opposition.[4]

Virtually all of this divisive legislative activity—eighty-one roll calls—pertained to the reform issues raised in Populist party platforms: railroad regulation, usury and interest regulation, labor legislation, tax reform, stockyard regulation, and so forth. Some Populists demonstrated great ingenuity in devising legislation to implement their national demands at the state level where their limited power applied. To counteract the credit shortage and decrease the influence of moneylenders, one Populist introduced a bill to put the state "into the moneylending business" by lending the principal of the state permanent school fund to individual citizens at low rates and on landed collateral. Another Populist sought to promote monetary inflation and unemployment relief by proposing Coxeyite legislation authorizing townships and cities to employ the jobless and pay them with county-issued notes to be redeemed by the state, a remarkable measure described by its sponsor as a test case for the great question of who controlled and issued money. Populists also enacted laws reflecting Debsian concerns, one providing for jury trials and the restriction of judicial authority in contempt-of-court cases and another authorizing municipal ownership of gas, water, and electric plants.[5]

Analysis of senators' votes on such proposals helps reveal the factors that influenced legislative behavior and the lines of division in public policymaking. Legislative analysts have found that voting cleavages often occur along partisan, regional, and occupational lines, thereby suggesting some possible explanations of behavior in the 1897 Kansas Senate. Indices of cohesion and disagreement are particularly helpful in understanding and describing the behavior of nominal groups, and I used them to determine whether voting patterns followed such divisions.[6]

Not surprising, given the nature of the legislation under consideration, the primary determinant of legislative voting was party. Although there usually was some Republican support for reform proposals, fifty-six of the eighty-one roll calls relating to reform questions and many other roll calls involving procedural, personnel, administrative, and miscellaneous matters resulted in substantial disagreement by party groupings. The partisan splits over reform issues are clearly revealed in the index of disagreement for Populists and Republicans over such issues as the initiative and referendum (100), election legislation (100), free silver resolutions (100, 100), taxation (100, 100, 92, 76, 65), government reform (100, 77), protective labor legislation (100, 83, 82, 81, 60), railroad regulation (94, 68, 64), stockyard regulation (92, 79), municipal ownership (89), interest and mortgage regulation (86, 76, 71, 70, 67, 65, 64), and banking and corporate regulation (100, 82, 66).

Another measure of the partisan division over reform legislation is provided by the calculation of agreement scores for each senator with the reform position for the eighty-one roll calls. On a scale of 0 (indicating opposition to all divisive reform) to 100 (indicating support for all reform), the average Populist scored 83 and the average Republican only 31. Republicans, on the one hand, constituted only 28 percent of all senators but provided 58 percent of all votes in opposition to reform proposals. Populists, on the other, constituted 68 percent of all senators but provided only 36 percent of the negative votes on reform bills. Such data refute the recent claims of one historian that there was no partisan response to such legislative proposals and that Populist legislators were no more inclined to support reform legislation than were members of the major parties.[7] Thus the typical Republican opposed, and the typical Populist endorsed, reform measures. This finding should hardly be surprising, but the necessity of demonstrating it indicates the impasse that afflicts Populist historiography.

The importance of party does not exclude the possibility that other determinants influenced legislative voting patterns in some fashion. Sectional differences, for instance, constituted a logical basis for voting decisions. There had been frequent conflict in Kansas, as in most western states, between the older and more developed eastern region and the remainder of the state, and historians have argued persuasively that the differential pattern of development provoked a political alignment in the 1890s best described as sectional.[8]

But sectional conflict rarely appeared in the 1897 senate. On fifteen roll calls a majority of eastern senators did oppose a majority of western senators, but in nearly every case the division was merely an artifact of partisan differences and the asymmetrical geographical distribution of Republicans and Populists. The index of disagreement revealed that party rather than region underlay the voting division. Only on two roll calls was this measure higher for regional than for party groupings. Neither of those roll calls dealt with reform issues. One reflected greater western support for, and more eastern opposition to, establishing a normal school in western Kansas. The other indicated that western more than eastern senators favored the death penalty, perhaps an indication of frontier justice but suggestive of little else. Indeed, indices of cohesion showed little unity in either regional group (24, 26, 6, 75), and neither roll call resulted in substantial regional disagreement (index figures of 34 and 25).[9]

Occupational influences were somewhat more apparent in legislators' voting decisions. Because of the small number of senators in specific nonagricultural occupations, I established nominal groups composed of farmers and nonfarmers. Fifteen roll calls produced significant disagreement between these broad occupational groupings. Here, too, most of the apparent disagreement reflected partisan differences and the fact that farmers were disproportionately Populists. Only on a roll call to restrict the power of local governments to borrow money and create indebtedness was the division among legislators along occupational lines clearly distinct from partisan influences. Farmers supported and nonfarmers opposed the bill. Such a measure had long been an agrarian demand and represented the rural reaction to the boom mentality of earlier years, when towns and counties had issued bonds to induce railroad construction and promote business enterprise. Many of these projects failed to materialize or collapsed in the subsequent depression, leaving the rural majority paying for the vanished dreams of business promoters. In the 1897 senate, farmers remembered the past, but lawyers, bankers, and merchants from the state's towns and villages still hoped to promote a boom for themselves.[10]

Only one other roll call significantly dividing legislators along occupational lines registered higher occupational than partisan disagreement, and it was indirectly related to the same concern. Farmer senators split evenly over a bill to prohibit railroad commissioners from having any personal economic interests in railroads, their cohesion index of 0 indicating the absence of a common farmers' perspective on the issue. But nonfarmers of all parties unanimously opposed the bill, suggesting again their common interest or involvement in promotional activities. Still, the occupational disagreement index (50) was virtually the same as the partisan one (46), for all Republicans opposed the bill. Three other bills, each reflecting the different economic interests of town and country, also provoked a majority of farmer senators to oppose a majority of nonfarmers and at disagreement levels greater than that indicated by partisanship, though slightly lower than herein defined as significant (37, 33, and 30). Farmers more generally supported a bill to levy a county rather than a district school tax and two efforts to impose tighter regulations on banking, whereas most nonfarmers opposed these measures. On all five roll calls, however, the relatively low level of cohesion among farmers (54, 0, 22, 4, 42) and, frequently, among nonfarmers (38, 100, 28, 70, 25) indicates the comparative unimportance of occupational considerations. Again the general conclusion is that party voting predominated in the legislature.[11]

It has often been suggested that Populists were older men, either literally or figuratively belonging to an earlier time. Recent research on the life cycle also suggests that some attention might be fruitfully directed to the connection between age and legislative behavior, a question once phrased by James C. Malin as "At What Age Did Men Become Reformers?" In the 1897 Kansas Senate, Populists were clearly older than members of the major parties, averaging forty-seven years old to forty-two for their opponents. The more appropriate question, however, is to what extent did age influence voting behavior. The answer: not much. Differences in average reform scores over eighty-one roll calls for legislators grouped into quintiles by age merely reflect the distribution of Populists and non-Populists among the quintiles. Agreement scores by individual roll calls for different age groups also reveal the complete insignificance of age as a legislative determinant.[12]

Nor do other individual characteristics of senators, as reported in the legislative directory, provide much insight into their voting behavior. Religion, frequently regarded as of decisive political importance by ethnocultural historians, seems to have had negligible effect on voting patterns. There were only three senators who claimed to be "liturgicals," too few to evaluate with any confidence, but the other senators divided into two large groups composed of pietists and of those who admitted to no religious affiliation at all. The average reform score for pietistic senators was 73.1 compared to 65.6 for the nonreligious and only 54.7 for the liturgicals. However, this apparent distinction only reflected the disproportionate Populist strength among the pietists. Religious differences in voting disappeared when party was considered: Populist pietists averaged 84.2 and nonreligious Populists averaged 83.4; Republican pietists averaged 29.0 and nonreligious Republicans averaged 30.0. Finally, no roll call showed substantial disagreement scores between the two large categorical groups. Even a roll call related to the cultural issue of prohibition failed to produce serious voting divisions along religious lines.[13]

Similarly, categorical groups composed of senators who attended college and those whose education was limited to a common school preparation showed no significant voting disagreement, not even over educational issues, such as establishing normal schools or mandating taxation policy for public schools.[14]

Although party was thus the most important voting determinant, partisan loyalty did not hold all senators with the same strength. Other factors occasionally influenced some legislators and cut across party lines. The saliency of specific voting determinants varied among senators according to the particular content of legislative proposals, and different issues generated different voting alignments. Since political parties tend to be coalitions of varying degrees of unity, it is important to examine the Populist legislative contingent to determine the fault lines within the party and the issues that provoked defection.

The most obvious determinant among Populist senators was their occupational status as farmer or nonfarmer. There was substantial disagreement among Populists along occupational lines on twelve roll calls, all focused on economic issues. These included three attempts to regulate interest rates and prohibit usury and one to tax mortgages, with the farmer Populists in favor of such legislation and their nonfarmer fellow partisans opposed. At times the disputes between the two groups became heated. One Populist farmer was "proud of the fact that I am not a lawyer"; Populist lawyer W. B. Crossan snapped, "All the honesty of the country is not confined to farmers, and . . . we should have the same friendship for the banking interests as we have for the farming interests." The sharpest disagreements between the two groups (index of 84 and 72) involved two other financial issues, with farmers strongly endorsing efforts to restrict the power of local governments to issue bonds and to have the state lend money to citizens at low rates of interest in order to decrease dependence on eastern capital. Nonfarmer Populists firmly opposed each proposal. On three roll calls over banking regulation and two involving railroad regulation, farmer and nonfarmer Populists disagreed substantially, with the farmers favoring stronger measures. Finally, Populist farmers favored (and nonfarmers spurned) levying a county school tax to equalize spending for town and country school districts.[15]

The greater farmer support for reform measures is also revealed in the average reform agreement scores over eighty-one roll calls. The merchant/lawyer Populists averaged 75.6 to their rural colleagues' 85.1. Constituting only 26 percent of the Populist senators, the nonfarmers provided 38 percent of total Populist opposition to reform measures. Moreover, they consistently furnished disproportionate opposition regardless of the type of issue involved although their opposition increased as the issues approached the classical Populist ones: 33 percent of all Populist opposition to labor-reform legislation, 37 percent of Populist opposition to railroad regulation, and 50 percent of all Populist opposition to interest and moneylending legislation.

Some historians have argued that the previous party affiliation of Populists influenced their political attitudes. Roll-call analysis offers limited confirmation. On eleven roll calls there was significant disagreement between groups of Populists divided along lines of partisan antecedents. Some of these voting alignments overlapped with, and are better explained by, the occupational divisions already noted. But several others are suggestive of possible important differences within the Populist coalition. On two of these roll calls, Populists of traditional third-party origins demonstrated far more support for railroad regulation, particularly for maximum freight-rate

legislation, than Populists of major-party antecedents, the majority
of whom opposed such legislation. Populists of third-party antecedents also significantly disagreed with Populists of major-party antecedents by supporting several bills that sought to regulate activities
of local elites, particularly one that prohibited county commissioners from depositing county funds in any bank in which they held an
interest.[16]

Perhaps these votes by Populists of third-party antecedents reflected their traditional outsider status, but they were also consistently more reformist than their colleagues. For all eighty-one roll
calls, the Populists of Union Labor and Greenbacker origins had an
average reform agreement score of 86.7, whereas former Republicans averaged 81.6 and former Democrats 76.5. The differential
was even greater in certain areas of traditional reform concern. On
roll calls involving both railroad regulation and interest and moneylending questions, third-party Populists averaged 18 points higher
than Republican-Populists and 23 and 26 points higher, respectively,
than Democratic-Populists. Perhaps Populists of third-party antecedents had been correct to doubt the commitment of latecomers to
reform.

At times Populist senators also divided along sectional lines. On
six roll calls there was substantial sectional disagreement between
eastern and western Populists. Several of these votes did not involve
reform issues, including those that most polarized the Populists by
sectionalism. On three different measures western Populists favored
establishing normal schools in western Kansas, but eastern Populists,
with a normal school already in their region, opposed establishing
more schools and called them unnecessarily extravagant in hard
times. Even among themselves, however, the western Populists demonstrated that local boosterism underlay attitude divisions on this
subject, for only half voted consistently; the others supported bills
for normal schools in or near their hometowns but opposed bills to
establish schools elsewhere in the region. Other apparent sectional
differences, especially on roll calls involving railroad regulation, are
better explained by the distribution of farmers or traditional third-
party men within the two sectional groupings of Populists.[17]

But there also was substantial disagreement between eastern and
western Populists, not related to underlying occupational or politi-

cal factors, on a deed of trust bill, reducing the redemption period and permitting sales of property without foreclosure by judicial proceedings. Regarded as "always . . . a Republican measure," it now was also supported by a majority of eastern Populists, who represented a well-settled area with relatively little mortgage debt and hoped to promote economic development by making conditions more attractive to potential investors. However, Populists from western Kansas, where mortgage indebtedness was extensive, overwhelmingly rejected the bill as harmful to their constituents' interests.[18]

Other individual characteristics of Populist senators had little apparent influence on their voting decisions. Divided into thirds by age, the Populist contingent showed no difference in supporting reform measures, each group averaging 83 percent over the eighty-one roll calls. Nor was education a measurable voting determinant. Categorical groups of Populists with a college background and those with only a common school education never substantially disagreed on any roll call, not even those dealing with educational issues. Religion also had little apparent influence. Nominal groups of pietistic Populists and those Populists not claiming any religious affiliation differed insignificantly on roll calls.

Constituency characteristics represent another possible influence on legislators' voting patterns. Correlations between legislative voting and measurable characteristics of Populists' respective districts shed some light on this type of determinant. The common perception of Populists as the farmers' representatives in politics was corroborated by the +.522 Pearson correlation coefficient between Populists' reform voting over eighty-one roll calls and the proportion of families in their districts that were engaged in agriculture. That is, the more rural the district, the more reformist was the voting behavior of its Populist senator. This relationship also held for subsets of issues. For instance, Populist reform voting on interest and mortgage legislation correlated at +.513 with this indicator of rural constituency. But correlations between Populists' reform voting in the senate and various indices measuring the economic distress of their districts, although positive, were of marginal or no significance.

The voting decisions of Populist senators were related to certain political characteristics of their constituencies, however. The stronger the Populists were in a district (measured by 1896 election results), the more reformist was their senator in his legislative votes, a correlation of + .301. A senator with strong popular support was less inclined to compromise Populist principles than one whose district was less unified. This tendency is also revealed in the much stronger correlation (+ .544) between Populist senators' reform voting and the proportion of their districts' Populist strength that was *not* composed of Democrats in the 1896 fusion campaign. The less dependent were the Populist senators upon Democrats or Democratic-Populists in their district electorate, the more reformist were their votes. This pattern reflects the greater conservatism of the Kansas Democrats and of their former partisans within the People's party and suggests the larger importance of political maneuvering among the factions of the People's party.[19]

Thus far analysis has been limited to categorical or nominal groups such as Populists and Republicans, farmers and nonfarmers. This approach involved classifying legislators on the basis of shared characteristics determined on an a priori basis. Although this procedure proved enlightening, another approach must be employed in order to understand legislative behavior. The second form of analysis involves empirically defined groups—legislators who by regularly voting together demonstrated in their legislative behavior shared attitudes. This mode of inquiry is particularly important because of the earlier use of reform-agreement scores. The latter measure can mask as well as reveal relationships: Two senators each scoring 50 on such a scale could in fact disagree on every roll call and, despite identical scores, hardly represent a shared attitude.

One technique to determine empirically based groups is cluster-bloc analysis, which requires the calculation of indices of interpersonal agreement for all possible pairs of legislators over the full gamut of roll calls. Arrangement of these scores in a matrix reveals clusters or blocs of senators who vote together. This technique requires specifying the minimum level of agreement in order to establish the limits of the cluster. The higher the minimum, the smaller and fewer any blocs will be, but progressively relaxing the minimum will expand the cluster. Thus the bloc structure will vary at different levels of agreement.[20]

Several striking facts emerge from this analysis. First, the majority of Populist senators were in accord at such high levels that to make useful distinctions I set the minimum level of agreement initially at ≥ 90 percent. This step revealed a cluster of four Populists, all farmers from western Kansas. Sixteen Populists agreed with at least one other Populist at ≥ 90 percent; no Republicans or Democrats agreed with anyone at that high level. Relaxing the agreement level to 85 percent doubled the size of the bloc to eight Populists, with an additional six Populists on the fringe, agreeing at that level with more than half but not all the members of the bloc. All fourteen of these Populists were farmers, ten from western Kansas.

Second, the nonfarmer Populists not only failed to register high levels of agreement with their rural colleagues, they also failed to agree with each other at high levels. No bloc begins to emerge from their ranks until the agreement level is reduced to 80 percent, and then only three of them cluster. At 75 percent another merchant and a farmer join this small bloc, but Populist agreement at that level is so generalized (the average interpersonal agreement score among Populists was 77.5 percent) that little further insight is gained, for the larger bloc contains virtually all remaining Populists. The tendency was for deviant Populists to agree strongly with no one at all, their voting patterns reflecting idiosyncratic factors. But although these Populists did not always vote with their fellow partisans, they were still less likely to vote with Republican senators.

Third, the Republicans demonstrated neither the high levels nor the range of interpersonal agreement apparent among the Populists. No Republicans voted together at a 90 percent rate. Not until an agreement level of 80 percent do even three Republicans emerge in a cluster, but at 75 percent all Republicans are in the cluster or at the fringe. At 65 percent all Republicans agree. Significantly, not one Populist agreed with even one Republican at that level, let alone approached inclusion into the Republican bloc by agreeing with all of them. One historian's recent argument that Populists and Republicans generally voted together on reform issues is invalid.[21]

Table 9.1 illustrates these points by summarizing the voting behavior of several groups of senators over the set of eighty-one roll calls. The first group represents the majority element of the Populists, the second includes Populists on the margin of Populist agreement, and the third contains a sample of Republicans. The percentages represent the means of all appropriate interpersonal agreement

Table 9.1. Average Agreement Scores 1897 Kansas Senate

	Majority Populists	Minority Populists	Republicans
Majority Populists	92.3		
Cooke			
Forney			
Lupfer			
Pritchard			
Minority Populists	64.8	75.5	
Crossan			
Hanna			
Ryan			
Shaffer			
Republicans	25.0	48.7	76.3
Battey			
Hessin			
Lamb			
Morrow			

scores. Neither Populist faction voted at high levels of agreement with the Republicans but instead voted more with each other; the minority Populists agreed considerably less among themselves than did the other Populists; and the Republicans showed virtually the same solidarity as did the Populist minority.

Although cluster-bloc analysis can reveal the existence and cohesion of groups, as well as the distance between them, other techniques are more helpful in identifying the attitudes and values around which grouping occurred. Guttman scale analysis is such a technique, designed to isolate groups on the basis of shared attitudes. The use of Guttman scaling assumes that, as Bogue has written, "legislators will vote for measures which in their minds represent only half a loaf because half is, after all, better than none." This is not always the case, particularly among ideological legislators. The only Populist to oppose the maximum freight-rate bill in the 1895 senate, for example, explained his vote by declaring that he "did not believe there was any way of reaching the railroads except by . . . government ownership." But as a rule, the assumption seems a safe one.[22]

Guttman scale analysis involves examining the patterns formed by legislators' responses to a set of intercorrelated roll calls and classifying legislators in terms of the extent of their support for the measures under consideration. The roll call with the fewest positive votes isolates the senators with the most extreme or radical views on the subject; the roll call with the largest number of positive votes reveals all senators with any sympathy toward the subject and identifies the remainder as the most conservative senators who voted against all proposals. Numerous positions between the extremes are possible. Although Guttman scales are typically constructed by determining the scalability of all roll calls sharing an apparent common issue, such as railroad legislation, those roll calls may be linked to others focused on different issues. Thus the common policy dimension as understood by the legislators themselves could escape notice. To eliminate this possibility and to test the likelihood that senators, rather than considering each roll call in isolation, shared general attitudes that regularly influenced their voting behavior, I determined scalability by calculating Yule's Q for each possible pair of roll calls, regardless of apparent issue content, and required each roll call to have a coefficient $> .90$ with every other one in the set.

See Table 9.2 for the results of this analysis. It is a skeletal representation of a Guttman scale fitting twenty-five roll calls and tapping a policy dimension among legislators that can best be described as a reform ideology. The roll calls that fit into this scale range over an apparent variety of issues: railroad, interest, bank, and stockyard regulation; taxation reform; prohibition of labor blacklisting; election reform; municipal ownership; and consumer protection. The significant features of this table are several. First, each Populist registers at a more "radical" scale position than any Republican or Democrat, voting the reform position on all or most roll calls from the least controversial to the most. Second, all Populists on scale type 8, reflecting the most radical group, are farmers, whereas the nonfarmer Populists dominate scale positions 3 and 4. Third, in light of this evidence of Populist factionalism, it is important to note that the most radical scale position contains more than one-third of all Populists; this was an irreducible core on all reform roll-call votes, and they were usually joined by most other Populists. The full scale shows relatively little voting differentiation across the complete set of twenty-five roll calls: Most Populists consistently demonstrated a reformist ideology toward all issues. Fourth, most Republicans were as consistent in making their voting decisions from a shared perspective of hostility to reform. Never supporting any of these diverse issues, most belonged to scale type 0, the most conservative position. Finally, the Democrats appear on the scale between the Populists and the Republicans, as might be expected from the fusion politics of the decade. Legislation touching the platform concerns of Populism thus did "activate ideological sensitivities" among senators, and serious ideological differences, not merely rhetorical hyperbole, divided parties over the role of government and the direction of the economy and society.[23]

One final matter for analysis involves the Populists' celebrated failure to enact a significant body of reform legislation in the 1897 senate. One explanation advanced focuses on their legislative inexperience and alleged lack of unity and skill in the legislative process. Roll-call analysis helps discount this possibility, for cohesion indices and party-support scores reveal that Populist senators demonstrated as much solidarity and unity in voting behavior over the full range of legislative issues as did their opponents. Another reason for Populist failure must be found.[24]

That explanation is suggested by the intraparty variation in party-support scores. All Republicans registered scores around their party average, but the standard deviation for Populists was twice as great; although a majority of Populists had extremely high party-support scores, a handful had significantly lower ones. These latter Populists were the same senators ranking at the lower positions of the Guttman scale portraying the radical-conservative dimension underlying voting decisions. The crucial importance of this group becomes clear upon examination of the fifteen roll calls in which reform legislation was defeated. On these roll calls, Republicans and Democrats voted as a solid bloc in opposition to the bills, casting only 7 reform votes out of a possible 195. When joined by the small group of conservative Populists, this bloc constituted a majority of the senate and defeated the proposed legislation. This Populist faction consisted largely of merchants and lawyers, although

Table 9.2. Radical/Conservative Continuum: Scale on Reform Issues

Senator	Party	Scale Type	1 Y	2 Y	3 N	4 Y	5 N	6 Y	7 Y	8 Y	1 N	2 N	3 Y	4 N	5 Y	6 N	7 N	8 N
Benson	Pop	8	+	e	+	+	+	+	+	+								
Cooke	Pop	8	+	+	+	+	+	+	+	+								
Forney	Pop	8	+	+	+	o	+	+	+	+								
Hart	Pop	8	+	+	+	+	+	+	+	+								
Householder	Pop	8	+	+	o	+	+	+	+	+								
Lupfer	Pop	8	+	+	+	o	+	+	+	+								
Mosher	Pop	8	+	+	+	+	+	+	+	+								
Pritchard	Pop	8	+	+	+	+	+	+	+	+								
Sheldon	Pop	8	+	+	+	+	+	+	+	+								
Titus	Pop	8	+	+	+	+	+	o	+	+								
Braddock	Pop	7		+	+	+	+	+	+	o	−							
Caldwell	Pop	7		+	+	o	o	+	+	+	o							
King	Pop	7		+	+	+	+	o	+	+	−							
Campbell	Pop	6			+	e	+	+	+	+	−	o						
Helmick	Pop	6			+	e	+	+	+	+	−	−		x				
Young	Pop	6			+	+	+	+	+	+	−	−						
Helm	Pop	5				+	+	o	+	+	−	−	−					
Jumper	Pop	5	x			+	o	o	+	+	e	−	−					
Reser	Pop	5				+	o	o	+	o	−	−	−					
Armstrong	Pop	4					+	+	+	o	o	−	o	−				
Hanna	Pop	4					+	+	+	+	−	−	−	−				
Ryan	Pop	4					+	+	+	+	−	−	−	−				
Shaffer	Pop	4					+	+	+	+	−	−	−	−				
Crossan	Pop	3						+	+	+	−	−	−	o	o			
Field	Pop	3						+	+	+	o	o	−	−	o			

Table 9.2. (continued)

Senator	Party	Scale Type	1 Y	2 Y	3 N	4 Y	5 N	6 Y	7 Y	8 Y	1 N	2 N	3 Y	4 N	5 Y	6 N	7 N	8 N
Lewelling	Pop	3						+	+	+	−	−	−	−	−			
Farrelly	Dem	2							+	+	−	−	−	−	−	o		
Zimmer	Dem	2						+	+	o	−	−	−	−	−			
Matthews	Rep	1								+	−	−	−	−	−	−	−	
Sterne	Rep	1								+	−	−	−	−	−	−	−	
Battey	Rep	0									−	−	−	o	−	−	−	−
Coleman	Rep	0									−	−	−	−	−	−	−	−
Fulton	Rep	0									−	o	−	−	−	−	−	−
Hessin	Rep	0									−	−	−	−	−	−	−	−
Johnson	Rep	0									−	−	−	−	o	−	o	−
Lamb	Rep	0									−	−	−	−	−	−	−	−
Morrow	Rep	0									−	−	−	−	−	−	−	−
Stocks	Rep	0									−	−	o	−	−	−	−	−
Wallack	Rep	0									−	−	−	−	−	−	−	−

+ = reform vote
− = vote against reform
o = absence, nonvoting
e/x = error or nonpattern vote

Seventeen more roll calls fit into this scale.
Coefficient of reproducibility = .99
Senator Harris omitted because of excessive absences.
Voting key:
1. Vote on Titus's amendment, providing for popular election of railroad commissioners, to S.B. 524
2. Vote on Titus's amendment, establishing maximum railroad freight rates, to S.B. 524
3. Vote to kill S.B. 8, taxing mortgages
4. Vote to reconsider killing S.B. 34, regulating interest and prohibiting usury
5. Vote on amendment, allowing corporations to avoid public scrutiny of their financial records, to S.B. 248
6. Vote on H.B. 43 to prevent blacklisting
7. Vote on S.J.R. 1 to amend the state constitution to establish the initiative and referendum
8. Vote on S.B. 446 to regulate banks

one lawyer and one editor generally supported the proposed reforms and a few Populist farmers (usually representing, however, the least rural constituencies of the farmer legislators) often voted against the legislation. This pattern suggests that ideological considerations — shared attitudes — rather than a narrow occupational identification determined legislative behavior, although ideology was itself in some fashion influenced by the rural perspective.[25]

Roll-call analysis also identifies the issues over which the Populist coalition splintered and thereby helps to explain the party's peculiar course and its ultimate demise. Populists in the Kansas Senate were most unified when voting on national issues, such as resolutions in favor of free silver or a federal income tax; on state issues affecting all of them equally, such as the establishment of the initiative and referendum; or on issues affecting virtually none of them directly, such as prohibiting labor blacklisting. But divergent groups emerged when the issues narrowed to specific programs of immediate relevance. These divisions among Populists appeared primarily over certain questions of economic activity at the state and local level. It would be more incomplete than inaccurate to characterize these disagreements as simply a split between radicals and conservatives, for the latter supported a variety of economic and political reforms and stood sharply to the left of their contemporaries in the major parties. The conflict would be better described as a division between those representing what the Populists called the "producing classes" and those interested in promoting economic development. The developers objected to any proposed restrictions on what they perceived as the engines of economic growth: eastern capital investment and the railroads. Bills introduced by producer-oriented Populists to tax mortgages, regulate interest rates, or lend state money to farmers all seemed, to developer Populists as much as to Republicans, to threaten the procurement of eastern capital investment in Kansas.[26]

Developer Populists also joined with Republicans to vote down bills to establish maximum railroad rates, to limit the return on railroad investments, or to prohibit railroad commissioners from having any personal investment in railroads. Similarly, they opposed a bill to restrict the power of local governments to create bonded indebtedness, a power they viewed as a major tool for economic development. The leader of these Populists was Sen. William A. Harris, who directed the defeat of railroad regulation and consistently supported the interests of creditors over debtors, arguing the necessity of attracting investment. Thus he helped defeat a bill to prohibit usury by describing it as vindictive toward moneylenders. His own legislation was designed to establish the deed of trust, to reduce the redemption period for property, and generally to "so shape the laws of the state as to protect alike the credit of the state and the money of honest investors."[27]

Many Populists denounced this group of senators for supporting the traditional positions of the major parties. "When Senator Harris favors high interest because he wants to encourage capital to come to Kansas," declared the *Norton Liberator*, "he announces he has not yet divested himself of the swaddling bands of old fogyism." Another Populist newspaper also complained that "Populists of certain districts in Kansas have sent men to the legislature who are more nearly Republicans than Populists." Indeed, most of the Populists who voted with the Republicans on developmental issues were merchants or distinctly entrepreneurial "farmers" like Harris, who was actually a civil engineer and a cattle breeder of national reputation who later moved to Chicago as president of the American Shorthorn Breeders' Association. Their producer-oriented opponents among the Populists were nearly all farmers. Advocates of the developers' point of view tried to ridicule such farmers as ignorant and unfit for public office. A newspaper in Harris's Leavenworth district, for example, attacked Sen. J. N. Caldwell as a Populist "transplanted from his hog pasture in Anderson County and never realizing the change . . . [with] more realization of shovelling corn than he has of law-making." The source of the criticism, however, was not the alleged ignorance or the real agricultural origins of such Populists, but the fact that they were consciously trying to change the direction of economic legislation.[28]

The importance of this division is clear in the summary of the voting behavior of several groups of senators on sixteen roll calls over "development" legislation (see Table 9.3). As with Table 9.1, the percentages given are the means of interpersonal agreement scores, and the groups represent samples of the majority element of the Populists, the marginal Populists, and members of the older parties. But whereas the ear-

Table 9.3. Average Interpersonal Agreement Scores on Development Issues

	Majority Populists	Minority Populists	Republicans	Democrats
Majority Populists	95			
Cooke				
Forney				
Lupfer				
Pritchard				
average development score: 9				
Minority Populists	17	80		
Crossan				
Hanna				
Ryan				
Shaffer				
average development score: 90				
Republicans	12	89	93	
Battey				
Hessin				
Lamb				
Morrow				
average development score: 97				
Democrats	30	77	83	79
Farrelly				
Zimmer				
average development score: 80				

lier cluster-bloc analysis over the full range of legislation indicated that deviant Populists' voting behavior still resembled that of their Populist colleagues more than that of the Republicans, that pattern is sharply reversed in this particular policy area. The majority Populists were closely united in near total disagreement with development policies (an average score of 9 on a scale of 0 to 100) and had little in common with either the minority Populists or the Republicans who voted solidly together and overwhelmingly supported the development position (scores of 90 and 97). The Democrats voted substantially in favor of development (a score of 80) but less so than the Republicans — as one might expect from a knowledge of general Democratic attitudes in the 1890s. Strikingly, however, the minority Populists were also more pro-development than the Democrats and even agreed with them far more readily than with their fellow Populists.

In sharing these promotional attitudes, and often town and commercial identifications, these Populists represented a bridge to the major parties and their traditional policies. It was through their efforts and persons, for example, that fusion typically was arranged, especially senators Harris, Lewelling, and W. H. Ryan with the Democrats and Senator Crossan with the Silver Republicans. Moreover, it was these more conservative Populist senators whom the party promoted politically: Harris was elected U.S. senator in 1897; Lewelling had been governor from 1893 to 1895; and incumbent governor John Leedy had been a leader of the conservative Populist group in the 1895 state senate. Their political prominence represented Populist attempts to appeal to a wider constituency and thereby achieve electoral success. As one Populist paper observed of these senators, "These 'conservative' Populists are largely composed of men whose political status was a matter of considerable doubt — who had been nominated because of their supposed ability to get votes." This practice, however, undermined rather than promoted the likelihood of securing Populist reform. The dilution of Populism for practical political reasons constituted a central weakness in the People's party, and the legislative behavior of those so chosen represented a concrete indication of how politics weakened Populism.[29]

This study has determined the practical policy objectives of Populists in power, specified the particular issues that divided legislators across and within party lines, and suggested the nature of the different groupings and their implications for the traditional political questions about Populism. Additional research along these lines, particularly of a cross-sessional nature, is obviously necessary, but these findings are suggestive. The majority of Populists worked, against fairly consistent Republican opposition, to fashion a legislative program that would enact their famous platform demands into law. A minority of Populists, sharing with the mass of the party most political and economic attitudes, also was tangentially related to the representatives of the major parties in terms of promotional attitudes and/or occupation and residence. On questions dealing with promoting or restricting economic development — ironically, as one Populist noted, "the things nearest to the Populistic heart"— this Populist minority deserted their party and its expressed principles. Although a minority, they wielded a decisive influence through their leadership positions and their strategic numbers in an electorate where Populists constituted a minority and in a senate chamber where their votes were needed. As one Populist senator complained of Harris, he "did all in his power to turn back the radical measures of his party." The nature and consequences of this division reveal the Populist tragedy that the methods by which they created a political coalition powerful enough to win elections often left it without the power to enact laws.[30]

10

NO RIGHTS ON THIS FLOOR:
THIRD PARTIES AND THE
INSTITUTIONALIZATION OF
CONGRESS

"If Christ came to Congress," wrote Alabama Populist congressman M. W. Howard in 1894, he would find a political institution corrupted and perverted, filled with hypocritical senators and representatives indifferent to public needs and popular demands, and teeming with contemptible lobbyists representing the "privileged classes." Howard depicted Congress as so thoroughly iniquitous that he projected a violent public retribution, involving bombs in both houses, the destruction of Congress, and the death of all members.[1]

Howard's remedy may have been singularly extreme, but his diagnosis of Congress was widely shared by other Populists and by Greenbackers as well. As members of radical third parties, representing western and southern farmers and workers, they confronted a Congress that had institutionalized the two-party system and had adopted procedures and norms that simultaneously obstructed the policy innovations they sought and promoted the power of the very political and economic interests against which their parties had been organized.

By the late nineteenth century, Congress was no longer primarily a deliberative body. In response to the growing volume and complexity of public business, and to developing political pressures, leadership had become increasingly centralized, symbolized by the expansive power of such Speakers as "Premier" John G. Carlisle and "Czar" Thomas B. Reed, and the committee system had taken over much of the work formerly performed by the House itself. As Woodrow Wilson observed of the House in 1885, "Committee work is everything and discussion nothing but 'telling it to the country.'" As the Speaker selected the members of the increasingly important committees, his power to control the flow of legislation was virtually complete. The Speaker further enhanced his power during the 1880s by expanding the authority of the Committee on Rules, to which he named himself and the chairs of the committees on Appropriations and Ways and Means. All three of these party leaders effectively controlled the course of legislation and made the Rules Committee "the formal, institutional vehicle through which the party system and the committee system were fused."[2]

In 1889, in the famous "Reed rules," Reed consolidated the Speaker's power by eliminating the "disappearing quorum" whereby representatives had prevented the House from conducting business simply by refusing to answer during quorum calls. Reed also assumed the authority arbitrarily to rule motions out of order as dilatory, further restricting the minority's ability to frustrate the majority's wishes as asserted by the Speaker. Believing that they should use their power, as Reed phrased it, to transform "party pledges into legislation," Speakers used the rules to impose discipline on their party members and to facilitate majority-party government.[3]

Comparable developments occurred in the Senate in the late nineteenth century as an assertive leadership emerged to establish partisan and procedural discipline in that body. In particular, from the mid-1880s, the Republican Steering Committee gained increasing control of the course of legislation by its power to determine committee assignments.[4]

In all of these ways, Congress was evolving into an institution less susceptible to minority influence, less open to new members and new parties, and less amenable to their attempts to represent their constituencies. Although previous scholars have recognized that these developments promoted the majority's ability to control legislative business, they have emphasized that such changes contributed to legislative efficiency and to institutional responsibility. They have taken little notice of the specific political context of these developmental changes or of their practical consequences for members of the minority and their policy objectives.

An examination of the Populists' activities in Congress provides a valuable perspective on the evolution of Congress as an institution, the influence of political parties on its operations, its role in popular consciousness, and its effectiveness as an institution of representative democracy. Roll-call analysis, the predominant methodology of behavioral research in legislative studies, is of little value in this effort, for the organizational attributes of Congress effectively excluded Populists from real participation and limited their roll-call voting to measures that scarcely reflected their own interests. But contemporary political scientists, perceiving the restrictions of roll-call analysis, have increasingly redirected attention to the influence of organizational factors on legislative operation and performance, public policy, and the behavior of legislators. Drawing from the work of such institutional analysts, while stressing the interactive nature of structural constraints and political decisions, this chapter illuminates both the nature of Congress as a political and governmental institution and the neglected congressional experience of the Populists themselves.[5]

Thirty-nine Populists were elected to fifty-eight terms in the House from 1890 to 1900 and an additional nine Populists served in the Senate, but they consistently encountered obstacles to the recognition of their party and to the achievement of their objectives in Congress. The tumultuous election of 1890 sent the first Populist contingent of nine representatives and two senators to Congress together with dozens of southern Democrats elected on the reform platform of the Farmers' Alliance, a rural organization that formed the basis for membership in the People's party. When the Alliance instructed its members to avoid any congressional caucus not committed to Alliance principles, the Populists moved to organize Congress along policy, rather than party, lines. Populists Benjamin Clover and Jerry Simpson of Kansas, in fact, arraigned the unresponsive character of the Democratic party as a motivating cause of the agrarian political revolt and urged the Alliance Democrats to join the independent caucus. But the southerners angrily rejected independent action and insisted upon adhering to the Democratic party as the best hope for securing reform, especially as it held a majority of seats in the new House.

The Populist plan collapsed amid such acrimony that Tom Watson, a Populist from Georgia, spoke of an "irrepressible conflict between factions." With the exception of Watson, all southern Alliance congressmen entered the Democratic caucus and were pledged to support Charles Crisp of Georgia for Speaker. As Crisp was a conservative who opposed Alliance reform demands, the Populists acidly observed that by subjecting themselves to the Democratic caucus the southerners obviously placed party before principles. The Populists then held their own congressional caucus, endorsed the Alliance resolution against old party caucuses, and chose Watson as their party's candidate for Speaker. In subsequent Congresses, Populist representatives consistently nominated and voted for their own independent candidate for Speaker.[6]

The Populists also failed in several attempts to persuade senators to surmount traditional party lines in organizing the upper house. Their most dramatic experience came in the Fifty-fourth Congress, when six Populists actually held the balance of power after the 1894 elections. As in 1891, the Populists appealed to reformers within the old parties by inviting all bimetallists to a meeting to discuss organizing the Senate on silver lines. But the silver meeting proved a failure. Of the fifty-two senators invited, only four attended, and they refused to leave their parties to secure silver legislation by acting with the Populists. Fred Dubois, a Silver Republican from Idaho, declared that "neither party will enter into any combination with the Populists" and suggested that it was more likely that Republicans and Democrats would reach an understanding on Senate offices and patronage in order to eliminate any Populist influence. William A. Peffer, a Kansas Populist senator, was not surprised by such comments. "As a matter of fact," he remarked, "the very thing I want to see, as a Populist, is a combination of the Democrats and the Republicans in the organization of the Senate. That will enable us to tell our people again, as we have told them in the past, that the two old parties are practically one." In Congress, as in the electoral arena, the Populists were outsiders, their very presence an indictment of both major parties and of politics as usual.[7]

The strength of party ties that prevented Senate reorganization along policy lines also precluded the realization of Dubois's scenario, and, ultimately, the Republicans organized the Senate when the Populists refused to vote on the issue at all. The Populists' abstention reflected their difficult predicament as a third party in a legislative body that incorporated the two-party system in its rule that required a majority of those voting to elect the chairs of committees. Once the senators of the major parties had rejected reorganization of the Senate on policy rather than on partisan lines, Populist senator Marion Butler explained, the Populists had only melancholy choices: Vote with the Republicans, an unacceptable course for an independent third party; vote with the Democrats, similarly unacceptable; or vote as Populists. But if they voted for their own candidates, the effect would be to deadlock the Senate and leave it under the Democratic organization of the preceding Congress—a virtual vote with the Democrats. By abstaining, the Populist senators allowed the forty-two Republicans to triumph over the thirty-nine Democrats, an outcome that William V. Allen, a Nebraska Populist, defended as a preferable result because the Republicans did have a plurality of the Senate as well as control of the House and therefore could be held responsible for the expected failure of Congress to respond to public needs, just as the Democratic majority had failed in the previous session. Whether the Populists voted or not, Allen concluded, "Evil was the result either way, and we chose what we considered the lesser evil." Democrats castigated the Populists for "collusion" with the Republicans, further indicating the awkward position of third-party adherents unable to be taken on their own terms.[8]

The Populists' marginal status in a Congress structured by the two-party system also appeared in the related area of committee assignments. The importance of committees was such that by 1891, according to the *Baltimore Sun,* new members began "immediately contriving means to obtain places on committees where they may best advance the interests of their constituents or further their personal ambitions." In the Senate, the task of making committee assignments was entrusted to committees appointed by the party caucuses. "Here a well-regulated system of promotions obtains, and conflicting claims are rare." The caucus committees reported their recommendations to the party caucuses, which, upon approval, then presented the lists to the vice-president who made the formal appointments. Populist senators Peffer and James Kyle tried to arrange independent recognition on committees, but neither of the major parties was willing to accept the Populist claim to independence, let alone to permit their own determination of committee positions. In the closely divided Congress, each major party instead attempted to attract the Populists as individuals into their respective camps through promises of favorable assignments, often approaching them on the basis of their former party affiliation. The *Sun* thought that Peffer, in particular, might gain desirable appointments "as a result of the efforts of the Republican and Democratic managers to land him on their respective sides." In the Republican caucus, a Montana senator, believing that Kyle "might be induced to act with" the GOP, urged his colleagues to place Kyle on important committees.[9]

But when the Populists refused to join either major party caucus, the two old parties agreed to ignore their committee requests. Peffer had hoped to be named to the committees on Finance, Agriculture, and Interstate Commerce in order to advance Populist reform objectives, but he failed to secure a seat on any of them. The Democratic caucus, concluding that Peffer's Republican origins made him unreliable, refused to name him to any committee. Eventually, the Republican caucus assigned him to several minor committees. The Republicans, in turn, doubting Kyle's "soundness on Republican principles" and "party questions," refused to give him any positions. After much discussion, the Democrats then finally agreed to take "me in out of the cold," Kyle reported, and named him to a few minor committees.[10]

In the deadlocked Senate of the Fifty-fourth Congress, Populists hoped that their balance-of-power position would produce better committee assignments. Determined to remain independent, however, they refused to request appointments from the steering committees of the old parties and derived little advantage from their position. Although Democrats complained that the Republicans had arranged for the Populists to abstain on the question of the Senate's organization by promising them choice committee assignments, Populist senator Allen denied that there had been any more negotiation between the Populists and the Republicans than "between the Populists and the Czar of Russia." The new committee assignments supported Allen's response, for the triumphant Republicans (as one noted) "treated the Populists just as the Democrats treated them in the last Congress." Still, by virtue of the close division between the major parties, the Populists gained the balance of power on fourteen committees, a position they gloried in, according to the *New York*

Times, and intended to exploit "in the interest of legislation which they favor[ed]." How successful they were depended on other factors.[11]

In the House, Populists received even less recognition on committees. In that body, the Speaker alone made all committee assignments, accepting only "such assistance and advice as he considers it advisable to take." In making his appointments, Crisp paid little attention to the wishes of the Populists, particularly singling out his fellow Georgian, Watson, who had had the temerity to run against him for Speaker. Crisp, Watson complained, "acted upon the idea that the House of Representatives is his private property," promoting his supporters and humbling his opponents. "Of course I was put just as low as the law allowed." The minor committees to which he was appointed would never even meet, he predicted. "There is nothing for them to do. They are simply pigeon holes in which dust accumulates and an occasional paper is filed away." Watson repeatedly expressed his frustration with being shunted aside and having little of consequence to do. "Maybe I can get the pages to let me help them bring up stationery, pens, ink, etc., and thus keep the rust off. The elevator man seems to be a good-natured outcast and possibly he may let me help him pull the cord." Watson's personal humiliation was not the source of his discontent, however; it was the consequent lack of representation for his constituents. "So fine a District as there is anywhere sends me here to work for it. Mr. Crisp out of personal spite places me where he thinks I'll never be heard of."[12]

The other Populist representatives were similarly relegated to minor committees and complained similarly, and these practices did not change during the course of the decade. In the Fifty-fourth Congress, John Bell of Colorado complained that "so far as the committees are concerned, the Populist members of this body have not a single important position. . . . Their committee assignments signify nothing." Democratic Speaker Crisp had been "hard on Populists," but Republican Speaker Reed treated them no better, and left them unable to advance the interests of their constituents. In the Fifty-fifth Congress, meeting in 1897, Bell renewed his charges on behalf of twenty-two Populists and another six fusionists, "the greatest representation of any third party in 40 years." With a constituency of 8 million people, and with "clearly enunciated principles, different in many essentials from any other political organization," the Populists told Reed that their party deserved separate recognition on all House committees, especially the powerful ones, such as Ways and Means.[13]

Reed not only rejected Bell's pleas but decisively demonstrated the Speaker's control over committee assignments by refusing to make any appointments beyond those of the Rules, Ways and Means, and Appropriations committees. While Ways and Means prepared what would become the Dingley Tariff, Reed declined to appoint any other committees for 131 days. His purpose was to restrict legislation to that desired by the House leadership. After the Republican majority passed the Dingley bill early in the session, the House waited months while the Senate debated the measure, unable to consider other action except by unanimous consent and simply meeting every third day to adjourn.[14]

The Democrats, rejecting "useless and captious opposition to Republican policies," did little to protest Reed's inaction. Populists, however, were furious, repeatedly demanding that Reed "appoint the committees and give Congress a chance to legislate." Simpson's arraignment of "Reed's autocratic and despotic methods" created a sensation, and soon the *Washington Post* referred to Simpson's "customary attack upon the Speaker for not appointing the committees." But Reed silenced his opposition and stood his ground.[15]

James B. Weaver, the 1892 Populist presidential candidate and a former Greenback congressman, summarized the Populist complaint against the Speaker's power to appoint committees: "It makes him an autocrat and enables him to mould legislation, stifle public sentiment, thwart the will of the majority, and defy the wishes of the people." The undemocratic consequences of such a power were matched only by its distorted effects upon public policy, a subject to which the Populists always returned: "Public sentiment is not observed. It is uniformly defied. . . . The wealthy and powerful gain a ready hearing, but the plodding, suffering, unorganized complaining multitude are spurned and derided."[16]

The growing power of the Speaker and the institutionalization of the House effectively worked against third parties in other crucial ways as well. The most crippling of these ways involved the Speaker's power to recognize representatives seeking to address the House.

Speakers had long used the right of recognition arbitrarily, but until 1881 a member had the right of appeal. In that year Speaker Samuel J. Randall ruled that the Speaker's right of recognition was absolute. Gradually the practice evolved of members having privately to submit their proposals to the Speaker in advance of attempting to introduce them as the only way to secure his recognition on the floor. That recognition would be awarded if the proposals met the Speaker's favor or could serve his purposes. Because the Speaker was chosen, in Reed's view, "not simply to preside over the deliberations of his fellow members, but to carry out party pledges and round up a successful legislative session," this tactic meant that members of a third party, whose very existence constituted a rejection of the principles and objectives of the major parties, would find it difficult to gain recognition in order to present their own distinctive measures.[17]

As a Greenback congressman in 1880, Populist leader Weaver figured in one of the most dramatic efforts to compel recognition from the partisan Speaker. For thirteen consecutive weeks, Weaver asked during the Monday call to be recognized to suspend the rules and place upon passage resolutions against the banking system. Devoted, as Weaver phrased it, "to the interests of the capitalistic classes," Speaker Randall regularly refused to recognize the Greenbacker. Crowds soon thronged the House gallery to watch the show, and the spectacle became the focus of national attention, culminating in a famous cartoon in *Harper's Weekly* depicting Weaver as a braying donkey with the Speaker turning his back on his challenger in order to avoid granting recognition. Weaver cleverly used the publication of this cartoon to gain the floor on a question of personal privilege, which the Speaker was not permitted to ignore.[18]

Similar scenes were frequently reenacted by Populist congressmen and Democratic and Republican Speakers in the 1890s. Even the tactic of rising to a question of personal privilege, however, often availed the Populists little. Simpson gained the House floor in one such instance only to have Speaker Reed rule him out of order as he began to speak. Another struggle between the two saw Reed rule Simpson out of order and refuse to entertain protests against his decision on the grounds that critical statements "are not conducive to order." Led back to his seat, Simpson shouted, "I have had great doubts lately whether I have any rights in this House." This episode, too, became the subject of a popular cartoon, appearing in the *Washington Post,* showing Reed sitting on Simpson with the help of a book labeled Rules.[19]

Most other Populists soon came to Simpson's conclusion that the House rules left them without any rights. Obtaining the floor when a sympathetic Democrat yielded to him, Bell vigorously attacked the rules that prevented him from gaining recognition on his own. Reed had refused to recognize him upon learning that he proposed to introduce currency legislation drawn up by the Populist caucus, Bell complained. "Had it been some little local measure or something that the Speaker approved he doubtless would have extended the courtesy." And because Bell was not a member of an important committee with privileged rights to the floor, he was able to speak only "by the courtesy of someone else," from whom he had to "beg the opportunity to address the House." This dismal experience demonstrated "the complete dependency of individual members on the will of the Speaker and the committees." Bell concluded, "Members of a new party are practically ostracized in the House and have no power under the rules to promulgate any of their principles."[20]

Other Populists could not even "beg" a chance to speak, and, instead, had to resort to canned speeches—remarks printed in the *Congressional Record* but never delivered on the floor of Congress. Nebraska Populist William Stark angrily described his canned speech as a "deception . . . made necessary by the rules of the House." "I had resolved that I would never 'can' a speech," he explained, "but rather than be deprived of all the rights to which the suffrages of the people of the Fourth district should entitle me, I avail myself of the only opportunity presented." Omer Kem, one of Stark's fellow Nebraska Populists, was even more bitter as he explained his "humiliating" recourse to canned speeches "because I was denied the privilege of being heard on the floor." Describing the House as "an arbitrary machine for smothering free speech and representing a part of the people only," Kem declared that the Populists "are denied the right of free speech by rules and practices more fitting for a monarchy than a republic." Weary and depressed by encountering the same frustration for six years, William Baker, a Populist from Kansas, cited his inability to secure recognition from the

Speaker when he declined to run for a fourth term, despite certain reelection.[21]

Populists were not the only ones who complained of the effects of the House rules. *Harper's Weekly* condemned Reed's rules for restricting access to the floor and limiting debate, discussion, and amendment. Democratic congressmen attacked them for constricting the rights of the minority, although Democratic Speaker Crisp effectively adopted them when he gained power. Even some Republicans considered challenging the rules. Republican congressman William Hepburn, for example, in 1896 described the Speaker's complete discretion over recognition as a violation of the constitutional principles that constituencies and their representatives have equal rights. He proposed to strip the Speaker of "the power arbitrarily to silence a constituency" by amending the rule in order to permit any member to rise and be recognized to speak.[22]

Many Republicans clamored to attack this proposition, but Speaker Reed slyly recognized Populist leader Bell. Bell strongly supported Hepburn's amendment by pointing out that the Populists "have stood here during the last four weeks and pleaded with the Speaker and with the members leading this House for the majority, and not one member of the Populist party has been permitted by them during this session the privilege of addressing the House." During one discussion on financial legislation, Bell had desperately tried to speak in order to protect his constituents' interests, "yet I could not get an opportunity to even breathe aloud upon that subject." By adopting rules that denied the equality of members, Bell continued, the House had "degenerated until it has become the body of bosses, the body of tyranny." Taking advantage of his rare opportunity to speak, Bell then combined his advocacy of Hepburn's amendment with what one reporter called "a Populistic harangue, during which he ran the gamut of isms preached by the Populists." Dismayed by "the object lesson just taught by 'indiscriminate recognition,'" Hepburn promptly withdrew his amendment to the amusement of all but the Populists.[23]

Excluded from important committees and from effective floor participation, Populists had little influence on legislation, and their opponents easily manipulated other congressional rules and procedures to obstruct the Populists' own legislative measures. And, as representatives of a third party, the very existence of which derived from a perception that the major parties failed to enact appropriate legislation, the Populists in Congress were exceptionally active in proposing measures to promote their constituents' interests. Senator Peffer, in particular, proved an indefatigable worker for Populist reform principles — "distinguishing himself [said one hostile observer] by the introduction of preposterous bits of legislation in the interest of unfortunate humanity in general." Observing "the mass of Pefferian bills which daily fall into the hopper," another reporter commented in 1894 that "the fecundity of Senator Peffer in the matter of introducing bills has passed into a proverb. No pent up Utica contracts his powers when it comes to subjects or the length at which they may be treated." Other Populists, in both Senate and House, were scarcely less active, introducing numerous proposals to implement their party's reform demands for the subtreasury, monetary inflation, income and inheritance taxes, railroad regulation, direct election, woman suffrage, unemployment assistance, land reform, and antimonopoly measures.[24]

But none of these distinctive measures became law. Many Populist proposals were reported adversely by committees dominated by their major-party opponents. The Republican chair of the Senate Finance Committee, for instance, marveling that Peffer's financial bills provided for "ten times more money than there is now in use by the whole world," dumped a pile of them on the desk of the Senate clerk with the remark that the committee reported them adversely.[25]

But most Populist proposals were not reported at all; they simply disappeared into the committees to which they were referred. "In the decorous depths of elegant committee rooms these bills sleep," lamented Watson, "and no man can bring them forth." Members of all parties frequently complained that they were unable to have a bill reported from committee, and Wilson described the process of sending a bill to committee as crossing "a parliamentary bridge of sighs to the dim dungeons of silence whence it will never return." The 1880 revision of House rules required a two-thirds vote to suspend the rules in order to pass a motion to discharge a committee from further consideration. The Reed rules adopted in 1890 made favorable action even more difficult by referring such motions without debate to the Committee on Rules, composed of men selected to impose the majority party's will on legislative business.[26]

Under these circumstances, Populist legislation had little chance to be considered, but Watson and his party colleagues valiantly tried. Their efforts for a bill to establish the subtreasury, the crucial early issue for the party, are instructive. When the Ways and Means Committee refused to take action on the subtreasury measure, Watson asked for unanimous consent to present a discharge resolution instructing the committee to report the bill. House Populists, he noted, had

> permitted both the Democrats and the Republicans to have considered measures here, month after month, by unanimous consent. We have observed that there is some sort of arrangement by which certain Democrats are recognized, and that certain Republicans have recognition. That is only fair, and I make no complaint of it. But . . . it should be remembered that there are three distinct parties in this House. We, the People's party, have not been recognized at all, and I submit to the fairness of the House on both sides that it is only right that we should have some recognition in these unanimous consents.

Until that was permitted, Watson warned, the Populists would object to all requests for unanimous consent and demand the regular order of business.[27]

Day after day, then, Watson and his major-party opponents skirmished, Watson asking unanimous consent for a discharge resolution and, when this was objected to, objecting himself to such requests by others. The nine Populist congressmen so successfully blocked the passage of bills by unanimous consent that a Democratic representative proposed that the Rules Committee report a new rule requiring the objection of ten or more members to prevent consideration of any measure by unanimous consent. Populist congressman John Davis described this as an attempt to authorize that powerful committee to change the meaning of the word "unanimous" in the dictionary. At last, House leaders asked for the objection to Watson's request to be withdrawn and for the discharge resolution to be approved. The Populist victory was small; the committee reported the subtreasury bill adversely, and the House took no further action on the measure.[28]

Populists remained concerned about the underlying issue of making Congress responsive. Watson once lectured liberal Democrats, frustrated by their inability to have their free silver and tariff reform bills reported, to "do as I did" and "put yourself in the way" until discharge motions were approved. Democrats responded by invoking the norm of "procedural reciprocity." One declared, "I do not regard myself as bigger than all the other members of the House," but Simpson retorted that was precisely the point at issue. "We are here as equals. No man and no committee has a right to ride ruthlessly over any member of this floor. We come here to discharge a public trust." Another Democrat nevertheless maintained that there was no practical way under the rules to require committees to report bills they did not want to report. With that Simpson had to agree: House leaders, he said, "did not want to have the rules in a shape that would enable you to compel them to report." Watson, too, conceded that Populist entreaties for committees to report legislation were futile. "We have no way to force action. We are powerless."[29]

In the Senate, despite the greater autonomy allowed its members, Populists encountered and denounced the same obstacles. Describing the Congress as "a government of the committee, by the committee, and sometimes for the committee," Allen complained that "the committee rooms are burial places" for Populist measures. "I have never been able to obtain thus far even an unfavorable report upon them so that I might have an opportunity to place the bills upon the calendar. . . . The purpose seems to be to have them die in the pigeonholes of the committee room, so the country will not know what has become of them." Repeatedly returning to the subject, Allen denied the legitimacy of committees killing legislation in this fashion; it was their duty, he maintained, to consider bills and to report them, favorably or adversely, within a reasonable time. "But as business is transacted here, . . . they will not give us the opportunity to place it before the Senate and take a vote upon it."[30]

Leaders of both established parties denied Populist charges, as one Democrat phrased it, "that there is a system of stifling legislation" in the Senate committees. Republican George Hoar self-righteously lectured Allen that Populists had as much power as Republicans since each senator had unlimited rights of speech and amendment as well as the authority to present any measure he desired. But Allen effectively cut Hoar short by asking whether he could "promise us that those measures will be reported back in one form or another to the Senate?" Hoar weakly admitted, "That is a very different question." Allen concluded, "I thought so." Hoar's Republican party, Allen noted, "having control of the important committees, has in its power to bury every Populist measure in this chamber and never let it see daylight again."[31]

Unable to advance their own legislation to the floor, Populists sought to promote their principles in other ways. One favored tactic involved proposing to amend pending measures in such a fashion as to implement Populist goals. This alternative was attractive, if limited, for House rules allowed any member to propose an amendment to legislation during its consideration in the Committee of the Whole and to speak for five minutes in support of the amendment. But if the Committee of the Whole was therefore "tolerant to the minority," in the words of one scholar, it remained "responsive to the majority" party, for the rules also permitted the partisan chair to reject amendments on the point of order that they were not germane. And since Populists tried to use amendments as substitutes for their own bills that they could not bring to the floor, opponents were quick to object. Kansas Populist Edwin Ridgely demonstrated the futility of this charade. After proposing an amendment to a naval bill requiring the appropriation to be paid in legal tender notes, thereby achieving the Populist goal of an inflated currency, he declined to argue against the inevitable point of order raised, maintaining, "I am satisfied that it would be sustained." Determined to raise issues of interest, Populists did not expect, nor did they receive, serious consideration, but they would not surrender. Their tenacity in this respect absolutely astounded many observers, including the editor of the *Detroit Tribune* who predicted that if the Ten Commandments were introduced the Populists would propose amendments to make them "conform to the Omaha platform."[32]

Stark later explained his initial amazement at seeing his colleagues use these "jump-up" speeches under the five-minute rule in the Committee of the Whole to discuss matters of little apparent relevance to the pending legislation. But "I soon learned that this was

the only way, under the iron rules of the House, . . . to obtain a
hearing on the matter they wished to present, and that they were
driven to adopt such subterfuge." Nevertheless, it was only a limited
hearing with no practical consequences for legislation, leaving the
Populists increasingly frustrated.[33]

A second tactic Populists pursued to gain attention for their principles involved introducing resolutions of inquiry. The rationale for
congressional investigations was to provide information for framing
legislation, but as Allan G. Bogue has noted, inquiries also had "legislative and political implications that often extended far beyond the
ostensible object of investigation." Populists clearly hoped that if
congressional obstacles prevented effective legislation, their inquiries into social, economic, or political conditions could serve to educate and arouse public opinion and to advance the party's interests.
The proposed objects of investigation revealed the Populists' goal of
dramatizing the necessity for reform: industrial conflict, railroad
rate-setting, tariff-protected industries, government ownership of
coal mines, business depression, stock manipulations, judicial conduct, railroad land grants, bank fraud, and many more. Some of
the Populists' proposed investigations were approved and even resulted in memorable reports, such as Senator Kyle's resolution instructing the U.S. commissioner of labor to investigate social, economic, and health conditions in the nation's urban slum areas.[34]

But most Populist resolutions of inquiry were rejected. Some were
never considered at all but instead ruled out of order on parliamentary grounds, such as Watson's proposal to investigate labor violence; others were voted down by an indifferent majority. Most were
sent to hostile committees, where they perished.[35]

The treatment accorded Peffer's resolution of inquiry into the
conduct of national banks was particularly instructive to the Populists. As the Panic of 1893 engulfed the nation, Peffer introduced a
resolution calling for the secretary of the treasury to inform the Senate whether the nation's banks were violating the law. Seeking to
shield the banks, both Republican and Democratic senators attacked Peffer's proposition, one Republican even insisting that
banks should not be made to "conform to the letter of the law."
Democratic Senate leader Arthur P. Gorman of Maryland conceded
that "it is the custom of this body to pass any resolution asking for

information from a Department of the Government that any Senator may think he requires in the discharge of his public duty, but I submit there are exceptions to all rules." Peffer expressed surprise, as one reporter phrased it, "at the sensitiveness of the Senators, and thought that the people were entitled to know whether the institutions which supplied currency were openly violating the law." Over Peffer's objections, Republicans and Democrats voted together to refer his resolution to the Senate Finance Committee, not to consider it, as Democratic senator David B. Hill said, but "for the purpose of suppressing it."[36]

Because their resolutions of inquiry were thus routinely killed, emasculated, or subverted by being referred to standing committees dominated by their opponents, Populists often proposed the creation of select committees of inquiry. At the least, the Populist sponsor might expect to get a committee less hostile to the intent of the resolution than the relevant standing committee. Still better, in accordance with congressional custom, he might be named to such a committee, thereby gaining more influence over the investigation than was possible with the standing committees from which he was generally excluded. Populists sought to guarantee their inclusion on select committees by specifying that the committee be composed of members from each political party. In 1892, for example, Peffer secured Senate approval of such a select committee to investigate the Homestead violence and, as a member, then took the lead in examining the sordid affairs of the Pinkerton agency. Populists also proposed select committees to investigate the use of money in elections, the feasibility of the initiative and referendum, the need and authority for government ownership of railroads, and other matters of public concern.[37]

But major-party politicians generally opposed giving Populists authority to investigate. Hill charged that Populists proposed investigations merely "to make political capital." And both Democrats and Republicans tried in various ways to kill such measures, either by refusing to consider them, by rejecting them, by referring them to standing committees for burial, or by substituting standing for select committees to carry out the proposed investigations. A final way to limit their efficacy was for the presiding officer to ignore precedent and to refuse to appoint any Populist to those committees that were established. For instance, Peffer's proposal for a select committee to investigate the depression of the mid-1890s was accepted, but neither Peffer nor any other Populist was named to the committee. To maximize the chances of having such investigations approved, Populists sometimes foreswore any interest in serving on the committees. But that action brought them no closer to achieving tangible results, for major-party politicians generally had little interest in investigating and exposing the conditions that attracted Populist concern. Without Peffer's presence, for example, the Select Committee to Investigate the Depression, chaired by Bourbon Democrat William F. Vilas of Wisconsin, never fulfilled its charge and failed to report.[38]

The third, and still more limited, method by which Populists tried to promote their principles in a hostile Congress was simply to exploit congressional practices to disseminate their ideas. This was achieved by reading articles, speeches, or other material into the *Congressional Record*, thereby making them available for free public distribution under members' franking privileges. Simpson helped to read into the *Congressional Record* an entire book by taking advantage of the House custom of granting unanimous consent to allow members to extend and to have printed remarks never made on the floor. Complaining that such tactics abused the practice of unanimous consent, Republican leader Julius C. Burrows of Michigan moved to strike the material from the *Congressional Record*. But one of Simpson's fellow "conspirators" responded with a statement that all Populist representatives could endorse: "Were it not for this liberty to print many a constituency would have no voice and never be heard on this floor on many important measures. Recognition by the Speaker or by the Chairman of the Committee of the Whole and division of time allowed to a committee for debate on a bill necessarily is influenced to a great extent by personal friendship and favoritism. All can not get time or recognition." With the Populists' unanimous support, Burrows's motion was tabled. Within a week, however, the Rules Committee reported a new rule, adopted without a roll-call vote, prohibiting "general leave to print remarks" in order to end the "abuses" of "the privileges of this House." Thus, again, Populist activities and opportunities were restricted by House rules and leadership.[39]

The only solace the congressional Populists could find in their predicament was that the consistent obstruction of their efforts served to "confirm previously formed opinions" that the two major parties and the government that they controlled were unresponsive to popular wishes and indifferent to popular needs — the beliefs that had called the third party into existence in the first place. With their beliefs confirmed by experience, Populists felt compelled by democratic ideology, as well as by partisan necessity, to attack the institution and procedures of Congress.[40]

Holding to a "citizen" or an "amateur" conception of representative government, Populists particularly and strenuously objected to what Nelson W. Polsby has described as the "institutionalization" of Congress: the growing professionalism and specialization of members, the increasing reliance on committees and formal rules, the rising importance of an apprenticeship period and of seniority. All such developments militated against the possibility that newcomers in general, and third-party radicals in particular, could participate effectively in Congress, as the Populists quickly learned. Populists necessarily regretted the developments by which Congress became more exclusive, more differentiated from the larger society, and less susceptible to its control. In both symbolic and substantive ways, Populists opposed the evolving institutionalization of Congress as undemocratic and as insulating Congress from its constituents and their concerns.[41]

Populists, for instance, condemned efforts to restrict public access to congressional proceedings, particularly those in the Senate, which they already regarded as "a most aristocratic body" out of "sympathy for the people." These steps toward what the *Washington Post* called "exclusiveness" included the Senate's decisions to expand the use of executive sessions closed to the public, to restrict the presentation of popular petitions, to close its chamber to visitors when not in session, and to reserve the Capitol elevator for its own members and to station guards to prevent "the common herd" from using the conveyance. Populists decried all these attempts at "shutting the people out of this place" and introduced resolutions to open virtually all Senate sessions to the public and to establish a special committee to receive petitions and hear testimony from citizen groups. "The building does not belong to the Senate nor to Senators," declared Peffer. "It belongs to the people." Senate leaders of both old parties, however, rejected Populist arguments. Committed to establishing institutional boundaries, they insisted that such restrictive rules were necessary for "the decent and orderly conduct of this body."[42]

Populists also rejected congressional norms of professionalism or personal conduct by attacking their opponents in language reminiscent of the virulent antebellum congressional debates. Early in his first term, Simpson denounced one member as "an iniquitous railroad attorney"—prompting outraged Republican protests that his language violated House rules. Simpson responded, "I am a new member, and not familiar with the rules, but that is the plain common sense of it as we talk in our country." Simpson gained experience with the rules but continued to speak plainly, once so contemptuously attacking Speaker Reed's supporters for abjectly doing his bidding in order to "get a good place on a committee" that furious Republicans insisted that he be banished from the House floor. Populists were also less than respectful when condemning their major-party colleagues as willing agents of corporations, banks, and the money power generally. California Populist Curtis Castle flayed Republicans for standing "here in these legislative halls with inflated lungs and idiotic sneers waiting for Wall Street to pull the string that they may fill the resonant air with the sound and fury of idiots."[43]

More disturbing to other members of Congress than the direct language the Populists employed was their willingness to raise such forbidden topics as the moral and financial misconduct of their colleagues—subjects that cast into doubt the desired decorum. As one Populist newspaper noted of Peffer's constancy in raising such troublesome issues, these discussions "his fellow senators consider entirely incompatible with 'senatorial courtesy.'" Here, too, the Populists' charges caused them at times to be ostracized and their remarks expunged from the *Congressional Record*. Populists, many of them prohibitionists, were particularly outraged by the ready availability and use of alcohol on Capitol Hill. When Watson complained of the existence of a barroom adjoining the Democratic caucus room and described drunken congressmen reeling about the House floor trying to debate crucial issues, there was an uproar in Congress. Democrats denounced Watson for impugning the integrity and moral character of congressmen, modestly maintaining, "The history of parliamentary proceedings from the beginning of civilization down to this day does not show an instance of as vile an attack upon a representative body." When Watson attempted to defend his comments he was hissed down, and Speaker Crisp ordered the sergeant-at-arms forcibly to seat him.[44]

The most sensational Populist arraignment of immoral conduct by congressmen appeared in Howard's book, *If Christ Came to Congress,* which described the Capitol as "the NATIONAL ASSIGNATION HOUSE as well as the NATIONAL SALOON." Basing his volume on the recent activities and highly publicized trial of the prominent Kentucky Democratic congressman William C. P. Breckinridge, which had scandalized all of polite America, Howard described congressmen as "moral lepers" engaged in gambling, sexual misconduct, and "bacchanalian revelry" in committee rooms and cloakrooms.[45]

Populists also questioned the financial integrity of their colleagues in the major parties. In the Senate, they raised the issue of members' compensation for travel expenses to congressional sessions. Both the law and the Senate's own rules restricted such compensation to actual expenses incurred on one round-trip a year. But in 1893, senators proposed to appropriate themselves an additional $175,000, an amount Populists considered extravagant as well as illegal. They found it particularly unconscionable to claim such money in the face of the common suffering during the dreadful depression of the time. Although one Democratic senator agreed with the Populists that members of Congress were not entitled to the appropriation, Republicans defended the measure, declaring that any senators who had "compunctions of conscience" could refuse the money, and ridiculed "the constant appeal that we hear to the dear people." The Populist proposal to reject the appropriation was overwhelmingly voted down.[46]

In the House, too, Populists were unable to persuade other congressmen to adhere to legal restrictions on their income. Watson urged the enforcement of the law providing that members not be paid when absent from Congress for any reason other than illness. He denounced representatives for collecting a salary from the public while attending to their law practice, banking interests, or politics at home. There was popular support for such a proposal even from such conservative newspapers as the *Chicago Tribune,* but the House overwhelmingly rejected it and sidestepped a roll-call vote that would have disclosed those favoring the illegal grab.[47]

Of larger importance to Populists, however, were the effects on public policy of their colleagues' financial interests and activities. Press reports of congressional corruption were common at the time, and even
Bradstreet's concluded that they "seriously affect[ed] the dignity and
integrity of Congress." It was hardly surprising that Populists, seeing
their reform measures systematically blocked, often concluded that
obstructionist Republican and Democratic members of Congress
might be corrupt. Peffer once introduced a resolution of inquiry into
widespread reports that senators were speculating in sugar-company
stocks on the basis of their inside knowledge of the Finance Committee's preparation of a new tariff. Declaring that the charges of misconduct were so frequent and specific as to raise serious questions about
the integrity of the Senate, Peffer expected that there would be no opposition to his motion to investigate. But Democratic leader Gorman
persuaded the Senate to "refuse to countenance inquiry into the acts of
its members," and the proposal was tabled.[48]

The audacity with which congressmen of the major parties rejected public scrutiny of their financial dealings also appalled the
Populists during the 1893 special session. In discussing a resolution
to form a select committee to determine whether any senator owned
stock in a national bank and would thus personally profit from the
repeal of the Sherman Silver Purchase Act, one Democrat maintained that members of Congress had a moral and legal right to
hold stocks that might be affected by their legislative decisions. This
bold candor in support of what seemed a manifest impropriety
shocked Senator Allen. With Congress already popularly accused of
"complicity with corporations and of suffering corporate power to
influence legislation," he contended, "the people have a right to
know what is going on here." Allen promptly introduced a measure
prohibiting any member of Congress from owning, buying, or sell-
ing any stock the value of which might be affected by a vote in Congress and prohibiting any member from owning or joining a national bank, board of trade, or stock exchange. Allen's bill died in
committee, but he reintroduced it in future sessions to the applause
of Populists in and out of Congress.[49]

Obviously convinced that some members of Congress were susceptible to special interests, Populists were alarmed by the presence and
activities of lobbyists, whom they found "haunting every crypt and

corner of the Capitol." The spectacle of lobbyists swarming about Congress was not merely an apparition of a fevered Populist imagination. Even the staid *Washington Post* reported that "representatives of manufacturing interests are as thick around the door of the Ways and Means Committee room as flies on a molasses barrel. . . . Nearly every interest affected by the [Wilson Tariff] bill, and that means every interest in the country, has a representative here now." Although most congressmen and business interests had come to accept and defend the role of lobbyists in providing needed information and expertise, the Populists regarded them as promoting the interests of the privileged at the expense of the general population. This conviction that lobbyists necessarily used corrupt means to achieve sordid ends was brought into sharp relief by the Populists' view of efforts to promote their own legislative goals.[50]

The Farmers' Alliance, for example, in 1890 established a legislative bureau that testified before the Senate Agricultural Committee on behalf of the subtreasury bill and coordinated a campaign to flood Congress with petitions favoring the measure. But "we are not lobbyists," Leonidas L. Polk, Alliance president, insisted. "We shall say our say and leave it with Congress." Lobbyists, he believed, were those who sought to induce Congress to provide preferential treatment for the classes—"the great magnates of the country, and Wall Street brokers, and the plutocratic power"—rather than equity for the masses. Populist representative Jeremiah Botkin of Kansas also described the problem as "the hired lobbyists of the corporations and trusts . . . working the National Congress . . . for every possible concession and advantage." Other Populists condemned as a "crime" the reception major-party congressmen gave to the "railroad lobbyists, tax lobbyists, bank lobbyists, and all the other lobbyists who infest this city and these Capitol grounds." To curb the evil, Populists introduced detailed bills prohibiting professional lobbying. A Populist newspaper praised these bills but held no illusions about their passage. "It is hardly probable," declared the *Farmers Tribune,* in suggesting how far Populist congressmen diverged from those of the major parties, "that a majority of our law-makers will aid legislation against the lobbyists."[51]

These attitudes and comments of Populist members of Congress suggest how little they were socialized into the legislative community. Populists were not ignorant of Congress and its formal and informal procedures; several were close students of the institution who thought deeply and wrote perceptively about its rules and traditions. Nor should scholars adopt the perspective of their contemporary opponents who tried to explain the Populists' behavior, reception, and lack of substantive achievement in Congress by deriding "Sockless Jerry" Simpson, "Whiskers Anarchy" Peffer, "Red Rooster" Kem, "Milkman" Otis, and their colleagues as unruly hicks. That criticism originated from fear and hatred of Populist principles more than from the appearance and behavior of men who were, by and large, shrewd and extraordinarily able. As a *Washington Post* reporter concluded, after studying the Populist congressional delegation, "No set of men ever merited less the ridicule that has been heaped upon them."[52]

In many personal characteristics often considered important in understanding legislative behavior, Populists scarcely differed from their contemporaries in the major parties. Using data from the *Biographical Directory of the American Congress,* Table 10.1 compares the educational, occupational, and political backgrounds of Populist House members with those of all representatives who entered Congress in the 1890s. In terms of educational experience, often indicative of social status as well, similar proportions of both groups enjoyed private secondary schooling, and 53.8 percent of the Populists had attended college compared to 62.3 percent of the larger number. As might be expected, Populists were much more likely to have occupational backgrounds in agriculture than were representatives of the major parties, but even so there were as many lawyers as farmers among the Populists, and Populists were more likely than other members of Congress to be editors and other professionals.

Populist farmers were scarcely hayseeds. John Otis, for example, was a dairy farmer who had graduated from Williams College and Harvard Law School; another Populist farmer, William A. Harris, was a civil engineer (a graduate of two colleges) and a cattle breeder of national reputation who later moved to Chicago as president of the American Shorthorn Breeders' Association. In terms of previous officeholding experience, Populist representatives were only slightly less active than the average rate for members entering Congress in the same years — and slightly more likely to have served in a judicial

Table 10.1. Characteristics of Representatives Entering Congress
1891–1900

	Populist Representatives	All Representatives
Education		
Percent with private secondary education	33.3	30.6
Percent attended college	53.8	62.3
Occupation		
Percent engaged in agriculture	38.5	8.2
Percent lawyers	38.5	60.3
Percent other professionals	15.4	9.7
Percent engaged in business	7.7	20.2
Prior Public Officeholding		
Percent holding local office	46.2	49.5
Percent holding state office	46.2	53.2
Percent holding judicial office	12.8	10.9
Percent holding no previous office	35.9	20.4
Percent with Military Experience	30.8	30.5
Noncommissioned service	20.5	13.7
Commissioned service	10.3	16.8
Median Age at Entry	49	45
Percent over 39 years old	76.9	70.9

Sources: Biographical Directory of the American Congress, 1774–1961 (Washington, D.C., 1961); Allan G. Bogue et al., "Members of the House of Representatives and the Processes of Modernization, 1789–1960," *Journal of American History,* 63 (1976): 275–302.

capacity. Few Republicans or Democrats could match the distinguished career of Populist Samuel Maxwell, who had been a justice on the Nebraska Supreme Court for a quarter of a century before entering Congress. The Populists' comparative inexperience reflected less an indifference to or an ignorance of public affairs than their own often lengthy commitment to minority political parties. Simpson claimed no previous officeholding experience, but he had twice unsuccessfully sought election to the Kansas legislature, as a Greenbacker in 1886 and as a Union Labor party candidate in 1888.

If Simpson had no prior legislative experience, many of his Populist colleagues did. Fully one-third of Populist House members in the 1890s had previously served in state legislatures. William Neville of Nebraska had been a legislator in two different states before being elected to Congress and would later serve in the legislature of a third. Experience in the less structured state legislatures, where debate and other forms of participation were often much more open, constituted little preparation for Congress, however, and another Populist felt compelled to use a canned speech to explain to his constituents how restrictive congressional procedures differed from practices in their state legislatures. Although the Populists as a group were not career politicians, they were hardly inexperienced, were as capable as members of the major parties, and were obviously not the simple hayseeds portrayed by their enemies.[53]

The Populists' outsider status in Congress derived, then, not from their alleged personal characteristics but from two other factors. First, with membership in one of the established major parties providing most of the cues for behavior, new members from third parties were little socialized into congressional norms of conduct. To be sure, some Populists could draw upon other resources in their attempts to fathom congressional practices. Shared military experiences sometimes provided a measure of assistance in assimilation. Senior Republican representative Bishop Perkins introduced Populist senator Peffer, his fellow veteran of the Eighty-third Illinois Infantry, to other members of Congress and showed him around the Capitol. A few western Populists were also aided by established major-party members from their own state delegations. Nebraska Populist Kem benefited from his close association with the rising young Democrat, William Jennings Bryan, an advocate and beneficiary of electoral fusion with Nebraska Populists. They traveled to Washington together, once rented rooms in the same hotel in the capital, and discussed legislative business. At times Bryan even yielded some of his own speaking time to Kem, who was unable to obtain separate recognition. But even this limited avenue of socialization was rare and apparently altogether closed to southern Populists, who were often bitterly despised by their region's congressional Democrats. In short, in a highly partisan legislative session, partisan bonds provided most of the cues for behavior as well as the opportunities for effective action, and by rejecting the major parties the Populists jumped the congressional traces.[54]

More important, Populists consciously rejected congressional rules of behavior, formal and informal, for they recognized what political scientists have since laboriously documented. Such norms and procedures are rarely politically impartial in their effects. In varying degrees, they promote institutional conservatism, deference to established leadership, moderation, and accommodation. Such "imperative rules and precedents," wrote Wilson in 1885, were difficult enough for new members, who were thereby "suppressed" and stripped of any "weight or title to consideration," but they were disastrous for members of a radical third party. Populists could not acquiesce in politics as usual under existing leadership and practices, for that was what their party had been created to oppose. They often concluded that congressional rules and norms functioned less to regularize the legislative process than to restrain political activity. As a Greenback congressman, Weaver had alluded to such political functions when he objected to Speaker Randall's decision to give floor priority to committee, rather than individual, members. "That rule," declared Weaver, aware that Greenbackers were excluded from important committees, "seems to have been made at the first appearance of the third party in the House." Populist congressmen similarly and repeatedly denied what Simpson termed "the pretext" that congressional rules and customs were designed simply to expedite legislative business. Too often, their purpose, and certainly their effect, was political.[55]

Populists therefore believed that their representational obligations to their constituents required them to reject congressional practices and customs. Each of the Populist senators, for example, announced his intention of ignoring the custom that new members should not speak. A Democratic senator defended the practice as a way for newcomers to gain experience and understanding before speaking out and predicted that the Populists would be squelched by peer pressure. The Populists, however, refused to be silenced by a tradition they condemned as "unreasonable." Peffer told a reporter that it was his "duty to tell the senate what he is here for and . . . he proposes to be heard, custom or not custom." Allen delivered his first speech within days of entering the Senate and spoke for fifteen hours, at the time the longest continuous speech ever delivered in Congress.[56]

Populists also attacked the growing importance of committees, one of the most obvious features of the institutionalization of Congress. Simpson expressed his astonishment that members surrendered their representative and legislative powers to committees "who can put a gag on us," and he urged his colleagues to reclaim their autonomy to "pass laws that will relieve the people." Greenbackers had similarly complained that congressional committees had "a veto power greater than that of the President," and now Populists proposed specific new rules to restrict that committee power over the legislative process. In the Senate, Allen sought to prevent committees from burying legislation by moving to require all bills to be reported within thirty days. (Allen's proposal was referred to the Rules Committee "and there," the *Washington Post* correctly predicted, "it will stay.") Populists also complained that there were too many committees, Howard describing at least one-third of them as useless. They were particularly outraged by proposals to increase the office space and staff for committees, denouncing the "reciprocity system" by which Democrats and Republicans agreed to support such measures for their own partisan and patronage purposes. North Carolina Populist congressman Alonzo Shuford not only opposed staff expansion but attempted to repeal the law authorizing the employment of clerks.[57]

Bell condemned another feature of committee government—the growing reliance on seniority in committee appointments and rank—that obviously excluded new members, and third-party congressmen in particular, from an effective legislative role. Analyzing the membership of committees, Bell found that three staunchly Republican states that regularly reelected their congressmen had in 1895 "more power in directing the business of the House of the American Congress than all of the other states in the Union. This is an offspring of the rule that they must be advanced according to their seniority on the committees." Twenty-six states had no committee chairmanships at all, but Iowa, Massachusetts, and Maine had seventeen. Their power made the House not a deliberative and representative body but "the body of bosses, the body of tyranny." Unable to gain important committee assignments and lacking seniority because he represented a new political party, the Populist could "do little for his constituents." His Colorado supporters had not sent him to Congress to have their interests represented by conservative Republicans from Maine or Massachusetts, Bell noted. "The things desired by these leaders are the very things that we do not want," the very things in fact that had provoked the formation of a new party in the first place, but their power under congressional rules prevented any effective recourse.[58]

Populists continually challenged such rules and procedures as impeding an effective democratic response to constituent needs through legislation. Led by Otis of Kansas, they even proposed a separate set of rules from those supported by Republicans and Democrats. Greenbackers had earlier demanded "absolute democratic rules for the government of Congress, placing all representatives upon an equal footing," and the Populists now tried to operationalize that concern. The Populists' rules clearly indicated a determination to democratize the internal workings of Congress, paralleling their effort to democratize the external electoral arena. Each member, Otis pointed out, represented the same number of constituents, was entrusted with the same constitutional authority, and was entitled to "equal privileges on this floor." But "the rules, customs, and precedents" of the House violated the principles of democratic government by conferring special privileges upon a few while robbing "the many of their just rights."[59]

To break this "parliamentary monopoly," Otis proposed three rules changes. The first sought to restrict the power of the Rules Committee by instituting a new Committee on Order of Business, to be composed of one representative elected from and by each state's congressional delegation. "It would not include merely a few individuals or represent simply the conceptions of a few men coming from only a few portions of this country." The second mandated that standing committees be elected by the full House membership rather than be appointed by the Speaker, a practice that violated "a principle of popular government" by making the House "ruled by one man." The final Populist recommendation was to have committee members elect their own chair rather than have him appointed by the Speaker. The Populists' proposed rules changes were solidly rejected without even a roll-call vote, confirming their worst fears about the responsiveness of the government and their own opportunities for effective representation.[60]

Unable to speak on the floor, to gain assignments to important or relevant committees, to introduce measures, have them reported, or bring them to a vote, the Populists grew increasingly frustrated with congressional rules and procedures. One Populist after another resorted to pathetic canned speeches to describe to their constituents how "the iron rules" of Congress operated to their fatal disadvantage. Kem was the most poignant in trying to explain to the Nebraska Populists why their representatives had not reformed the government and economy: "We not only do not have the power to inaugurate any measure, but we do not even have the power to be heard on measures others inaugurate." Populists should know, he continued, that their representatives in Congress "have no rights on this floor . . . which the powers that be are bound to respect."[61]

In 1897, Populist participation in Congress began to change significantly. They introduced progressively fewer bills and resolutions having to do with their party's reform principles. They virtually stopped the practice of introducing motions of inquiry. Their rates of nonvoting rose remarkably. In some measure, this transformation reflected the changing personnel in the party's congressional delegation and external political circumstances. Some of the party's early leaders were replaced by less radical politicians, whose policy interests were often more narrowly focused and whose election depended upon their maintaining a fusion coalition with the still more conservative Democrats in their state's electorate. The most dramatic example of this process was the 1897 displacement in the Senate of the indefatigable Peffer by Harris, a relatively conservative Populist who held little interest in Populism's original reform objectives and whose career as a state legislator was marked by absenteeism and what one reporter termed "old fogyism." The crushing disappointment of the presidential election of 1896, in which Populists subordinated their party and its principles by fusing on the Democratic candidacy of Bryan, may also have helped to produce the lethargy of congressional Populists by 1897. But the tensions of such external political factors had always been present. Peffer, in fact, traced the "poisonous political drug" of fusion to the first congressional election of Simpson in 1890 and complained that as early as 1893 conservatives were replacing radicals in the Populist congressional delegation and the "silver glare" was obscuring other Populist legislative objectives.[62]

Most of the reason for the change in the Populists' congressional behavior by 1897 must be attributed to factors within Congress itself, to the institutional obstacles that produced growing frustration, estrangement, and disappointment among Populists attempting to achieve reform in Congress. This explanation is particularly evident in two significant exceptions to the Populists' waning reform agenda and decreasing reform activity, both of which indicated their dissatisfaction with Congress itself. First, Populists introduced a series of bills to establish more effective popular control of members of Congress through regulating campaign practices and finances and by providing for the popular election of senators. In supporting the latter, Simpson seized the occasion to attack as well "the system of rules" that made the House even less susceptible to popular influence and participation than the indirectly elected Senate.[63]

The second exception reflected a still deeper mistrust of the partisan, hostile Congress and a conviction that representative government was perhaps too rigid or corrupt to be reformed. To help its readers evaluate the state of Congress in 1897, for instance, one Iowa Populist newspaper carried two articles. The first wondered "whether it will ever again be possible for the people to govern themselves through representatives." The second forcefully concluded that "representative government is a failure." The solution the Populist editor proposed for the problems of congressional obstruction, corruption, and misrepresentation was direct popular rule through the initiative and referendum. Members of the Populist delegation reached a similar conclusion from their own inability to influence Congress. One of Peffer's final measures was a proposed constitutional amendment mandating a popular referendum on all important legislation. Other Populists in 1897 and thereafter repeatedly supported the initiative and referendum in order to "destroy the pernicious influence and effects of the trust and monopoly lobby that infests legislative halls and too often influences the people's representatives to vote for measures against the public welfare."[64]

The dramatic increase of nonvoting among Populists was also tied to developments within Congress itself. Some of it reflected growing absenteeism among Populists who saw that vigilant attendance had no practical effect; some stemmed from decisions to abstain as a deliberate way to emphasize that congressional activity was not particularly relevant to what they saw as the needs of the nation or the wishes of their constituents. Such deliberate nonvoting was initially apparent with respect to the Dingley Tariff constructed by the Republican majority in the first session of the Fifty-fifth Congress. With few exceptions, Populists in each house abstained from voting on the measure, and the Populist joint caucus then issued an address to explain their behavior. Declaring that no tariff legislation could solve the problems created by "a contraction of money and the rule of monopolies," the Populist address condemned both major parties for manipulating the tariff question in order to divert popular attention from their failure to deal with such larger issues in Congress. By refusing to vote, the Populists were refusing to participate in this callous effort to avoid taking the necessary action on "the real and vital issues between the people and concentrated wealth." The abstaining that began with the tariff, however, soon expanded. After the beginning of the second session of the Fifty-fifth Congress, many Populist representatives simply stopped voting on roll calls, and the practice of refusing to vote continued in the Fifty-sixth Congress, beginning in 1899.[65]

Simpson left Congress in 1899, defeated and downcast. Asked about his future plans, he alluded to Howard's book on Congress and announced his intention to write one of his own, to be entitled *If the Devil Came to Congress.* Simpson never wrote it, but he would have argued that the devil was simply going home. Populists had campaigned on the contention that the government was unresponsive to farmers and workers, dominated by the two-party system that placed party position before public interest, and susceptible to corporate influence. They should not have been surprised by what they found once elected to Congress.[66]

NOTES

CHAPTER 1. THE POLITICAL LIMITS OF WESTERN POPULISM

1. For valuable recent historiographical surveys, see William F. Holmes, "Populism: In Search of Context," *Agricultural History* 64 (Fall 1990): 26–58, and Worth Robert Miller, "A Centennial Historiography of American Populism," *Kansas History* 16 (Spring 1993): 54–69.

2. Robert C. McMath, Jr., *American Populism: A Social History, 1877–1898* (New York, 1993), 154. See also Donna A. Barnes, *Farmers in Rebellion: The Rise and Fall of the Southern Farmers Alliance and People's Party in Texas* (Austin, 1984); Scott G. McNall, *The Road to Rebellion: Class Formation and Kansas Populism, 1865–1900* (Chicago, 1988); and Jeffrey Ostler, *Prairie Populism: The Fate of Agrarian Radicalism in Kansas, Nebraska, and Iowa, 1880–1892* (Lawrence, Kans., 1993).

3. *Ottawa Journal and Triumph,* October 25, 1894, and *Hutchinson Alliance Gazette,* September 19, 1890. For elaboration of this argument, see Peter H. Argersinger, "Pentecostal Politics in Kansas: Religion, the Farmers' Alliance, and the Gospel of Populism," *Kansas Quarterly* 1 (Fall 1969): 24–35 (also Chapter 3 of this book). For the Southwest, see Robert C. McMath, Jr., "Populist Base Communities: The Evangelical Roots of Farm Protest in Texas," *Locus* 1 (Fall 1988): 53–63.

4. Ostler, *Prairie Populism,* 134, 150, 156–157, 160–162, 172; Stanley B. Parsons, *The Populist Context: Rural versus Urban Power on a Great Plains Frontier* (Westport, Conn., 1973), 77–78; Kenneth E. Hendrickson, Jr., "Some Political Aspects of the Populist Movement in South Dakota," *North Dakota History* 34 (Winter 1967): 80; W. P. Harrington, "The Populist Party in Kansas," *Collections of the Kansas State Historical Society* 16 (1925): 407. See also Robert C. McMath, Jr., "Preface to Populism: The

Origin and Economic Development of the 'Southern' Farmers' Alliance in Kansas," *Kansas Historical Quarterly* 42 (Spring 1976): 62–63.

5. *Independence Star & Kansan,* December 9, 1898; Katherine B. Clinton, "What Did You Say, Mrs. Lease?" *Kansas Quarterly* 1 (Fall 1969): 54n; *Fort Scott Daily Monitor,* August 14, 1890. Gene Clanton has argued that Lease was "psychologically incapable of cooperating with Democrats" because of her "deep resentment against the Democratic party" (see Clanton, "Intolerant Populist? The Disaffection of Mary Elizabeth Lease," *Kansas Historical Quarterly* 34 [Summer 1968]: 195–196).

6. *Topeka Daily Capital,* January 24, 1891, and *Atchison Daily Champion,* July 25, 1890.

7. *Fort Scott Daily Monitor,* April 2, 1890.

8. Quoted in O. Gene Clanton, *Kansas Populism: Ideas and Men* (Lawrence, Kans., 1969), 268.

9. Goff (Kans.) *Advance,* June 23, 1892. For the importance of political sectionalism and its effects on western Populism, see particularly Peter H. Argersinger, *Populism and Politics: William Alfred Peffer and the People's Party* (Lexington, Ky., 1974), esp. 83–91, 97–98, 103, 112–120, 144–147, 147, 150, 303–304.

10. Walter T. K. Nugent, *The Tolerant Populists: Kansas Populism and Nativism* (Chicago, 1963), 93, and Raymond C. Miller, "The Populist Party in Kansas" (Ph.D. diss., University of Chicago, 1928), 222–225.

11. John M. Peterson, "The People's Party of Kansas: Campaigning in 1898," *Kansas History* 13 (Winter 1990–1991): 250–251, 256–257, and Nugent, *Tolerant Populists,* 220.

12. Terrence J. Lindell, "Populists in Power: The Problems of the Andrew E. Lee Administration in South Dakota," *South Dakota History* 22 (Winter 1992): 354, and Hendrickson, "Some Political Aspects," 86. For another Populist governor's comparable attempts to satisfy ethnic claims to patronage, see Nugent, *Tolerant Populists,* 146–147.

Patronage and related issues were also important in Populist efforts to include and retain black voters in their party coalition; see William H. Chafe, "The Negro and Populism: A Kansas Case Study," *Journal of Southern History* 34 (August 1968): 402–419. In most of the West, however, blacks were not particularly numerous and as a consequence, in McMath's careful words, "Racism posed no *tactical* dilemma for western Populism as it did in the South" (see McMath, *American Populism,* 122). For a recent account of the political problem in the South, see Gregg Cantrell and D. Scott Barton, "Texas Populists and the Failure of Biracial Politics," *Journal of Southern History* 55 (November 1989): 659–692.

13. James E. Wright, *The Politics of Populism: Dissent in Colorado* (New Haven, Conn., 1974), 251–252. See also Barnes, *Farmers in Rebellion,* 114–116, 119–120, 131–133; Lawrence Goodwyn, *Democratic Promise: The Populist Moment in America* (New York, 1976), 213–243; Ostler, *Prairie Populism,* 68–69, 147–149, 152–153, 170–171.

14. For the 1890 campaign in Kansas, see Peter H. Argersinger, "Road to a Republican Waterloo: The Farmers' Alliance and the Election of 1890 in Kansas," *Kansas Historical Quarterly* 33 (Winter 1967): 443-469 (also Chapter 2 of this book). For the larger political context of that campaign, see also Argersinger, *Populism and Politics,* 12-32.

15. Hendrickson, "Some Political Aspects," 81-83. For parallel developments in Nebraska, see Ostler, *Prairie Populism,* 114-115, 118-120, 123.

16. See Peter H. Argersinger, "The Value of the Vote: Political Representation in the Gilded Age," *Journal of American History* 76 (June 1989): 59-90.

17. Peter H. Argersinger, " 'A Place on the Ballot': Fusion Politics and Antifusion Laws," *American Historical Review* 85 (April 1980): 287-306.

18. *Minneapolis Tribune,* October 13, 19, 24, 1892; William Joseph Gaboury, *Dissension in the Rockies: A History of Idaho Populism* (New York, 1988), 54.

19. *Clear Lake Advocate* quoted in *Brookings County Press* (Brookings, S. Dak.), November 2, 1893, and *Montana Silverite* (Missoula), March 8, 1895.

20. John F. Willits to B. F. Oldfield, July 20, 1897, Kansas Biographical Scrapbook, 175: 27, Kansas State Historical Society, Topeka.

21. Worth Robert Miller, *Oklahoma Populism: A History of the People's Party in the Oklahoma Territory* (Norman, 1987), 137-138; Garnett (Kans.) *Journal,* May 20, June 10, 1892; Pleasanton (Kans.) *Herald,* July 8, 22, 1892.

22. *Washington Post,* May 27, 1892; J. A. Edgerton to Marion Butler, January 11, 1897, Marion Butler Papers, Southern Historical Collection, University of North Carolina, Chapel Hill; Gaboury, *Dissension in the Rockies,* 123-124. For the 1892 Kansas Populist campaign, see Argersinger, *Populism and Politics,* 120-150 (also Chapter 5 of this book, "Party Officials and Practical Politics").

23. *Topeka Daily Capital,* June 26, 1892; *Kansas City Star,* June 2, 1901; *Leavenworth Herald,* August 18, 1894; *American Non-Conformist* (Indianapolis), November 15, 1894.

24. John D. Hicks, *The Populist Revolt: A History of the Farmers' Alliance and the People's Party* (Minneapolis, 1931), 236.

25. Clanton, *Kansas Populism,* 296n; Gaboury, *Dissension in the Rockies,* 122; *Atchison Daily Champion,* December 14, 1890; *Des Moines Farmers Tribune,* March 3, 1897.

26. Winterset (Iowa) *Review,* June 2, 1897. For a full account of this incident, see Peter H. Argersinger, "To Disfranchise the People: The Iowa Ballot Law and Election of 1897," *Mid-America* 63 (January 1981): 18-45, (also Chapter 6 of this book).

27. Wright, *Politics of Populism,* 211, and Gaboury, *Dissension in the Rockies,* 295.

28. *Topeka Daily Capital,* July 20, 1892, and Argersinger, *Populism and Politics,* 72–77, 184–191.

29. Herman Taubeneck to W. S. Morgan, January 29, 1895, Davis Waite Papers, Colorado State Archives, Denver, and Argersinger, "Party Officials and Practical Politics."

30. *Montana Silverite,* March 8, 1895; *People's Party Paper* (Atlanta), May 8, 1896; Davis Waite manuscript speech, 1897, Waite Papers.

31. See Robert Durden, *The Climax of Populism: The Election of 1896* (Lexington, Ky., 1965), esp. 72, 76–78, 99.

32. *People's Party Paper,* November 13, 1896; *Topeka Advocate,* July 14, 1897; Hicks, *Populist Revolt,* 380–402.

33. An exception in the West was Montana, which enacted an Australian ballot law in 1889 through the heroic efforts of Will Kennedy, who later became the first gubernatorial candidate of the Montana People's party. See William L. Lang, "The People's Tribune: Will Kennedy of *The* (Boulder) *Age,*" paper presented at the Pacific Northwest History Conference, Victoria, B.C., April 24, 1981. Gene Clanton kindly provided a copy of this paper.

34. Gaboury, *Dissension in the Rockies,* 122.

35. *Laws Passed at the Eighth Session of the General Assembly of the State of Colorado . . . 1891* (Colorado Springs, 1891), 143, and *Laws, Joint Resolutions, and Memorials, passed by the Legislative Assembly of Nebraska . . . 1891* (Lincoln, 1891), chap. 24, 239.

36. Erik Falk Petersen, "The Struggle for the Australian Ballot in California," *California Historical Quarterly* 51 (Fall 1972): 227–243, and *Laws of Nevada, 1893,* chap. 106.

37. *St. Paul Pioneer-Press,* April 25, 1891; A. L. Maxwell to Henry D. Lloyd, September 13, October 18, November 1, 3, 23, 1894, Henry D. Lloyd Papers, State Historical Society of Wisconsin, Madison. The petitions in support of Populist nomination papers in Illinois' Tenth Congressional District were over twenty feet long (Cuba [Illinois] *People's Press,* October 21, 1892).

38. Peterson, "Struggle for the Australian Ballot," 238–239; Donald E. Walters, "The Feud between California Populist T. V. Cator and Democrats James Maguire and James Barry," *Pacific Historical Review* 27 (August 1958), 290–291; Harold F. Taggart, "Thomas Vincent Cator: Populist Leader of California," *California Historical Society Quarterly* 27 (1948): 311–318; *Eaton v. Brown,* 31 Pacific Reporter 250.

Populists rarely benefited from the judiciary, an important (and often partisan) feature of their political context, but historians have devoted little attention to the subject. For some indications of its role, however, see Peter H. Argersinger, "Regulating Democracy: Election Laws and Dakota Politics, 1889–1902," *Midwest Review* 5 (Spring 1983): 1–19 (also Chapter 7 of this book). See also R. Douglas Hurt, "The Populist Judiciary: Election Reform and Contested Offices," *Kansas History* 4 (Summer 1981): 130–

141; Michael J. Brodhead, *Persevering Populist: The Life of Frank Doster* (Reno, Nev., 1969); Michael J. Brodhead, "Populism and the Law: Some Notes on Stephen H. Allen," *Kansas Quarterly* 1 (Fall 1969): 76-84.

39. *State v. Stein* (Nebr.), 53 N.W. Rep. 999. For studies of the effects of these ballot provisions in specific state political contexts, see Argersinger, "To Disfranchise the People," and "Regulating Democracy"; for the wider political context of such laws, see "'A Place on the Ballot.'"

The New party of the 1990s is attempting to revive the legal possibility of double-listing as a means of promoting progressive political action (Joel Rogers to Peter H. Argersinger, November 1, 1991; the New party, "Building the New Majority," April 13, 1992.

40. *State v. Anderson* (Wis.), 76 N.W. Rep. 482, and *Des Moines Farmers Tribune*, March 17, June 23, 1897. See especially the experience of Iowa Populists in Argersinger, "To Disfranchise the People."

41. *Kalamazoo Weekly Telegraph*, March 20, 1895; *Des Moines Farmers Tribune*, January 5, 1898.

42. For similar observations on "the test in the West," see Gene Clanton, *Populism: The Humane Preference in America* (Boston, 1991), 105, 117-118; McMath, *American Populism*, 182-183, 193-195; Hicks, *Populist Revolt*, 274-300.

43. Lindell, "Populists in Power," 361-364.

44. Argersinger, *Populism and Politics*, 161-162; Nugent, *Tolerant Populists*, 149; Clanton, *Kansas Populism*, 138-139.

45. Argersinger, *Populism and Politics*, 164-165; Nugent, *Tolerant Populists*, 156-157; *Girard Western Herald*, August 14, 1895.

46. Robert W. Cherny, *Populism, Progressivism, and the Transformation of Nebraska Politics, 1885-1915* (Lincoln, Nebr., 1981), 48, and Parsons, *Populist Context*, 83-85. For the alienation of Henry Loucks and other important South Dakota Alliance officials by the patronage policies of Populist governor Lee, see Lindell, "Populists in Power," 355. Loucks, too, soon returned to the GOP. For a nearly verbatim denunciation of the influence of "jackleg lawyers and town loafers" and Democratic interests in the Kansas People's party by a former state president of the Farmers' Alliance, who similarly withdrew from the party, see Argersinger, *Populism and Politics*, 143. For growing conflict between rural and more urban interests among California Populists, see John T. McGreevy, "Farmers, Nationalists, and the Origins of California Populism," *Pacific Historical Review* 58 (November 1989): 471-495.

47. Lindell, "Populists in Power," 355, and D. Jerome Tweton, "Considering Why Populism Succeeded in South Dakota and Failed in North Dakota," *South Dakota History* 22 (Winter 1992): 335-336.

48. Argersinger, *Populism and Politics*, 282, 297-298. For the effect of the prohibition issue on the Iowa People's party, see Herman C. Nixon, "The Populist Movement in Iowa," *Iowa Journal of History and Politics* 24 (January 1926): 26-28, 57-58, 71-72.

49. See Peter H. Argersinger, "The Most Picturesque Drama: The Kansas Senatorial Election of 1891," *Kansas Historical Quarterly* 38 (Spring 1972): 43-64 (also Chapter 4 in this book).

50. William A. Peffer, *Populism, Its Rise and Fall* (Lawrence, Kans., 1992), 75; Hendrickson, "Some Political Aspects," 84-85, 89; Daryl Webb, " 'Just Principles Never Die': Brown County Populists, 1890-1900," *South Dakota History* 22 (Winter 1992): 388. For an account of the maneuvering over the election of Palmer in Illinois and Kyle in South Dakota that stresses its destructive consequences for third party action, see Roy V. Scott, *The Agrarian Movement in Illinois, 1880–1896* (Urbana, Ill., 1962), 103-115.

51. *Topeka Advocate*, December 16, 1896, and Argersinger, *Populism and Politics*, 276-281.

52. Gaboury, *Dissension in the Rockies*, 228-257, 412-415, and *Des Moines Farmers Tribune*, February 3, 1897. For another instance of significant Democratic influence in the choice of Populist senators, see Paola E. Coletta, "William Jennings Bryan and the Nebraska Senatorial Election of 1893," *Nebraska History* 31 (September 1950): 183-203.

53. *Appleton's Annual Cyclopedia, 1898* (New York, 1898), 143. At least Teller supported silver; in North Carolina, the political dynamics generated by election laws and coalition politics caused Populists to help elect Gold Republican Jeter Pritchard to the U.S. Senate. See James L. Hunt, "The Making of a Populist: Marion Butler, 1863-1895," Part 3, *North Carolina Historical Review* 72 (July 1985): 317-343.

54. Argersinger, *Populism and Politics*, 156-157; Peffer, *Populism, Its Rise and Fall*, 82; William E. Parrish, "The Great Kansas Legislative Imbroglio of 1893," *Journal of the West* 7 (October 1968): 471-490.

55. Carroll H. Wooddy, "Populism in Washington: A Study of the Legislature of 1897," *Washington Historical Quarterly* 21 (April 1930): 109-112, and Claudius O. Johnson, "George Turner, Part I: The Background of a Statesman," *Pacific Northwest Quarterly* 34 (July 1943): 256-263.

56. *Daily Oregon Statesman*, January 27, 1893; David B. Griffiths, "Populism in Wyoming," *Annals of Wyoming* 40 (April 1968): 66; Robert W. Larson, *Populism in the Mountain West* (Albuquerque, N.Mex., 1986), 96.

57. *Daily Oregon Statesman*, January 3, 20, 1893; Taggart, "Thomas Vincent Cator," 317; Harold F. Taggart, "The Senatorial Election of 1893 in California," *California Historical Society Quarterly* 19 (1940): 66; R. Hal Williams, *The Democratic Party and California Politics, 1880–1896* (Stanford, Calif., 1973), 164-166.

58. *Montana Silverite*, March 22, 1895, and Gaboury, *Dissension in the Rockies*, 140.

59. McNall, *Road to Rebellion*, 251-252; Wright, *Politics of Populism*, 162-163; *Daily Oregon Statesman*, February 22, 1893.

60. Gaboury, *Dissension in the Rockies,* 75; Miller, *Oklahoma Populism,* 48; Cherny, *Populism and Nebraska Politics,* 37.

61. Gaboury, *Dissension in the Rockies,* 133.

62. See Peter H. Argersinger, "Ideology and Behavior: Legislative Politics and Western Populism," *Agricultural History* 58 (January 1984): 43-58 (also Chapter 8 in this book).

63. *Daily Oregon Statesman,* January 25, 1895; *Washington Standard* (Olympia), January 25, 1895, quoted in Stephen Henry Peters, "The Populists and the Washington Legislature, 1893-1900" (Master's thesis, University of Washington, 1967), 39-40; *Topeka State Journal* quoted in *Topeka Advocate,* March 6, 1895.

64. Carl H. Chrislock, "The Alliance Party and the Minnesota Legislature of 1891," *Minnesota History* 35 (September 1957): 297-312, esp. 304, 312, and Martin Ridge, *Ignatius Donnelly: The Portrait of a Politician* (Chicago, 1962), 279-283. Chrislock also notes that, under the circumstances, a successful legislative program would have required "the arts of compromise rather than the techniques of political evangelism" (p. 305). But it seems likely that the evangelical campaign of 1890 by which Populists drew partisans from the major parties may have itself created conditions and expectations that prevented Populist legislators from compromising with (equally obdurate) Democrats and Republicans. That is, the necessary methods of mobilizing a third party may have impeded effective governance after the election.

For the Colorado legislature, where even at their strongest in the 1893 session Populists were a minority in each house, see Wright, *Politics of Populism,* esp. 162, 165, 177. For the efforts and frustrations of the Populist minority in Idaho legislatures, see Gaboury, *Dissension in the Rockies,* 72-84, 131-141.

65. *Topeka Daily Capital,* June 16, 1892.

66. *Topeka State Journal,* February 27, 1893. For the legislative war, its partisan and extraconstitutional resolution, and the political use Republicans gained from it by their domination of its reporting, see especially Parrish, "Legislative Imbroglio of 1893."

67. *Seattle Post-Intelligencer,* November 5, 1896, March 14, 1897; *Portland Sunday Oregonian,* November 15, 1896; Wooddy, "Populism in Washington," 113-117; Gaboury, *Dissension in the Rockies,* 257-263 (quotations on 262, 263). For Oklahoma's 1897 fusionist legislature, in which "Democrats sidetracked or gutted much of the Populist-sponsored reform program" and which left Populists dismayed and discredited, see Miller, *Oklahoma Populism,* 162-167 (quotation from 164).

The 1897 South Dakota legislature was an exception to this general tendency of fusionist bodies, for it enacted significant reform laws, particularly dealing with elections and railroads, although the latter were frustrated by permanent court injunctions and most of the former were repealed by subsequent Republican legislatures.

68. *Norton Liberator,* March 12, April 2, 1897; *Topeka Advocate,* March 24, 1897; Peter H. Argersinger, "Populists in Power: Public Policy and Legislative Behavior," *Journal of Interdisciplinary History* 18 (Summer 1987): 81-105 (also Chapter 9 of this book).

69. Peter H. Argersinger, "No Rights on this Floor: Third Parties and the Institutionalization of Congress," *Journal of Interdisciplinary History* 22 (Spring 1992): 655-690 (also Chapter 10 of this book).

70. Quoted in Miller, *Oklahoma Populism,* 180.

CHAPTER 2. ROAD TO A REPUBLICAN WATERLOO

1. *Kansas City* (Mo.) *Star,* November 5, 1890.

2. W. P. Harrington, "The Populist Party in Kansas," *Collections of the Kansas State Historical Society* 16 (1925): 411.

3. D. O. McCray, "The Administrations of Lyman U. Humphrey," *Transactions of the Kansas State Historical Society* 9 (1905-1906): 424.

4. Raymond C. Miller, "The Background of Populism in Kansas," *Mississippi Valley Historical Review* 11 (March 1925): 470.

5. Ibid., 475.

6. Harrington, "Populist Party in Kansas," 408 (Harrington mentions that this same condition prevailed for cotton and livestock, in fact, for "all farm products").

7. Miller, "Background of Populism," 478, and Harrington, "Populist Party in Kansas," 408.

8. Walter T. K. Nugent, *The Tolerant Populists* (Chicago, 1963), 53.

9. Quoted in Harrington, "Populist Party in Kansas," 405-406; this is based on an account of W. F. Rightmire, which, later in the narrative, is open to some question.

10. Nugent, *Tolerant Populists,* 58.

11. Fred E. Haynes, *Third Party Movements since the Civil War* (Iowa City, 1916), 240; this belief of Haynes can be accepted in only a limited sense.

12. Quoted in W. F. Rightmire, "The Alliance Movement in Kansas," *Transactions of the Kansas State Historical Society* 9 (1906): 2. Rightmire, in fact, states that, despite this resolution, the Kansas Alliance was organized "for a distinct political purpose." This idea might have been in the minds of a few organizers but certainly was not widely held at first among Alliance members. Moreover, *The Constitution for Subordinate Alliances,* sec. 4, p. 6, stated that "there shall not be any political or religious test for membership." Rightmire's assertion is also doubtful in light of future happenings among certain suballiances and individual members.

13. Quoted in Harrington, "Populist Party in Kansas," 407.

14. Ibid., 409.

15. See S. M. Scott, *The Champion Organizer of the Northwest* (McPherson, Kans., 1890), for full examples of this interesting and often

humorous process of organizing a suballiance. Discounting Scott's personal vanity, it is still significant to note the tempo of his action through the period covered. The 100,000-member March estimate of the *Farmers' Advocate* is perhaps a little inflated, for the report of the national secretary of the Farmers' Alliance indicated a total membership in July 1890 of 1,269,500 in twenty-two states, and Kansas was credited with 100,000 members. The *Daily Monitor* (Fort Scott, Kans.) of March 14, 1890, quoted Benjamin H. Clover as saying there were 70,000 Alliance men in Kansas in 1,800 suballiances.

16. *Fort Scott Daily Monitor,* March 14, 1890.

17. Ibid., March 19, 1890. The platform decided upon demanded the abolition of national banks, free silver coinage, free sugar, lumber, and coal, and government ownership of the railroads and telegraph and objected to all taxation that promoted the interests of one class at the expense of another.

18. *Lawrence Daily Journal,* March 11, 1890. On March 16, 1890, the *Lawrence Daily Journal* quoted the *Atchison Globe* with approval: "They now say that Peffer will succeed Ingalls in the senate. Who in the hello is Peffer?"

19. *Fort Scott Daily Monitor,* March 21, 1890.

20. *Lawrence Daily Journal,* March 19, 1890.

21. Ibid., March 4, 1890.

22. Ibid., March 7, 1890.

23. Ibid., March 19, 1890.

24. *Atchison Weekly Times,* March 22, 1890.

25. *Lawrence Daily Journal,* March 26, 1890.

26. Kirk Mechem, ed., *Annals of Kansas, 1886–1925, 2 vols.* (Topeka, Kans., 1954), 1: 103. The farmers had already petitioned Kansas railroads (January 16, 1890) for an emergency rate in order to move the corn crop; the existing rate had been determined when corn sold for 2.5 times more than it had in January (ibid., 92). The Interstate Commerce Commission in hearings in Topeka on March 20, 1890, claimed to have found "no great dissatisfaction" with freight rates to eastern markets (ibid., 94).

27. Quoted in Harrington, "Populist Party in Kansas," 410.

28. *Lawrence Daily Journal,* March 28, 1890.

29. Quoted by Rightmire, "Alliance Movement," 5 (John D. Hicks, *The Populist Revolt* [Minneapolis, 1931], 155, has the last two phrases reversed).

30. *Lawrence Daily Journal,* March 27, 1890.

31. *Fort Scott Daily Monitor,* March 26, 1890.

32. Ibid., March 29, 1890. This convention in all likelihood was merely a county convention.

33. Ibid., March 30, 1890.

34. *Lawrence Daily Journal,* March 19, 1890.

35. Ibid., March 27, 1890.

36. Quoted in *Fort Scott Daily Monitor,* March 26, 1890.

37. Ibid., March 29, 1890.

38. Ibid., April 2, 1890.

39. "A majority vote of all members present entitled to vote shall decide any question before any Alliance unless otherwise specified" (By-law no. 3, *Constitution for Subordinate Alliances,* 10).

40. *Fort Scott Daily Monitor,* April 12, 1890.

41. Ibid., April 13, 1890.

42. Ibid., April 19, 1890.

43. Ibid., June 6, 1890.

44. Ibid., May 27, 1890.

45. Ibid., May 28, 1890.

46. Ibid., June 6, 1890.

47. Ibid., April 25, 1890.

48. Ibid., June 6, 1890.

49. Ibid, June 6-10, 1890, and *Annals of Kansas,* 1: 105.

50. William A. Peffer, *The Farmer's Side, His Troubles and Their Remedy* (New York, 1891), 156, 157.

51. The following discussion is based primarily on Nugent, *Tolerant Populists,* 65-70.

52. Hicks, *Populist Revolt,* 156.

53. At least it was according to Peffer (*Farmer's Side,* 157). The *Fort Scott Daily Monitor,* June 13, 1890, mentioned the presence of delegates from the "Industrial Union" and the "Industrial Grange."

54. Hicks, *Populist Revolt,* 427, 428.

55. *Fort Scott Daily Monitor,* June 13, 1890.

56. Harrington, "Populist Party in Kansas," 411.

57. *Fort Scott Daily Monitor,* July 18, 1890.

58. Ibid., July 23, 1890, and Harrington, "Populist Party in Kansas," 412.

59. *Fort Scott Daily Monitor,* July 13, 1890.

60. To become a member of the Farmers' Alliance, one must have been a citizen of Kansas for at least the preceding six months and "a farmer, a farm laborer, mechanic, country school teacher, country physician, or country minister of the gospel" (*Constitution for Subordinate Alliances,* 6).

61. *Topeka Daily Capital,* August 13, 1890.

62. *Fort Scott Daily Monitor,* August 14, 1890.

63. Nugent, *Tolerant Populists,* 73.

64. The *Topeka Daily Capital,* August 12, 1890, phrased it thus. The paper claimed there was a "deal" in the making between the Democrats and Populists whereby both were to nominate Robinson for governor; for this concession the Democrats supposedly were to refrain from making a nomination in the Third Congressional District and to support B. H. Clover. The Democrats, as it developed, did not nominate anyone to oppose

Clover. As the Populist convention opened, the *Daily Capital*, August 13, 1890, claimed that the Democrats "manipulated the People's party" and that the nomination of Robinson was "cut and dried."

65. Harrington, "Populist Party in Kansas," 413. Harrington also quoted a resolution passed by the Populists in June as a hindrance to fusion: "We will not support for office any member of our organizations who will accept a nomination from either of the old parties, but will consider such member a traitor to our cause" (p. 411).

66. *Fort Scott Daily Monitor*, August 14, 1890.

67. Nugent, *Tolerant Populists*, 73. German voters, by and large, were politically "wet."

68. *Fort Scott Daily Monitor*, August 14, 1890.

69. Quoted in ibid., August 20, 1890.

70. Ibid., July 6, 1890.

71. Ibid., September 4, 1890.

72. Ibid., August 7, 1890.

73. Ibid., September 10, 1890.

74. Harrington, "Populist Party in Kansas," 413.

75. The Republicans demanded in their platform the free coinage of silver, the free ballot, an increased volume of currency, the prohibition of alien ownership of large blocs of land, antigrain-speculation legislation, and the election of railroad commissioners by the vote of the people (*Fort Scott Daily Monitor*, September 5, 6, 1890). The Democratic platform deplored paternalism in government and ecclesiasticism in public affairs and favored the free coinage of silver and the regulation of the railroads (ibid., September 10, 1890).

76. Nugent, *Tolerant Populists*, 74. The point, however obvious, was essential: "When the party platforms and candidates were all before the people in the late summer of 1890, clear choices on the basis of merit were not easy. All promised about the same thing and the tickets exhibited a mixture of men, ranging from ability to incompetence in proportions too nearly equal for any one safely to make charges against the other" (James C. Malin, *A Concern about Humanity: Notes on Reform* [Lawrence, Kans., 1964], 38).

77. *Fort Scott Daily Monitor*, July 16, 1890.

78. Quoted in ibid., July 6, 1890.

79. Ibid., September 30, 1890.

80. Ibid., October 2, 1890.

81. *Kansas City Star*, November 3, 1890.

82. Quoted in Peffer, *Farmer's Side*, 159.

83. Quoted in Harrington, "Populist Party in Kansas," 413. The Olathe Citizens' Alliance resolved "to not support any newspaper that will not publish the report of our proceedings when requested to do [so] by any of its officers and that does not show a tolerant spirit towards us in our demands for all classes of depressed laborers" (*Topeka Daily Capital*, June 12, 1890).

84. Quoted in Malin, *Concern about Humanity,* 194.

85. Harrington, "Populist Party in Kansas," 414, and *Topeka Daily Capital,* October 1, 1890.

86. *Fort Scott Daily Monitor,* October 16, 1890.

87. Quoted in ibid., October 4, 1890.

88. Supplement in ibid., October 21, 23, 1890.

89. Ibid., November 1, 1890.

90. Ibid., October 11, 1890, and *Annals of Kansas,* 1: 109.

91. *Fort Scott Daily Monitor,* October 16, 1890.

92. *Kansas City Star,* October 23, 1890.

93. Ibid., October 30, 1890. Willits did, in fact, receive 106,972 votes—startling evidence of the extent of the Alliance-Populist organization.

94. Quoted in the *Kansas City Star,* November 1, 1890.

95. *Kansas City Star,* October 30, 1890.

96. *Topeka Daily Capital,* November 6, 1890.

97. Peffer, *Farmer's Side,* 157. The Republicans had a 42,000-vote majority over all opposition combined in 1888 and were some 60,000 votes short of achieving a majority in 1890. Peffer determined from the election results that the People's party consisted of 45,000 normally Republican voters, 35,000 Democrats, 33,000 Union-Labor men, and 2,000 Prohibitionists.

98. Nugent, *Tolerant Populists,* 92.

CHAPTER 3. PENTECOSTAL POLITICS IN KANSAS

1. See Allan G. Bogue, "Social Theory and the Pioneer," *Agricultural History* 34 (January 1960): 30-33.

2. L. B. Wright, *Culture on the Moving Frontier* (New York, 1955), 168-197.

3. James C. Malin, "The Kinsley Boom in the Late Eighties," *Kansas Historical Quarterly* 4 (May 1935): 174.

4. General Assembly of the Presbyterian Church, *25th Annual Report of the Board of Home Missions* (New York, 1895), 31.

5. *Church at Home and Abroad* (September 1892), 244.

6. *Baptist Home Mission Monthly* (February 1891), 35; *Journal of Proceedings, 33rd Annual Convention of the Protestant Episcopal Church of Kansas* (1892), 74, 89; Presbyterian Church, *Report, Board of Home Missions* (1894), 26-27; J. M. Moeder, *Early Catholicity in Kansas* (Wichita, Kans., 1937), 66; *Report of the Woman's Board of Missions of the Interior* (Chicago, 1896), 61.

7. *Journal of the Episcopal Church, Kansas* (1895), 71; Presbyterian Church, *Report, Board of Publication and Sabbath School Work* (1894), 12-13; Congregational Churches in Kansas, *Memorial Volume* (Kansas City, Kans., 1904), 19, 45-48.

8. *Report, Woman's Board of Missions* (1895), 57, and (1893), 59; Presbyterian Church, *Report, Board of Home Missions* (1897), 24, and (1891), 271; R. J. McGinnis to the American Home Missionary Society (AHMS), April 10, 1893, and F. B. Wilson to AHMS, April 24, 1893, American Home Missionary Society Papers, Hammond Library, Chicago Theological Seminary; *Baptist Home Mission Monthly* (May 1896), 174, and (August 1896), 285.

9. *Baptist Home Mission Monthly* (April 1889), 94, and *Journal of the Episcopal Church, Kansas* (1898), 96, and (1892), 33–34.

10. To use the phrasing of C. B. Goodykoontz, *Home Missions on the American Frontier* (Caldwell, Idaho, 1939), 419.

11. W. R. Bair to AHMS, June 10, 1893, and W. E. Brehm to AHMS, April 24, 1893; AHMS Papers.

12. *Church at Home and Abroad* (June 1894), 500, and S. D. Storrs to AHMS, May 8, 1893, AHMS Papers.

13. *Baptist Home Mission Monthly* (February 1891), 35, and *The Spirit of Missions* (May 1894), 179.

14. *Report, Woman's Board of Missions* (1897), 67; *Journal of the Episcopal Church, Kansas* (1892), 33–34, 89; (1894), 73; (1898), 96; Congregational Churches, *Memorial Volume*, 47; Presbyterian Church, *Report, Board of Home Missions* (1894), 27; L. P. Broad to AHMS, April 7, 1893, AHMS Papers; *Church at Home and Abroad* (September 1892), 244. Religious organizations of course did provide some direct relief to the destitute settlers, yet their efforts were distinctly secondary to uncoordinated secular labors, and all were inadequate. Some organizations apparently aided their frontier ministry while refraining from any effort to assist their frontier congregations. Not until 1895 did the Congregational superintendent actively seek assistance for the "multitudes . . . too poor," for example (*Home Missionary* [July 1895], 151).

15. See especially *Report, Woman's Board of Missions* (1896), 61–62.

16. Presbyterian Church, *Report, Board of Home Missions* (1897), 32. For a fuller discussion, see Peter H. Argersinger, "The Divines and the Destitute: Organized Religion in Drought and Depression on the Agricultural Frontier," *Nebraska History* 51 (Fall 1970): 303–318.

17. W. A. Peffer, "The Farmers' Alliance," *Cosmopolitan*, April 1891, 698.

18. Walter T. K. Nugent, *The Tolerant Populists* (Chicago, 1963), 58.

19. *Frank Leslie's Illustrated Newspaper*, February 28, 1891; Annie Diggs, *The Story of Jerry Simpson* (Wichita, Kans., 1908), 64; S. M. Scott, *The Champion Organizer of the Northwest* (McPherson, Kans., 1890), 8, 94–95; *Minutes of the Gove County Farmers' Alliance, 1890*, Kansas State Historical Society, Topeka; Farmers' Alliance, *Constitution for Subordinate Alliances* (Topeka, 1890); *Topeka Advocate*, December 2, 1891, March 30, 1892, December 11, 1895.

20. W. A. Peffer, *The Farmer's Side* (New York, 1891), 149-154; *Kansas Farmer* (Topeka), June 7, 1882; *Voice of True Reform* (Topeka, 1891), 50.

21. *Topeka Mail,* June 6, 1890.

22. *Proceedings of the Alliance Women's Association of Barton County, Kansas* (Great Bend, Kans., 1891), 2-3. Women did have equal membership in the regular Alliance organization and took an active role therein, it being (with the churches) one of a very few social outlets for frontier women.

23. See N. J. Demerath, *Social Class in American Protestantism* (Chicago, 1965), xxii-xxiii, and C. P. Loomis and J. A. Beegle, *Rural Sociology* (New York, 1957), 203-210, 227.

24. *Atchison Daily Champion,* June 17, 1890.

25. *Topeka Mail,* June 6, July 4, 1890; *Atchison Daily Champion,* June 17, 1890; *Voice of True Reform,* 49.

26. Scott, *Champion Organizer,* 12-13, passim.

27. Ibid., 150. See Joachim Wach, *Sociology of Religions* (Chicago, 1944), 37-42, and F. R. Kramer, *Voices in the Valley: Mythmaking and Folk Belief in the Shaping of the Middle West* (Madison, Wis., 1964), 177-181.

J. Rogers Hollingsworth has made some incisive observations as to the role of Populism in reaffirming traditional values for alienated Kansas farmers; see his "Commentary; Populism: The Problem of Rhetoric and Reality," *Agricultural History* 39 (April 1965): 82-85. In leaving their old party, however, they lost a major vehicle for transmitting those traditional values. The primary burden, then, had to be borne by religion. But as organized religion proved unresponsive to the needs of the people, Populism incorporated the roles of both, serving as a political party and as the primary source for the reaffirmation of traditional rural religious values.

28. F. H. Olmstead, *The Alliance Nightingale* (Douglass, Kans., 1890); Scott, *Champion Organizer,* 180-187; Diggs, *Simpson,* 83-84; *Kansas Farmer,* June 7, 1882; *Proceedings of the Fourth Annual Meeting of the Farmers' Alliance of Kansas* (Topeka, 1892), 23.

For insights into the relationship between economic distress and religious experience, see A. T. Boisen, *Religion in Crisis and Custom: A Sociological and Psychological Study* (New York, 1955); J. B. Holt, "Holiness Religion: Cultural Shock and Social Reorganization," *American Sociological Review* 5 (1940): 740-747; R. R. Dynes, "Church-Sect Typology and Socio-Economic Status," *American Sociological Review* 20 (1955): 555-560; H. R. Niebuhr, *The Social Sources of Denominationalism* (New York, 1929).

29. Peffer, "Farmers' Alliance," 696.

30. Diggs, *Simpson,* 81-82; Scott, *Champion Organizer,* 119; *Proceedings, Alliance Women's Association,* 2-3.

31. *Lawrence Journal-Tribune,* June 17, 1890.

32. *Voice of True Reform,* 1-4; Mary Lease, *The Problem of Civiliza-*

tion Solved (Chicago, 1895), passim; *Hutchinson Alliance Gazette,* February 6, 1891.

33. L. D. Lewelling, "Problems before the Western Farmer," *North American Review* (January 1895): 18-20; *Voice of True Reform,* 2, 15-20; Percy Daniels, *Problems of Taxation* (Topeka, 1894), 21, and *A Lesson of Today and a Question of Tomorrow* (Girard, Kans., 1892), 10.

34. *Congressional Record,* 53d Cong., 1st sess., 583.

35. James H. Lathrop, *The Phonograph of Human Liberty* (Topeka, Kans., November 1902).

36. Percy Daniels, *Cutting the Gordian Knot* (Pittsburg, Kans. 1896), 62-63, 85; *Appendix to Congressional Record,* 53d Cong., 3d sess., 71, 256; ibid., 2d sess., 54, 506.

37. *New York Independent,* February 16, 1893.

38. *Voice of True Reform,* 15-20; *Topeka Advocate,* August 29, 1894; Farmers' Alliance Clippings, vol. 1, Kansas State Historical Society; *Dawn* (Boston), September 1891, 6, and July 1890, 167; *Nationalist* (Boston), September 1890, 114.

39. *Topeka State Journal,* July 13, 1894; *Topeka Advocate,* September 5, 1894, March 30, April 6, 1892; *Hutchinson Alliance Gazette,* September 19, 1890; *Topeka Daily Capital,* May 17, 1892; *Pleasanton Herald,* April 8, 1892.

40. *The Great Quadrangular Debate* (Salina, 1894), and Lease, *Problem of Civilization,* 5-6, 322. One Populist wanted even more emphasis upon the general aims of the movement and less upon the specific objectives. He argued for a Populist platform "that talks less about silver and more about salvation; less about finance and more about religion" and sought a platform with "principles in it by which we can live more acceptably in the sight of the Lord" (*Topeka Daily Capital,* June 13, 1894). In 1890 the Populist platform recognized God as sovereign, as the source of all "just powers of government," and declared that "all human enactments ought to conform" to God's will. Both old parties avoided the subject.

41. *New York Independent,* September 10, 1896, February 16, 1893; *Topeka Mail,* October 31, 1890; *Atchison Daily Champion,* November 16, 1890.

42. *Journal of the Episcopal Church, Kansas* (1893), 25-26.

43. *Minutes of the General Association of Congregational Ministers and Churches of Kansas* (Wichita, Kans., 1893), 31-34; *Report, Woman's Board of Missions* (1894), 66; L. P. Broad to AHMS, April 1, 7, 1893, AHMS Papers; *Church at Home and Abroad* (July 1893), 42; *Topeka Advocate,* March 30, 1892.

44. Broad to AHMS, March 29, April 1, 7, 1893, AHMS Papers; *Chicago Advance,* May 11, 1893; *Home Missionary* (July 1893), 159, and (July 1894), 158-159.

45. Wichita *Kansas Commoner,* April 28, 1892.

46. *Topeka Advocate,* February 17, March 2, 1892; W. A. Peffer, *The Way Out* (Topeka, 1890), 38; Kansas, *Senate Journal* (Topeka, 1895), 25;

clipping dated July 22, 1897, in John Davis Scrapbooks, vol. F, Kansas State Historical Society.

47. Percy Daniels, *The Midnight Message of Paul Revere* (Pittsburg, Kans., 1896), 2, and *A Crisis for the Husbandman* (Girard, Kans., 1889), 58–59.

48. *Atchison Daily Champion*, August 16, 1890; *Hutchinson Alliance Gazette*, September 26, 1890, January 23, 1891; E. S. Waterbury, *The Legislative Conspiracy in Kansas* (Topeka, 1893), 59; Lease, *Problem of Civilization*, 14; G. Campbell, *Island Home* (Parsons, Kans., 1894), 22.

49. Waterbury, *Legislative Conspiracy*, 1–7, 58–59; *Hutchinson Alliance Gazette*, November 21, 1890; Frank Doster letter in Farmers' Alliance Clippings, vol. 1, and unidentified clipping, Populist Party Clippings, vol. 1, Kansas State Historical Society.

50. See, e.g., *Report of the Woman's Home Missionary Society of the Methodist Episcopal Church* (1895–1896), 143; *Home Missionary* (April 1896), 612, and (July 1896), 144, 161; *Home Mission Monthly* (November 1900), 317.

51. W. A. White, *Stratagems and Spoils* (New York, 1901), 207, 214.

52. R. M. Manley, "The Farmers' Alliance," *New Kansas Magazine*, 1: 2 (Atchison, March 1892): 5–6.

CHAPTER 4. THE MOST PICTURESQUE DRAMA

1. Albert R. Kitzhaber, "Götterdammerung in Topeka," *Kansas Historical Quarterly* 18 (August 1950): 243–278, and James C. Malin, "Some Reconsideration of the Defeat of Senator Pomeroy of Kansas, 1873," *Mid-America* 47 (January 1966): 47–57.

2. J. J. Ingalls to Mr. Croffut, October 25, 1890, John J. Ingalls Papers, Kansas State Historical Society, Topeka, and Peter H. Argersinger, "Road to a Republican Waterloo: The Farmers' Alliance and the Election of 1890 in Kansas," *Kansas Historical Quarterly* 33 (Winter 1967): 443–469 (also Chapter 2 of this book).

3. *Harper's Weekly*, February 7, 1891, 103.

4. Ingalls to Croffut, October 25, 1890, Ingalls Papers, and *Topeka Daily Capital*, November 14, 1890.

5. *Topeka Daily Capital*, November 9, 13, December 9, 1890, and *Kansas Farmer* (Topeka), December 10, 1890.

6. George Glick to Grover Cleveland, November 27, 1890, George Innes to Cleveland, December 2, 1890, and W. A. Peffer to George Innes, November 29, 1890, Grover Cleveland Papers, Library of Congress; *Topeka Daily Capital*, November 13, 1890.

7. *Atchison Daily Champion*, August 27, September 9, and (quoting the *Emporia Republican*) October 8, 1890, and *Topeka Daily Capital*, August 14, November 13, 1890.

8. *Topeka Daily Capital*, November 8, 9, 1890.

9. *Kansas Farmer,* November 19, December 3, 10, 1890, and *Fort Scott Daily Monitor,* November 25, 1890.

10. Innes to Cleveland, November 29, 1890, Cleveland Papers; *Atchison Daily Champion,* December 14, 1890; *Topeka Daily Capital,* November 18, 1890.

11. Bird City (Kans.) *News,* November 20, 1890, and *Topeka Daily Capital,* December 11, November 13, 19, and (quoting the *St. Louis Globe-Democrat)* 11, 1890.

12. *Topeka Daily Capital,* December 12, 1890.

13. Ibid., January 8, 1891.

14. *Kansas Farmer,* January 7, 21, 1890.

15. Ibid., December 3, 10, 17, 24, 31, 1890; *Atchison Daily Champion,* December 23, 1890, January 2, 1891; *Topeka Daily Capital,* December 26, 1890; *Topeka Mail,* December 12, 1890.

16. See S. N. R. in *Kansas Farmer,* December 3, 1890, and *Alliance Echo* (Sharon Springs, Kans.) quoted in ibid., December 17, 1890.

17. *Kansas Farmer,* December 3, 1890; *Topeka Daily Capital,* December 5, 12, 1890; *Atchison Daily Champion,* December 7, 1890.

18. *Topeka Mail,* November 14, 1890; *Topeka Daily Capital,* December 5, 1890, January 4, 6, 9, 1891; *Atchison Daily Champion,* January 7, 1891.

19. *Atchison Daily Champion,* January 11, 1891; *American Non-Conformist* (Winfield, Kans.), January 15, 1891; *Topeka Daily Capital,* January 4, 1891.

20. *American Non-Conformist,* January 15, 1891; *Kansas Farmer,* January 7, 1891; *Girard Western Herald,* January 17, 1891; *Topeka Populist,* December 3, 1892; *Topeka Daily Capital,* January 6, 9, 1891; *Kansas City* (Mo.) *Star,* January 28, 1891.

21. Nelson Acres to Cleveland, November 13, 1890, Cleveland Papers.

22. Edward Carroll to George Innes, November 29, 1890, Cleveland Papers.

23. *Topeka Daily Capital,* January 6, 9, 14, 15, 24, 1891.

24. Ibid., January 7, 15, 1891, and *Kansas Farmer,* December 31, 1890, January 7, 1891.

25. *Kansas City Star,* January 29, 1891, and *Chicago Tribune,* January 28, 1891.

26. *Kansas City* (Mo.) *Journal* in *Topeka Daily Capital,* January 2, 1891; *Kansas Farmer,* January 7, 1891; *Atchison Daily Champion,* January 10, 1891; M. W. Wilkins to Ignatius Donnelly, January 22, 1891, Ignatius Donnelly Papers, Minnesota Historical Society, St. Paul.

27. *Kansas Farmer,* January 7, 1891, and *Kansas City Star,* January 28, 1891.

28. *Kansas City Star,* January 29, 1891.

29. *Atchison Daily Champion,* December 23, 1890, January 2, 1891, and *Topeka Daily Capital,* January 13, 20, 1891.

30. *Topeka Daily Capital,* January 3, 11, 13, 14, 15, 1891, and *Atchison Daily Champion,* January 17, 1891.

31. Ingalls to J. W. Steele, January 3, 1891, Ingalls Papers, and Ingalls to J. A. Halderman, January 7, 1891, J. A. Halderman Papers, Kansas State Historical Society.

32. *Topeka Daily Capital*, January 13, 1891; *Topeka Mail*, January 23, 1891; Burton J. Williams, "John James Ingalls: A Personal Portrait of a Public Figure" (Ph.D. diss., University of Kansas, 1965), 275-276; James C. Malin, *Confounded Rot about Napoleon* (Lawrence, Kans., 1961), 106-109.

33. *Kansas Farmer*, January 21, 1891; *Atchison Daily Champion*, January 16, 17, 1891; *Topeka Daily Capital*, January 15, 1891; Williams, "Ingalls," 276.

34. *Topeka Daily Capital*, January 3, 1891.

35. Williams, "Ingalls," 277; Malin, *Confounded Rot*, 79; *Topeka Daily Capital*, January 3, 1891.

36. *Kansas City Star*, January 13, 21, 29, 1891; *Chicago Tribune*, January 26, 1891; *Topeka Advocate*, October 2, 1895; *Topeka Daily Capital*, January 13, 1891; *Atchison Daily Champion*, January 17, 30, 1891; Acres to Cleveland, November 13, 1890, and Glick to Cleveland, November 27, 1890, Cleveland Papers.

37. *Atchison Daily Champion*, January 18-20, 1891, and *Topeka Daily Capital*, January 21, 1891.

38. *Topeka Daily Capital*, January 28, March 21, 1891; Williams, "Ingalls"; *Topeka Advocate*, October 2, 1895.

39. *Topeka Advocate*, October 28, November 4, 1891, and Malin, *Confounded Rot*, 109.

40. *Topeka Daily Capital*, January 15, 18, 1891.

41. *Kansas City Star*, January 17, 20, 1891; *Fort Scott Daily Monitor*, January 21, 1891; *Topeka Daily Capital*, January 22, 1891; G. J. McQuaid to George C. Angle, January 21, 1891, George C. Angle Papers, Spencer Research Library, University of Kansas, Lawrence.

42. Wilkins to Donnelly, January 22, 1891, Donnelly Papers.

43. *Topeka Daily Capital*, January 23, 1891.

44. Ibid., January 24, 25, 1891; *Kansas City Star*, January 23, 24, 1891; Malin, *Confounded Rot*, 109.

45. See John Livingston to Benjamin Harrison, February 6, 1891, and enclosed clippings, Benjamin Harrison Papers, Library of Congress.

46. Kansas, *Senate Journal, 1891* (Topeka, 1891), 126, 140-142, 151-156, 160-168, 176, and Kansas, *House Journal, 1891* (Topeka, 1891), 138-140.

47. Kansas, *Senate Journal*, 162, and *Topeka Daily Capital*, January 24, 25, 1891.

48. Kansas, *Senate Journal*, 162; *Chicago Tribune*, January 26, 1891; *Topeka Daily Capital*, January 15, 20, 25, 1891; *Kansas City Star*, January 26, 1891.

49. *Atchison Daily Champion*, January 27, 1891; *Kansas City Star*, January 21, 26, 1891; Peffer to Innes, November 29, 1890, and Carroll to Innes, November 29, 1890, Cleveland Papers.

50. *Atchison Daily Champion,* January 27, 1891.

51. *Topeka Daily Capital,* January 22, 1891.

52. Ibid., January 24, 1891, and *Kansas City Star,* January 23, 1891.

53. *Topeka Daily Capital,* January 25, 1891, and *Kansas City Star,* January 24, 1891.

54. *Kansas City Star,* January 26, 1891.

55. *Topeka Daily Capital,* January 27, 1891.

56. *New Orleans Daily Picayune,* January 27, 1891.

57. *Kansas City Star,* January 27, 1891; *Topeka Daily Capital,* January 27, 1891; *Kansas Farmer,* February 11, 1891.

58. *Topeka Daily Capital,* January 27, 1891, and *Kansas City Star,* January 27, 1891.

59. *Kansas City Star,* January 27, 1891.

60. A. J. R. Smith in *Topeka Populist,* December 3, 1892; cf. Frank McGrath in *Topeka Daily Capital,* March 21, 1891.

61. *Kansas City Star,* January 27, 28, 1891.

62. Ibid., January 27, 28, 1891, and *Fort Scott Daily Monitor,* January 28, 1891. For an account of this election as a struggle between radical and moderate groups, see David Rothman, *Politics and Power: The United States Senate, 1869–1901* (Cambridge, Mass., 1966), 173. Rothman's interpretation, facts, and political labels all reveal at best a superficial examination of this election.

63. *Topeka Daily Capital,* January 28, 1891.

64. Ibid.

65. *Kansas City Star,* January 28, 1891.

66. *Topeka Daily Capital,* January 28, 29, 31, 1891; *Topeka Mail,* January 30, 1891; Kansas, *House Journal,* 191-197.

67. *Chicago Tribune,* January 29, 1891. For another description of the scene as "a great campmeeting in the height of religious excitement," see the *Kansas City Journal,* January 28, 1901.

68. *Topeka State Journal,* January 29, 1891; *Topeka Daily Capital,* January 29, 1891; Stuart Noblin, *Leonidas LaFayette Polk, Agrarian Crusader* (Chapel Hill, N.C., 1949), 228; *National Economist* (Washington, D.C.), February 7, 1891; *Atchison Daily Champion,* January 29, 1891; *Journal of the Knights of Labor* (Philadelphia), February 5, 19, 1891.

69. *Kansas City Star,* January 29, 1891.

70. *Harper's Weekly,* February 7, 1891, 103.

71. Quoted in *Topeka Daily Capital,* February 3, 1891.

72. *Topeka Daily Capital,* January 30, 1891.

CHAPTER 5. PARTY OFFICIALS AND PRACTICAL POLITICS

1. *Pleasanton Herald,* February 12, March 11, 1892, and *Wichita Weekly Beacon,* April 15, 1892.

2. Van Prather to Charles Robinson, January 10, 1892, Charles Robin-

son Papers, Kansas State Historical Society, Topeka; *Topeka Daily Capital,* March 22, April 3, 5, 20, 26, 1892; Paola (Kans.) *Times,* May 5, 1892; *Miami Republican* (Paola), May 6, 1892.

3. George Glick to Grover Cleveland, March 2, 10, 17, April 21, May 9, 1892, Grover Cleveland Papers, Library of Congress; *Wichita Weekly Beacon,* February 26, April 1, 1892; *Girard Western Herald,* April 16, 1892.

4. *Topeka Daily Capital,* April 5, 1892, and Kansas City (Mo.) *Journal,* April 13, 1892.

5. *Topeka Daily Capital,* April 5, 1892.

6. *Kansas Agitator* (Garnett), May 26, 1892.

7. *Washington Post,* May 27, 1892, and *Topeka Advocate,* May 26, 1892.

8. *Pleasanton Herald,* January 15, March 18, April 1, 1892; *Paola Times,* May 5, 1892; *Wichita Weekly Beacon,* June 10, 17, 1892; *Topeka Daily Capital,* May 12, 1892; *Leavenworth Evening Standard,* July 11, 13, 16, 1892.

9. *Kansas City Journal,* April 12, 1892, and *Kincaid Kronicle,* June 17, 1892.

10. *Kansas Democrat* (Topeka), July 18, 1892; *Leavenworth Evening Standard,* June 1, 1892; Kansas City (Mo.) *Star,* June 1, 2, 1892; *Topeka Daily Capital,* May 18, June 2, 1892; J. M. Jones to Charles Robinson, April 28, 1892, Robinson Papers; *National Economist* (Washington, D.C.), June 25, 1892.

11. *Kansas City Journal,* April 12, 1892; *Topeka Daily Capital,* May 24, 1892; Prather to Robinson, January 10, 1892, and Jones to Robinson, April 28, 1892, Robinson Papers; Glick to Cleveland, March 17, 1892, Cleveland Papers.

12. *Wichita Weekly Beacon,* April 15, 1892; *Topeka Daily Capital,* May 24, 1892; *Washington Post,* May 24, 1892; *Kansas City Star,* June 2, 11, 1892.

13. *Kansas City Star,* June 2, 3, 1892, and *Topeka Daily Capital,* June 3, 1892.

14. *Leavenworth Evening Standard,* June 3, 6, 1892; *Kansas City Star,* June 3, 1892; *Topeka Daily Capital,* June 9, 1892.

15. *Kansas City Star,* June 6, 9, 1892; *Topeka Daily Capital,* May 17, 25, 26, 1892.

16. U. C. Spencer to John G. Otis in *National Economist,* June 25, 1892.

17. *Kansas City Star,* June 14, 1892; *Topeka Daily Capital,* June 15, 1892; *Emporia Tidings,* June 18, 1892; *National Economist,* June 25, 1892.

18. *National Economist,* June 25, 1892; *Emporia Weekly Republican,* June 23, 1892; *Topeka Daily Capital,* June 18, August 20, 1892; *Washington Post,* June 17, 1892.

19. *Kansas City Star,* June 13, 14, 1892; *Wichita Weekly Beacon,* April

22, June 17, 1892; *Washington Post,* May 23, 1892; *Topeka Daily Capital,* June 5, 1892.

20. *Kansas City Star,* June 13–16, 1892, and *Wichita Daily Beacon,* June 15, 1892.

21. *Lawrence Daily Journal and Evening Tribune,* June 7, 1892; *Topeka Daily Capital,* June 16, 17, 18, 1892; *Topeka Advocate,* June 22, 1892; *Topeka State Journal,* July 6, 1892.

22. *Leavenworth Evening Standard,* June 17, 1892; *Wichita Weekly Beacon,* June 24, 1892; *Garnett Journal,* July 15, 1892.

23. *Topeka Daily Capital,* July 5, 7, August 19, 1892.

24. Ibid., May 18, June 4, 1892, and *Wichita Weekly Beacon,* July 1, 1892.

25. J. B. Chapman to Robinson, March 26, 1892, Robinson Papers; *Topeka Daily Capital,* April 3, 5, June 8, 1892; *Leavenworth Evening Standard,* June 1, 1892; *Wichita Weekly Beacon,* May 6, 1892.

26. *Garnett Journal,* May 20, June 10, 1892; *Kincaid Kronicle,* June 17, 1892; *Kansas Agitator,* June 23, 1892.

27. *Topeka Daily Capital,* June 22, 23, 1892; *Kansas Agitator,* June 23, 1892; *Kincaid Kronicle,* June 24, 1892.

28. *Washington Post,* June 27, 1892; *Wichita Weekly Beacon,* July 1, 1892; *Pleasanton Herald,* March 18, July 8, 22, 1892; *Topeka Daily Capital,* July 9, 1892.

29. *Kansas Agitator,* July 7, 14, 1892, and *Kincaid Kronicle,* July 15, 1892.

30. *Kansas Agitator,* July 14, 1892.

31. *Pleasanton Herald,* August 19, 1892; *Topeka Daily Capital,* March 16, August 16, 21, 1892; *Topeka Advocate,* August 24, 1892; *Kansas City Star,* August 16, 1892. For Breidenthal, see also James C. Malin, *A Concern about Humanity* (Lawrence, Kans., 1964), 211–213; Walter T. K. Nugent, *The Tolerant Populists* (Chicago, 1963), 137–138; *Kansas City Star,* January 26, 1891.

32. *Kincaid Kronicle,* August 19, 26, 1892; *Kansas Agitator,* September 1, 1892; *Topeka Daily Capital,* June 26, August 18, 28, 1892.

33. See especially *Kansas Agitator,* May 26, 1892, and *Topeka Populist,* March 3, 1893.

34. *Pleasanton Herald,* July 22, 1892; *Topeka Daily Capital,* July 20, 1892; *Girard Western Herald,* July 15, 29, 1892.

35. *Topeka Daily Capital,* June 26, July 28, August 14, 27, 31, September 1, 4, and passim, 1892.

36. *Marion Advance,* October 1, 8, 1892; *Goff Advance,* June 23, 1892; *Topeka Daily Capital,* September 29, 1892.

37. Fred E. Haynes, *James Baird Weaver* (Iowa City, 1919), 346, 356–361; Herman C. Nixon, "The Populist Movement in Iowa," *Iowa Journal of History and Politics* 24 (January 1926): 25–26; Weaver to W. J. Bryan, September 1, 30, 1894, W. H. Lanning to Bryan, September 18, 22, 1894,

M. B. Gearon to Bryan, October 3, 1894, C. J. Smyth to Bryan, October 13, 1894, C. D. Casper to Bryan, March 6, 1893, William Jennings Bryan Papers, Library of Congress; Paola E. Coletta, *William Jennings Bryan: Political Evangelist* (Lincoln, Nebr., 1964), 99–103; *American Non-Conformist* (Indianapolis), August 2, 1894; and *National Watchman* (Washington, D.C.), June 15, 22, 1894.

38. *Topeka Advocate,* August 22, 1894; *National Watchman,* June 15, 22, July 20, August 3, 10, 1894.

39. Haynes, *Weaver,* 362–365, and Weaver to Bryan, November 9, 1894, Bryan Papers.

40. *Southern Mercury* (Dallas), November 29, 1894; *St. Louis Post-Dispatch,* November 27–29, 1894; P. W. Couzins to H. D. Lloyd, December 30, 1894, Henry D. Lloyd Papers, State Historical Society of Wisconsin; Joseph C. Sibley to Davis Waite, December 13, 1894, Davis Waite Papers, Colorado State Archives.

41. Taubeneck to Lloyd, December 10, 1894, Lloyd Papers, and *National Watchman,* November 30, 1894.

42. *Non-Conformist,* December 6, 1894; *National Watchman,* November 30, December 7, 1894; Henry L. Loucks to Waite, July 30, 1895, Waite Papers; W. M. Stewart to H. E. Taubeneck, December 25, 1894, William M. Stewart Papers, Nevada State Historical Society, Reno.

43. *Southern Mercury,* November 29, 1894; *Topeka Advocate,* December 12, 19, 1894; Donnelly to Waite, December 14, 1894, Waite to Robert Schilling, December 17, 1894, Waite Papers; Waite to Donnelly, December 11, 1894, George F. Washburn to Donnelly, December 22, 1894, Ignatius Donnelly Papers, Minnesota Historical Society.

44. Thomas F. Byron to Lloyd, April 8, 1895, Lloyd Papers; *Washington Post,* December 30, 1894; *St. Louis Post-Dispatch,* December 26–30, 1894; *Southern Mercury,* January 10, 1895.

45. *National Watchman,* January 11, 25, 1895.

46. Taubeneck to W. S. Morgan, January 10, 29, 1895, Waite Papers.

47. Weaver to Donnelly, January 13, 1895, Donnelly Papers; *Topeka Daily Capital,* February 15, 1895; Kansas Biographical Scrapbook, 137: 106, Kansas State Historical Society; *Chicago Tribune,* June 15, 1899; *Non-Conformist,* June 27, 1895; *Topeka Advocate,* February 20, 1895.

48. *National Watchman,* February 22, 1895.

49. *Kansas Commoner* (Wichita), February 14, 1895; *Topeka Advocate,* February 20, 1895; *Non-Conformist,* March 14, 1895; *Kansas City Star,* February 22, 23, 1895.

50. *Washington Post,* February 28, 1895; *Topeka Advocate,* March 13, 1895; *Non-Conformist,* March 7, 1895; *Southern Mercury,* March 7, 1895.

51. *Southern Mercury,* June 27, July 11, 1895; Haynes, *Weaver,* 365–373; Thomas F. Byron to Lloyd, April 8, May 5, 28, 1895, Lloyd Papers; Waite to Donnelly, April 22, 1895, Donnelly Papers.

52. *Topeka Advocate,* October 30, 1895, and *Southern Mercury,* October 10, 1895.

53. W. J. Bryan to Waite, December 2, 1895, Waite Papers; Marion Butler to Bryan, January 8, 1896, and J. B. Weaver to Bryan, December 31, 1895, January 3, 1896, Bryan Papers; W. M. Stewart to Ignatius Donnelly, December 20, 1895, Stewart to H. E. Taubeneck, December 12, 16, 1895, Stewart Papers; *St. Louis Post-Dispatch,* January 17, 1896; G. C. Clemens, *An Appeal to True Populists* (Topeka, 1896).

54. Paul Van Dervoort to Waite, January 20, 1896, Ralph Beaumont to Waite, January 19, 1896, Waite Papers; *St. Louis Post-Dispatch,* January 16–20, 1896; *Non-Conformist,* January 23, 1896.

55. Beaumont to Waite, January 19, 1896, Waite Papers; *Topeka Advocate,* January 22, 1896; *Southern Mercury,* January 30, 1896.

56. *Southern Mercury,* February 27, April 23, May 7, June 11, 1896; Taubeneck to Donnelly, February 29, 1896, Donnelly Papers; Stewart to Sylvester Pennoyer, March 13, 26, 1896, Stewart Papers; *Topeka Advocate,* April 29, 1896; *Des Moines Leader,* April 23, 1896; *Kansas City Star,* March 18, 19, 1896.

57. *Kansas Semi-Weekly Capital,* March 24, 1896.

58. Ibid., and Stanley L. Jones, *The Presidential Election of 1896* (Madison, 1964), 169–173.

59. *People's Party Paper,* June 26, 1896; *St. Louis Post-Dispatch,* June 20, 1896; Taubeneck to Donnelly, June 20, 1896, Donnelly Papers; Elmer Ellis, *Henry Moore Teller* (Caldwell, Idaho, 1941), 269–272; *Chicago Tribune,* July 1, 1896; Butler to Stewart, July 6, 1896, Stewart Papers.

60. Lloyd to R. I. Grimes, July 10, 1896, Lloyd Papers.

61. *Kansas Semi-Weekly Capital,* July 14, 21, 24, 1896; Stewart to Butler, July 14, 1896, Stewart Papers; *St. Louis Post-Dispatch,* July 15, 18, 19, 1896; *St. Louis Globe-Democrat,* July 20, 1896.

62. *Kansas City Star,* July 17, 19, 1896, and *St. Louis Post-Dispatch,* July 20, 1896.

63. Quoted in Martin Ridge, *Ignatius Donnelly: The Portrait of a Politician* (Chicago, 1962), 341.

64. Jones, *Election of 1896,* 320–326; G. L. McKean to Marion Butler, September 16, 1896, Marion Butler Papers, Southern Historical Collection, University of North Carolina.

65. Davis Waite manuscript speech, 1897, Waite Papers.

66. Supplement to *Girard Independent News,* April 14, 1898.

67. *Chicago Tribune,* June 29, 1899.

68. McKean to Butler, September 16, 1896, Butler Papers.

Chapter 6. To Disfranchise The People

1. L. E. Fredman, *The Australian Ballot: The Story of an American Reform* (East Lansing, Mich., 1968); Jerrold G. Rusk, "The Effect of the Aus-

tralian Ballot Reform on Split Ticket Voting, 1876-1908," *American Political Science Review* 64 (December 1970): 1220-1238; Richard Jensen, *The Winning of the Midwest: Social and Political Conflict, 1888-1896* (Chicago, 1971), 9, 29, 40-43. There has been, of course, considerable attention paid to electoral legislation in the South. For one recent account, see J. Morgan Kousser, *The Shaping of Southern Politics: Suffrage Restriction and the Establishment of the One-Party South, 1880-1910* (New Haven, Conn., 1974).

2. For the most recent discussion, see Thomas B. Colbert, "Political Fusion in Iowa: The Election of James B. Weaver to Congress in 1878," *Arizona and the West* 20 (Spring 1978): 25-40.

3. H. G. McMillan to James S. Clarkson, September 5, 1896, James S. Clarkson Papers, Library of Congress; Thomas R. Ross, *Jonathan Prentiss Dolliver: A Study in Political Integrity and Independence* (Iowa City, 1958), 128.

4. Herman C. Nixon, "The Populist Movement in Iowa," *Iowa Journal of History and Politics* 24 (January 1926): 100; *Des Moines Farmers Tribune,* November 11, 1896; McMillan to Clarkson, September 5, 1896, Clarkson Papers; Fred E. Haynes, *Third Party Movements since the Civil War with Special Reference to Iowa* (Iowa City, 1916), 370-371.

5. *Sioux City Journal,* October 17, November 4, 11, 12, 1896.

6. *Des Moines Farmers Tribune,* November 4, 11, 18, 1896, January 13, 1897, and *Dubuque Daily Herald,* November 10, December 18, 31, 1896.

7. *Sioux City Journal,* January 2, 1897, and James S. Clarkson to Jonathan P. Dolliver, November 25, 1896, Jonathan P. Dolliver Papers, State Historical Society of Iowa, Iowa City.

8. *Chicago Tribune,* February 8, 1897, and *Dubuque Daily Herald,* January 7, 1897. The legislature was overwhelmingly composed of Republicans, forty-two in the Senate, compared to eight Democrats and Silver Republicans, and seventy-eight in the House, compared to twenty-two Democrats and silverites (*Iowa Official Register, 1897* [Des Moines, 1897], 33-36).

9. *Dubuque Daily Herald,* February 14, 1897; Iowa, *Journal of the Senate, Extra Session, . . . 1897* (Des Moines, 1897), 117; Des Moines *Iowa State Register,* January 30, 1897.

10. Des Moines *Iowa State Register,* April 2, February 17, 1897; *Sioux City Journal,* February 17, 1897; *Dubuque Daily Herald,* February 14, 1897.

11. Des Moines *Iowa State Register,* February 5, 19, 1897.

12. *Dubuque Daily Herald,* February 13, 14, 1897; Winterset (Iowa) *Review,* February 17, 1897; Des Moines *Iowa State Register,* February 13, 1897. Politicians in neighboring Minnesota had earlier estimated that first place on the state ballot was worth an additional 5,000 votes (*Minneapolis Tribune,* October 12, 1892).

13. Des Moines *Iowa State Register,* February 13, 19, January 30, 1897.

14. *Winterset Review,* March 31, February 17, 1897; *Des Moines Farmers Tribune,* February 3, 1897; and Des Moines *Iowa State Register,* February 18, 19, 1897.

15. Des Moines *Iowa State Register,* February 19, 1897, and *Journal of the Senate,* 276.

16. *Indianola Record,* quoted in *Winterset Review,* March 3, 1897; Des Moines *Iowa State Register,* February 20, March 6, 1897; *Dubuque Daily Herald,* January 30, February 17, 21, March 12, 1897; *Sioux City Journal,* March 24, 1897. Moreover, the minor parties' problems with the election law would only begin with the antifusion provision, which would remove them from the ballot and end their legal existence should they fuse with another party. Another provision of the ballot law would require them to petition to regain the right to appear on the ballot in the future, a procedure especially onerous for organizations with limited funds and personnel (*Sioux City Journal,* March 10, 1897).

17. *Des Moines Farmers Tribune,* March 17, 1897; Des Moines *Iowa State Register,* March 20, 26, 1897; *Sioux City Journal,* March 29, 1897; *Journal of the Senate,* 426, 528, 574–584.

18. *Des Moines Farmers Tribune,* February 3, March 10, 31, 1897; *Dubuque Daily Herald,* February 7, 1897; *Sioux City Journal,* March 11, 1897; *Winterset Review,* March 31, 1897.

19. Des Moines *Iowa State Register,* May 13, 1897.

20. *Winterset Review,* May 19, 26, 1897, and *Dubuque Daily Herald,* May 28, 1897.

21. Quoted in Des Moines *Iowa State Register,* June 2, 1897.

22. *Des Moines Farmers Tribune,* May 26, 1897, and *Winterset Review,* June 2, 1897.

23. *Des Moines Farmers Tribune,* June 9, 23, 1897; *Sioux City Journal,* June 17, 1897; Des Moines *Iowa State Register,* June 20, 1897.

24. *Des Moines Farmers Tribune,* June 30, 1897; Des Moines *Iowa State Register,* June 23, 24, 1897; *Winterset Review,* June 23, 1897.

25. *Des Moines Farmers Tribune,* June, 30, 1897, and Des Moines *Iowa State Register,* June 24, 1897.

26. Des Moines *Iowa State Register,* June 24, 1897.

27. *Des Moines Farmers Tribune,* June 30, 1897.

28. *Davenport Democrat* and *Burlington Gazette* quoted in *Sioux City Journal,* June 30, 1897; *Des Moines Farmers Tribune,* June 30, 1897; *Dubuque Daily Herald,* June 25, 27, 1897.

29. Des Moines *Iowa State Register,* July 8, August 11, 1897, and *Sioux City Journal,* July 8, 1897.

30. *Des Moines Farmers Tribune,* July 14, 1897; *Winterset Review,* June 30, 1897; Des Moines *Iowa State Register,* July 1, 11, 14, 17, 30, 1897.

31. Des Moines *Iowa State Register,* July 14, 17, 23, 1897; A. W. C. Weeks to Lemuel H. Weller, August 10, July 5, 1897, Lemuel H. Weller Papers, State Historical Society of Wisconsin, Madison.

32. *Winterset Review,* July 28, 1897; Weeks to Weller, July 12, 1897, and James Bellangee to Weller, July 25, 1897, Weller Papers.

33. *Des Moines Farmers Tribune,* August 3, 11, 1897.

34. Ibid., August 3, 18, 1897.

35. Des Moines *Iowa State Register,* August 1, 15, 1897.

36. Ibid., August 19, 20, 1897; *Des Moines Farmers Tribune,* August 25, 1897; Peter H. Argersinger, *Populism and Politics: William Alfred Peffer and the People's Party* (Lexington, Ky., 1974), 289-292.

37. Des Moines *Iowa State Register,* August 12, 1897; *Des Moines Farmers Tribune,* June 2, August 3, 25, 1897; *Dubuque Daily Herald,* July 29, 1897.

38. *Des Moines Farmers Tribune,* May 5, 1897; Des Moines *Iowa State Register,* July 23, August 19, 1897; *Dubuque Daily Herald,* July 25, 1897; Cyrenus Cole to Leslie M. Shaw, undated but after Shaw's August 1897 gubernatorial nomination, Cyrenus Cole Papers, State Historical Society of Iowa, Iowa City.

39. *Sioux City Journal,* May 26, 1897, and Des Moines *Iowa State Register,* August 31, 1897.

40. *Dubuque Daily Herald,* May 13, September 17, 1897; *Des Moines Farmers Tribune,* June 2, 1897; Des Moines *Iowa State Register,* September 4, 1897.

41. Des Moines *Iowa State Register,* September 4, 7, 10, 1897, and *Winterset Review,* September 8, 15, 1897.

42. Des Moines *Iowa State Register,* September 8, 17, 18, 1897.

43. *Des Moines Farmers Tribune,* September 15, 22, 29, 1897; *Dubuque Sunday Herald,* September 26, 1897; *Winterset Review,* September 29, 1897.

44. *Dubuque Daily Herald,* September 23, October 14, 17, 1897.

45. Ibid., October 22, 28, 1897.

46. Ibid., October 28, 29, 1897; *Des Moines Farmers Tribune,* November 10, 1897; *Winterset Review,* November 3, 1897.

47. Charles Schaeffer to William B. Allison, September 30, 1897, William B. Allison Papers, Iowa State Department of History and Archives, Des Moines, and Des Moines *Iowa State Register,* September 24, 25, 1897.

48. *Des Moines Farmers Tribune,* November 10, 24, 1897, and *Dubuque Daily Herald,* December 4, 19, 1897.

CHAPTER 7. REGULATING DEMOCRACY

1. James Willard Hurst, "Old and New Dimensions of Research in United States Legal History," *American Journal of Legal History* 23 (January 1979): 20.

2. One scholar has even argued that the special characteristic of legal historians is their "insistence on a radical separation between law and poli-

tics"; see Morton J. Horwitz, "The Conservative Tradition in the Writing of American Legal History," *American Journal of Legal History* 17 (July 1973): 281.

3. Austin Ranney, *Curing the Mischiefs of Faction: Party Reform in America* (Berkeley, Calif., 1975), 61, 74.

4. *Minneapolis Tribune,* October 23, 1892.

5. Actually, North Dakota's constitution required the Australian ballot, and its first legislature passed an Australian ballot bill in 1889, but the bill was stolen before it reached the governor for his signature—indicating serious opposition to the measure.

6. *New York Times,* October 25, 1892.

7. *Laws Passed at the Second Session of the Legislative Assembly . . . of North Dakota . . . 1891* (Bismarck, 1891), chap. 66, 171–184; *Laws Passed at the Second Session of the Legislature of . . . South Dakota . . . 1891* (Pierre, 1891), chap. 57, 152–166; Yankton (S.Dak.) *Press and Dakotan,* October 20, November 12, 17, 1892; *Brookings County Press* (Brookings, S.Dak.), October 13, 1892.

8. *Mandan Times* quoted in Jamestown *North Dakota Capital,* November 18, 1892; *Jamestown* (N.Dak.) *Daily Alert,* October 20, 1892; *Yankton Press and Dakotan,* October 20, 29, November 3, 24, 1892; *Brookings County Press,* November 3, 1892; *Fargo Forum,* November 8, 1892.

9. *Yankton Press and Dakotan,* October 20, 1892, November 16, 1893.

10. Des Moines *Iowa State Register,* October 12, 1892; *Laws Passed, North Dakota, 1891,* 178; Jamestown *North Dakota Capital,* May 6, 13, June 3, 1892.

11. *New York Times,* December 15, 29, 1892, and *Bismarck Daily Tribune,* December 27, 28, 1892.

12. Jamestown *North Dakota Capital,* March 18, 1892; *Laws Passed, North Dakota, 1891,* chap. 66. The *Jamestown Daily Alert* reacted to this plan to "'monkey' with the ticket" by describing it as an "injustice," although conceding that the partisan "temptation to juggle with the Australian ballot is great" (see issues of September 30 and October 13, 14, 1892).

13. *Eaton v. Brown,* 31 Pacific Reporter 250. The North Dakota attorney general ruled, however, that the Populists could appear on the 1892 ballot under the heading "Independent Party" because a party with that name had captured the requisite 5 percent of the vote in the 1890 election (Jamestown *North Dakota Capital,* March 18, April 8, 1892). In this way the Populists in North Dakota officially became, and subsequently had to remain, the "Independents." For North Dakota's reaction to the California court decision and recognition of its applicability to the North Dakota ballot, see Jamestown *North Dakota Capital,* October 21, 1892 (misdated October 12, 1892), and *Jamestown Daily Alert,* November 5, 1892.

14. *Sioux Falls Argus-Leader,* November 15, 1892, and *Laws Passed, South Dakota, 1891,* 153–154.

15. *Yankton Press and Dakotan,* November 17, 1892, January 12, 1893.

16. *Brookings County Press,* October 20, 1892; *Laws Passed, South Dakota, 1891,* 153–155; *Yankton Press and Dakotan,* October 13, November 10, 1892, October 19, November 2, 1893; *Pierre Daily Capital,* October 11, 1894; *Lucas et al. v. Ringsrud,* 53 Northwestern Reporter 426.

17. Kenneth E. Hendrickson, Jr., "The Public Career of Richard F. Pettigrew of South Dakota," South Dakota Department of History, Pierre, *Report and Historical Collections* 34 (1968): 217.

18. *Brookings County Press,* September 29, 1892.

19. *Clear Lake Advocate* quoted in ibid., November 2, 1893.

20. *Brookings County Press,* September 15, 1892, and *Yankton Press and Dakotan,* September 8, 15, November 3, 1892.

21. *New York Times,* September 19, 29, 1892.

22. Ibid., October 21, 1892, and Hendrickson, "Pettigrew," 222, 233–234.

23. *New York Times,* October 21, 1892.

24. Ibid., October 19, 25, 1892, and *Brookings County Press,* October 13, 1892.

25. *Minneapolis Tribune,* October 16, 1892.

26. Ibid., October 18, 19, 1892, and John D. Hicks, "The People's Party in Minnesota," *Minnesota History Bulletin* 5 (November 1924): 545.

27. Actually, Republicans also elected the secretary of state, but only with the fusion assistance of the Prohibitionists.

28. *State v. Stein,* 53 Northwestern Reporter 999, and Lincoln *Nebraska State Journal,* November 15, 16, 17, 1892.

29. *Laws Passed at the Third Session of the Legislature of . . . South Dakota . . . 1893* (Pierre, 1893), 137–141; *Yankton Press and Dakotan,* November 17, December 22, 1892, March 9, 23, 1893; *Brookings County Press,* November 24, 1892; *Sioux Falls Argus-Leader,* November 15, 1892, January 3, 1893; *South Dakota House Journal* (Pierre, 1893), 862, 1113; *South Dakota Senate Journal* (Pierre, 1893), 283–286, 581, 1006.

30. *Eaton v. Brown,* 31 Pacific Reporter 250; *Sioux Falls Argus-Leader,* November 4, 1893; *Yankton Press and Dakotan,* November 24, December 8, 1892; *De Smet Independent* quoted in *Brookings County Press,* November 2, 1893. In its 1893 legislative session, North Dakota adopted the party-column ballot but eliminated the provision for straight-ticket voting, perhaps with the intention of forcing fusionists to confront directly the necessity of voting outside their party, thereby provoking roll-off and scratched tickets (see Jamestown *North Dakota Capital,* November 4, 1892).

31. *Sioux Falls Argus-Leader,* August 3, 29, 1894, and *Pierre Daily Capital,* October 16, 24, 1894.

32. *Sioux Falls Argus-Leader,* August 18, 1894.

33. Ibid., September 5, 6, 1894.

34. Ibid., August 29, September 7, 14, October 23, 1894.

35. *Brookings County Press,* October 19, 1893.

36. *Vallier v. Brakke,* 64 Northwestern Reporter 180.

37. *Sioux Falls Argus-Leader,* November 13, 1894; *Parmley v. Healy,* 64 Northwestern Reporter 186; *McKittrick v. Pardee,* 65 Northwestern Reporter 23.

38. *Sioux Falls Argus-Leader,* August 18, 1896.

39. *Kimball Graphic* quoted in ibid., August 25, 1896.

40. Sioux City (Iowa) *Journal,* October 17, 1896; *Pierre Daily Capital,* October 23, 1896; *Sioux Falls Argus-Leader,* August 18, September 1, 1896; *Vallier v. Brakke,* 64 Northwestern Reporter 180; *McKittrick v. Pardee,* 65 Northwestern Reporter 23.

41. *Sioux City Journal,* November 15-21, December 26, 1896; Arthur Brooks, "The Administration of Andrew E. Lee, Governor of South Dakota, 1897-1901" (Master's thesis, University of South Dakota, 1939), 18-19.

42. *Chicago Tribune,* January 4, 1897, and *Sioux City Journal,* November 19, 30, 1896.

43. *South Dakota Senate Journal* (Pierre, 1897), 43-44.

44. Ibid., 1263-1264, 1282-1283; *South Dakota House Journal* (Pierre, 1897), 713, 1275-1280; *Laws Passed at the Fifth Session of the Legislature of . . . South Dakota . . . 1897* (Pierre, 1897), 170-171.

45. *Laws Passed, South Dakota, 1897,* 173-176, and *Sioux City Journal,* March 27, April 4, 1897. See also *South Dakota House Journal* (Pierre, 1899), 1283.

46. *Yankton Press and Dakotan,* March 18, May 6, 1897.

47. *Laws Passed at the Fifth Session of the Legislative Assembly . . . of North Dakota . . . 1897* (Bismarck, 1897), 117-119. In another action of political and ideological significance, the 1897 North Dakota legislature repealed the Edwards Precinct Law, which had established rules for allowing citizens to vote despite moving from one local precinct to another. In its place a firm ninety-day residence requirement was established, which disfranchised more than one hundred residents of Fargo alone in the next election (see *Fargo Forum and Daily Republican,* November 10, 1898).

48. Winterset (Iowa) *Review,* March 31, 1897, and *State v. Falley,* 76 Northwestern Reporter 996.

49. *Bismarck Daily Tribune,* November 12, 1898.

50. Ibid., October 23, 31, November 1, 2, 12, 1898, and *Fargo Forum and Daily Republican,* November 14, 1898.

51. *Bismarck Daily Tribune,* November 8, 1898, and *New York Times,* April 6, 1900.

52. *Appleton's Annual Cyclopedia, 1901* (New York, 1902), 747; *Bismarck Daily Tribune,* March 8, 9, 1901; *North Dakota Senate Journal* (Bismarck, 1901), 568; *North Dakota House Journal* (Bismarck, 1901), 512.

53. Literature on the primary and its consequences is vast; see especially V. O. Key, Jr., *American State Politics: An Introduction* (New York, 1956).

54. *Brookings County Press,* December 1, 1898, and *Yankton Press and Dakotan,* June 30, 1898.

55. Valley Springs (S.Dak.) *Vidette,* quoted in *Sioux Falls Argus-Leader,* November 19, 1898, and *Brookings County Press,* November 17, 1898.

56. *Brookings County Press,* December 1, 1898.

57. Quoted in *Sioux Falls Argus-Leader,* March 7, 1899.

58. Brooks, "Administration of Lee," 48; *Brookings County Press,* December 22, 1898, January 12, 26, February 9, 23, 1899; *South Dakota House Journal* (1899), 586, 596-597, 1563-1564; *South Dakota Senate Journal* (Pierre, 1899), 973.

59. *South Dakota House Journal* (1899), 1283, 1562; *South Dakota Senate Journal* (1899), 1508; *Sioux Falls Argus-Leader,* March 7, 8, 10, 1899.

60. *Sioux Falls Argus-Leader,* March 8, 1899.

61. *South Dakota House Journal* (Pierre, 1901), 1415, and *South Dakota Senate Journal* (Pierre, 1901), 1283.

62. *Sioux Falls Argus-Leader,* June 26, 28, 1902.

63. Ibid., June 26, 1902.

64. Ibid., June 28, 1902.

65. Samuel P. Hays, "The Politics of Reform in Municipal Government in the Progressive Era," *Pacific Northwest Quarterly* 55 (October 1964): 169, and *Sioux Falls Argus-Leader,* March 4, 1901.

66. *Sioux Falls Argus-Leader,* June 28, 1902.

67. *Chamberlain v. Wood,* 88 Northwestern Reporter 109, 113.

68. *Miller v. Schallern,* 79 Northwestern Reporter 865-866.

69. *Chamberlain v. Wood,* 88 Northwestern Reporter 109, 113-114.

CHAPTER 8. IDEOLOGY AND BEHAVIOR

1. Karel D. Bicha, "The Conservative Populists: A Hypothesis," *Agricultural History* 47 (January 1973): 9-24; Bicha, "Western Populists: Marginal Reformers of the 1890s," *Agricultural History* 50 (October 1976): 626-635; Bicha, *Western Populism: Studies in an Ambivalent Conservatism* (Lawrence, Kans.: Coronado Press, 1976). Bicha himself sees his position as distinct from the 1950s' view, but Gene Clanton has described his work as a "determined" effort "to sustain the 1950s revisionists," and David S. Trask has termed it "a restatement of the 1950's analysis of Populism." See Bicha, *Western Populism,* 14; Clanton, "Populism, Progressivism, and Equality: The Kansas Paradigm," *Agricultural History* 51 (July 1977): 563, n.10; Trask, review of *Western Populism* in *Nebraska History* 59 (Spring 1978): 151-153.

2. In the other chapters of the book, focused on four individual politicians, Bicha offers little convincing support for the claim that Populism was conservative. Bicha describes the relatively conservative William V. Allen as having little connection with the Populist party or program and as

being virtually "a non-Populist"; conversely, he describes Davis Waite as believing in "near socialism" and as being the only one of the four to adhere to Populist dogma (Bicha, *Western Populism*, 43, 44, 52, 70). As for Bicha's discussion of Populists in Congress, see Gene Clanton, "Congressional Populism: Ambivalent Conservatism or Democratic Promise," paper presented at the Seventy-fifth Annual Meeting of the Organization of American Historians, Philadelphia, April 3, 1982.

3. Three important exceptions in Populist historiography are Sheldon Hackney, *Populism to Progressivism in Alabama* (Princeton, N.J., 1969); Stanley B. Parsons, *The Populist Context: Rural versus Urban Power on a Great Plains Frontier* (Westport, Conn., 1973); and James E. Wright, *The Politics of Populism: Dissent in Colorado* (New Haven, Conn., 1974).

4. Walter T. K. Nugent, review of *Western Populism* in *Agricultural History* 51 (October 1977): 797.

5. Bicha, *Western Populism*, 77, 92, 101, and 93-100 (for convenience the citations will be to Bicha's book rather than to the article in *Agricultural History* though there is no substantial difference in the argument).

6. Bicha, *Western Populism*, 79 (emphasis in original).

7. Ibid., 79, 80, 86, 104.

8. Ibid., 78.

9. James C. Malin, *A Concern about Humanity* (Lawrence, Kans., 1964), 41; Peter H. Argersinger, *Populism and Politics: William Alfred Peffer and the People's Party* (Lexington, Ky., 1974), 173; Pierre (S.Dak.) *Daily Capital*, June 16, 18, 1894; *Idaho Daily Statesman* (Boise), August 22, 1896; *Spokane Spokesman-Review*, August 14, 1896; *Appleton's Annual Cyclopedia, 1890* (New York, 1891), 782, *1892* (New York, 1893), 614, and *1894* (New York, 1895), 556.

10. Kansas, *House Journal, 1891* (Topeka, 1891), 490, 527; Kansas, *Senate Journal, 1891* (Topeka, 1891), 574-576.

11. South Dakota, *House Journal, 1895* (Pierre, 1895), 959; Washington, *House Journal, 1895* (Olympia, 1895), 244-245; *Spokane Spokesman-Review*, February 8, 1895. Moreover, Populists overwhelmingly supported woman suffrage in the 1893 Colorado legislature while both Republicans and Democrats opposed the measure, and Populist legislators also supported the issue in the 1891 Nebraska legislature (see Wright, *Politics of Populism*, 164, and Parsons, *Populist Context*, 135-136).

12. Bismarck (N.Dak.) *Daily Tribune*, March 4, 1893; North Dakota, *House Journal, 1893* (Bismarck, 1893), 844-848, 801-821; North Dakota, *Senate Journal, 1893* (Bismarck, 1893), 551-555.

13. Kansas, *Senate Journal, 1895* (Topeka, 1895), 534, 852, 903. Populists supported this bill by a vote of 17 to 2; Republicans and Democrats also favored the measure but by a weaker proportion (8 to 4). The Republican House of Representatives took no action on the bill.

14. Norton (Kans.) *Liberator*, June 15, 1894. The limited evidence available also suggests that on the popular level Populists voted favorably

on woman suffrage referenda while members of the old parties did not (Wright, *Politics of Populism*, 203, found this for Colorado and my own work confirms it for Kansas).

15. *Topeka Daily Capital*, June 16, 1892, August 6, 1896; *Spokane Spokesman-Review*, August 14, 1896; *Topeka State Journal*, February 19, 20, March 8, 1897; *Omaha Morning World-Herald*, August 6, 1896. For some of the background for the Populist position on insurance reform, see H. Roger Grant, *Insurance Reform: Consumer Action in the Progressive Era* (Ames, Iowa, 1979), esp. 20.

16. *Topeka Daily Capital*, March 5, 1895; Kansas, *Senate Journal, 1897* (Topeka, 1897), 154, 889–896; *Topeka State Journal*, March 6, 1897. Nebraska Populists also demanded municipal ownership in their 1894 platform (*Appleton's Annual Cyclopedia, 1894*, 506).

17. *Topeka Advocate*, January 16, 1895, and *Topeka State Journal*, January 23, 1895.

18. Bicha, *Western Populism*, 92, 101.

19. Ibid., 80. Without giving any indication of the number of "duplicates," Bicha used the figures of 10 out of 1,500.

20. Nebraska, *House Journal, 1891* (Lincoln, 1891), 1976–1978 and references for House Bills 20, 24, 69, 87, 146, 149, 155, 171, 313.

21. Bicha, *Western Populism*, 83; Nebraska, *House Journal, 1891*, 1078, passim. Bicha had assured his readers that "bills withdrawn from consideration in deference to similar bills are not included in the table" (*Western Populism*, 101).

22. See Nebraska, *House Journal, 1891*, 962, and Bicha, *Western Populism*, 96.

23. Bicha, *Western Populism*, 86; South Dakota, *House Journal, 1897* (Pierre, 1897), 713, 1275–1280; South Dakota, *Senate Journal, 1897* (Pierre, 1897), 1263–1264, 1282–1283.

24. Bicha, *Western Populism*, 82 (emphasis in original).

25. *Topeka Daily Capital*, June 16, 1892. Bicha claimed that the senate rejected only two Populist bills that had passed the house, both regulating railroads, but his own table indicates that another bill, regulating interest rates, passed the house but not the senate (*Western Populism*, 82, 96). The bills specified by the Populist platform Bicha apparently overlooked altogether.

26. Quoted in Argersinger, *Populism and Politics*, 47. Indeed, the Republican governor did veto a Populist bill to regulate coal weighing that did get past the senate.

27. Allan G. Bogue, "American Historians and Legislative Behavior," in *American Political Behavior: Historical Essays and Readings*, ed. Lee Benson, et al. (New York, 1974), 109–110. This excellent essay is a good introduction to the study of legislative behavior. For useful elaboration, see Lee F. Anderson, Meredith W. Watts, Jr., and Allen R. Wilcox, *Legislative Roll-Call Analysis* (Evanston, Ill., 1966).

Bicha did make a brief effort at roll-call analysis. Unfortunately his selective use of indices of cohesion and agreement obscures rather than clarifies important data on individual legislators. Moreover, by reporting a mathematically impossible pair of scores he again casts doubt on the validity of his conclusions and reported data (see *Western Populism*, 103, and for Bicha's attitude toward the two Kansas sessions, see 80–82).

28. Reform is here defined in terms of all the issues to which Populists pledged themselves in platforms and campaign promises, including such issues as woman suffrage. To evaluate whether bills had reform content, regardless of their title, extensive analysis of many newspapers was undertaken, especially an examination of the various Topeka newspapers that carried lengthy reports of daily legislative activity. Only by such traditional historical research in "impressionistic" sources can the actual substance of legislation be determined. When bills could not be identified as to their content in this fashion they were necessarily excluded from the analysis. For instance, lack of information about the specific content of a Populist bill relating to township assessors and the 1895 state census caused it to be omitted even though it resulted in the highest Riker coefficient of significance. Finally, the legislative context of bills had to be considered. For example, a Republican-sponsored effort to initiate a constitutional amendment to prohibit railroad passes was widely viewed as a bluff, to delay for several years the reform that was otherwise possible through immediate statutory action. Opposition to this proposal was thus considered the reform position. This interpretation is strengthened by the fact that the Republicans voted against (and the Populists for) a proposal to prohibit railroad passes by law (*Topeka Daily Capital*, February 22, 1895; *Topeka Advocate*, February 27, 1895; Kansas, *Senate Journal, 1895*, 658, 806).

29. Though all these thirty-five roll calls, to say nothing of the larger number of bills introduced, correspond to Bicha's notion of reform, he did not record any proposed legislation from this 1895 session as reformist.

30. Cf. Bicha, *Western Populism*, 102. The index of disagreement (the obverse of the index of likeness) is calculated by determining the difference between the percentage of yea votes cast by each group on a roll call. The index varies from 0 to 100. Following the example of Allan G. Bogue, "Bloc and Party in the United States Senate: 1861–1863," *Civil War History* 13 (September 1967): 221–241, I am regarding index of disagreement scores of 40 and above as indicating significant disagreement.

31. Bicha, *Western Populism*, 14; *Topeka State Journal*, January 9, 1895; *Topeka Daily Capital*, February 19, 1895; R. H. Semple, "The Legislature of 1895," *Agora* 4 (April 1895): 263; J. W. Parker, "The Legislature of 1895," *Agora* 4 (April 1895): 254; *Topeka Advocate*, February 27, 1895.

32. Cf. Bicha, *Western Populism*, 25.

33. *Topeka State Journal*, January 15, 16, 1895; *Topeka Daily Capital*, February 5, 1895; Kansas, *Senate Journal, 1895*, 802. Populists had also demanded in the 1892 Washington State platform the establishment of free

employment offices (see Stephen Henry Peters, "The Populists and the Washington Legislature, 1893–1900" [Master's thesis, University of Washington, 1967], 20).

34. *Topeka State Journal,* February 2, 5, 25, 1897; *Topeka Daily Capital,* March 2, 1897; Kansas, *Senate Journal, 1897,* 311, 414, 781, 852.

35. *Topeka State Journal,* February 13, 16, March 4, 6, 1897; *Leavenworth Times,* March 7, 1897; Kansas, *Senate Journal, 1897,* 39, 45, 84, 154, 340, 889. The 1896 Populist state convention had resolved in favor of jury trials in all cases and opposed injunction and contempt proceedings (*Appleton's Annual Cyclopedia, 1896,* 373). Bicha regarded none of these bills as reform legislation.

36. Astonishingly, Bicha ignored all these roll calls. Indeed, he declared that of a group of Populist reform proposals only one ever came to a vote and it was defeated. But that roll call actually involved only a substitute proposal offered as an amendment, and the bill itself was passed on a roll-call vote recorded two pages later in the *Senate Journal* (see Bicha, *Western Populism,* 81, 142n, and Kansas, *Senate Journal, 1897,* 789–794).

37. For a full discussion of this more detailed analysis, see Peter H. Argersinger, "Populists in Power: Public Policy and Legislative Behavior," paper presented at conference, "The Variety of Quantitative History," California Institute of Technology, March 24–26, 1983 (also Chapter 9 of this book).

38. Cf. Bicha, *Western Populism,* 80.

39. See Argersinger, *Populism and Politics,* 282–285; O. Gene Clanton, *Kansas Populism: Ideas and Men* (Lawrence, Kans., 1969), 201–205; Walter T. K. Nugent, *The Tolerant Populists: Kansas Populism and Nativism* (Chicago, 1963), 204–205.

40. *Topeka Daily Capital,* March 3, February 6, 1895.

41. *Leavenworth Standard,* March 16, 1897. The objectionable section prohibited banks from lending money to their own stockholders on their stock as collateral. See also *Leavenworth Times,* March 14, 1897, for another example of tampering with a mortgage law. Nor was this problem limited to Kansas. North Dakota witnessed perhaps the worst case in its 1893 legislative session when thirteen bills disappeared altogether after passage, prompting the *Fargo Forum* (March 6, 1893) to add a new category to its summary of legislative activity: "Lost, Stolen, or Strayed." The disappearing bills, like those tampered with in the Kansas sessions, involved efforts at reform: railroad regulation, especially, and banking regulation but also the Australian ballot and other regulatory legislation. "It is supposed," the *Forum* concluded dryly, "that Colonel Dodge, attorney for the Great Northern," knew "something about" the disappearance of the bills to regulate railroads, but "as there is no law providing for the punishment of a member or employee who steals or 'loses' a bill, nothing is likely to be done about it."

42. *Topeka State Journal* quoted in *Topeka Advocate,* March 6, 1895.

This was a routine bill appropriating for the state normal school the funds that had accrued from its own endowment. For elaboration of this argument that partisanship dictated the defeat of reform measures, see the comments of legislators themselves in Parker, "Legislature of 1895," 253; Semple, "Legislature of 1895," 267; Ed. O'Bryan, "Legislature of 1895," *Agora* 4 (April 1895): 257.

43. *Topeka Advocate*, March 13, 1895, and Kansas, *House Journal, 1895* (Topeka, 1895), passim.

44. W. P. Harrington, "The Populist Party in Kansas," *Collections of the Kansas State Historical Society* 16 (1925): 444; *Appleton's Annual Cyclopedia, 1897*, 435; Clanton, *Kansas Populism*, 201.

45. Bicha, *Western Populism*, 80, 87, 92, and Clanton, *Kansas Populism*, 200. The Rice index of cohesion ranges from 0 to 100 and is calculated by determining the absolute difference between the percentage of group members voting yea and the percentage voting nay on any single roll call. The party-support score is simply the percentage of times a senator voted with the majority of his party on those roll calls with a Populist/Republican disagreement index ≥ 50.

46. One such lawyer, though classified by the *Senate Journal* as a Populist and here so treated, was in fact only a Silver Republican endorsed by Populists in the 1896 fusion campaign. His lack of commitment to Populist reform, indicated by his Silver Republican affiliation, was substantiated by his legislative voting performance. Additionally, the two Democrats in the senate, though endorsed by the Populists and regarded as Popocrats in the 1896 fusion election—and often participants in the Populist legislative caucus—were not reliable allies either. This suggests that Bicha's functional equation of Populists and fusionists is untenable and misleading (see Bicha, *Western Populism*, 101). Indeed, one scholar investigating the 1897 Washington state legislature has found support for these points. The major reason for that Populist legislature's failure to enact much reform legislation was the factional split within the People's party between mid-roaders and fusionists and the ability of the Republican minority to form combinations to defeat legislation it disliked (see Peters, "Populists and the Washington Legislature," 93–95).

47. *Kansas Agitator* (Garnett), April 2, 1897; *Topeka Advocate*, March 3, 10, 1897; *Norton Liberator*, March 12, April 16, 1897; *Kansas Semi-Weekly Capital* (Topeka), March 16, 1897; Clanton, *Kansas Populism*, 296n.

CHAPTER 9. POPULISTS IN POWER

1. James Turner, "Understanding the Populists," *Journal of American History* 67 (September 1980): 356.

2. Bruce Palmer, *"Man Over Money": The Southern Populist Critique of American Capitalism* (Chapel Hill, N.C., 1980), xvi.

3. Allan G. Bogue, "American Historians and Legislative Behavior," in *American Political Behavior: Historical Essays and Readings*, ed. Lee Benson et al. (New York, 1974), 109. Bogue's thoughtful essay represents perhaps the best introduction to the historical study of legislative behavior. For useful elaboration, see Lee F. Anderson et al., *Legislative Roll-Call Analysis* (Evanston, Ill., 1966). Three important exceptions to the neglect of legislative analysis in Populist historiography are Sheldon Hackney, *Populism to Progressivism in Alabama* (Princeton, N.J., 1969); Stanley B. Parsons, *The Populist Context: Rural versus Urban Power on a Great Plains Frontier* (Westport, Conn., 1973); James E. Wright, *The Politics of Populism: Dissent in Colorado* (New Haven, Conn., 1974).

4. Also excluded were roll calls on legislative proposals the actual substance of which could not be determined even after extensive investigation of a large number of newspapers, particularly the various Topeka newspapers that carried lengthy reports of daily legislative activity. By repetitive motions I refer to repeated roll calls raising substantially the same point on the same bill and provoking the same voting alignment time after time. The Republican minority adopted this procedure as a stalling tactic to prevent the Populist majority from acting (see *Topeka Daily Capital*, February 6, 1897).

5. *Topeka State Journal*, February 13, 16, March 4, 6, 1897; *Leavenworth Times*, March 7, 1897; Kansas, *Senate Journal, 1897* (Topeka, 1897), 39, 45, 84, 154, 340, 889–896.

6. For excellent recent examples of such suggestive legislative analyses, see Ballard C. Campbell, *Representative Democracy: Public Policy and Midwestern Legislatures in the Late Nineteenth Century* (Cambridge, Mass., 1980), and Allan G. Bogue, *The Earnest Men: Republicans of the Civil War Senate* (Ithaca, N.Y., 1981). The Rice index of cohesion ranges from 0 to 100 and is calculated by determining the absolute difference between the percentage of group members voting yea and the percentage voting nay on any single roll call. The index of disagreement (the obverse of the index of likeness) also varies from 0 to 100 and is the difference between the percentage of yea votes cast by each group on a roll call. Following the example of Bogue, *Earnest Men*, I regard index of disagreement scores >40 as indicating significant disagreement.

7. For elaboration of this point, see Peter H. Argersinger, "Ideology and Behavior: Legislative Politics and Western Populism," *Agricultural History* 58 (January 1984): 43–58 (also Chapter 8 of this book).

8. See, for example, O. Gene Clanton, *Kansas Populism: Ideas and Men* (Lawrence, Kans., 1969), 28–29. Clanton also emphasizes important differences between central and western Kansas, but by the 1890s western Kansas had become so depopulated that it had virtually no representation in the

senate, one senator representing eighteen counties in the southwest and another representing thirteen counties in the northwest, both districts extending into central Kansas. For purposes of analysis, therefore, the forty senators were grouped into two blocs, twenty-two representing the more established eastern third and 18 representing the remainder of the state.

9. Senate Bills (S.B.) 129, 153, Kansas, *Senate Journal, 1897*, 311, 535.

10. S.B. 147, ibid., 291. Kansas had the largest increase in public debt of any state in the 1880s. For aspects of this boom, see James C. Malin, "The Kinsley Boom of the Late Eighties," *Kansas Historical Quarterly* 4 (February and May 1935): 23–49, 164–187. Parsons, *Populist Context*, emphasizes this same conflict between villagers and farmers over questions of economic promotion in Nebraska. For suggestive observations on the legislative reflection of the conflict between developers and producers, see Allan G. Bogue, "To Shape a Western State: Some Dimensions of the Kansas Search for Capital, 1865–1893," in *The Frontier Challenge: Responses to the Trans-Mississippi West,* ed. John G. Clark (Lawrence, Kans., 1971), 203–234.

11. Amendment to S.B. 524, S.B. 111, amendments to S.B. 446, Kansas, *Senate Journal, 1897,* 641, 852, 945–946, and *Topeka State Journal,* February 19, 1897.

12. James C. Malin, "At What Age Did Men Become Reformers?" *Kansas Historical Quarterly,* 29 (1963): 250–266. Malin's clever and imaginative article has a different focus from this chapter. He treats reformers in the Kansas legislatures simply as members of self-described reform parties and does not examine their actual voting behavior.

13. Although ethnoculturalists focus on the pietist-liturgical dichotomy, they emphasize the pietistic perspective as underlying the reform movements of the nineteenth century. Thus the relative absence of liturgical senators should not altogether prevent testing the role of religion. But many of the most evangelical Populists were exceedingly hostile to organized religion, and thus to the problem of possible nonreporting of affiliations must be added the problem of measuring religious attitudes by this method. For Populist views toward religion and churches, see Peter H. Argersinger, "Pentecostal Politics in Kansas: Religion, the Farmers' Alliance, and the Gospel of Populism," *Kansas Quarterly* 1 (Fall 1969): 24–35 (also Chapter 3 of this book). The prohibitionist roll call was on House Bill (H.B.) 3, Kansas, *Senate Journal, 1897,* 638–639.

14. Again, as with religion, a substantial number of legislators did not report their educational background, a fact that should suggest caution about any conclusions here.

15. *Topeka State Journal,* January 20, February 10, 19, 1897; *Leavenworth Times,* February 3, 10, 20, 1897; roll calls on S.B.s 34, 8, 147, 3, 446, 72, 524, 111, Kansas, *Senate Journal, 1897,* 398–399, 527–528, 569–570, 291, 833, 945–946, 555–559, 371, 641, 852.

16. S.B. 524, S.B. 121, H.B. 442, S.B. 446, Kansas, *Senate Journal, 1897,* 641, 678, 349, 1126, 555.

17. Eastern Populist opponents of bills to establish additional normal schools believed that the purpose of such legislation was primarily "the aggrandizement of the local representative or senator" (Kansas, *Senate Journal, 1897,* 586–587). In Nebraska, too, legislatures continually wrangled "over new state institutions, especially normal schools, a favorite device to promote community growth" (Robert W. Cherny, *Populism, Progressivism, and the Transformation of Nebraska Politics, 1885–1915* [Lincoln, 1981], 72).

18. *Topeka Daily Capital,* February 18, 1897, and S.B. 85, Kansas, *Senate Journal, 1897,* 744. For the advantages of the deed of trust in the creditor's eyes, see Allan G. Bogue, "To Shape a Western State," 217, and *Money at Interest: The Farm Mortgage on the Middle Border* (Ithaca, N.Y., 1955), 17.

19. For the debilitating effect of Democratic influence and fusion on the People's party, see Peter H. Argersinger, *Populism and Politics: William Alfred Peffer and the People's Party* (Lexington, Ky., 1974).

20. The index of interpersonal agreement is the frequency with which each legislator agrees with every other legislator over the roll calls on which they both vote. Thus, absences are excluded from the calculations. Senators absent for more than half the roll calls are omitted.

21. Karel Bicha, *Western Populism: Studies in an Ambivalent Conservatism* (Lawrence, Kans., 1976), 79, 80, 86, 104.

22. Bogue, *Earnest Men,* 350, and *Topeka Daily Capital,* February 14, 1895. An incident in the 1897 legislature, involving the same analogy that Bogue employed, supports the validity of this assumption. Forty-four Populists formally protested against a gutted railroad bill but still voted for it after being told by a colleague that if they did not realize "a half loaf is better than none" their constituents would replace them with politicians who did (Clanton, *Kansas Populism,* 204). For an excellent explanation of the logic of Guttman scale analysis, see Bogue, *Earnest Men,* 345–351.

23. The quote is from Bicha's sentence in *Western Populism,* 80, denying what Table 9.2 demonstrates. Thus perhaps there was some truth in the rhetoric of an earlier Republican who concluded that "all Populists are not socialists . . . but all socialists . . . are Populists" (*Topeka State Journal,* January 24, 1893).

24. The charge of Populist failure was exaggerated. The 1897 Kansas legislature passed laws providing for stockyard regulation, ballot reform, banking regulation, a state grain-inspection department, a school textbook commission, regulation of life insurance companies, taxation of deficiency judgments, municipal ownership, antitrust legislation, railroad regulation, conservation, and a series of labor protections from anti-Pinkerton and antiscrip provisions to antiblacklisting, protection of unions, and improved health and safety conditions for miners. Even so, as Clanton has noted, "the

party's supporters had a right to expect greater things" (Clanton, *Kansas Populism*, 201, 89, 199, 294n.; Bicha, *Western Populism*, 80, 87, 92; Wright, *Politics of Populism*, 162-163). The party-support score is the percentage of the time a senator voted with his party majority when the parties were polarized at a disagreement index ≥ 50. For those forty-five roll calls, Republicans averaged 92 percent; Populist party loyalty was 87 percent. For all eighty-one roll calls, Populist cohesion averaged 70.4 to 65.7 for Republicans.

25. The conservative bloc of nine Populists had an average reform score of only 21 on these crucial questions; the other Populists averaged 79.

26. *Topeka State Journal*, February 19, 1897; *Leavenworth Times*, February 3, 10, 20, 1897; S.B.s 3, 8, 34, Kansas, *Senate Journal, 1897*, 398-399, 452, 526-528, 570-571, 833.

27. *Topeka State Journal*, January 14, 1897; *Topeka Daily Capital*, February 6, 1897; S.B.s 524 (and amendments), 147, 85, Kansas, *Senate Journal, 1897*, 641, 648, 677, 678, 291, 52, 728-730, 744.

28. Norton (Kans.) *Liberator*, February 26, 1897; *Topeka Advocate*, March 3, 1897; *Leavenworth Times*, March 14, 1897. In an important article, Walter Nugent established that, among Kansas politicians in 1891-1893, Republicans and Democrats were much more likely to be urban oriented than were Populists, who were overwhelmingly farmers. By carefully examining individual mortgage transactions and land purchases, he also demonstrated that Populists, generally, were more "yeoman-like" and less entrepreneurial and speculative than Republicans and Democrats (see Walter T. K. Nugent, "Some Parameters of Populism," *Agricultural History* 40 [October 1966]: 255-270). Nugent's profile of the typical Populist and his economic attitudes seems comparable to the rural orientation and "producer" attitudes that I have attributed to the Populist majority in the 1897 senate. By adopting more entrepreneurial and prodevelopment attitudes and by being disproportionately urban oriented, therefore, members of the Populist minority diverged in significant ways from most Populists and resembled their Republican senatorial colleagues.

29. *Topeka Advocate*, March 24, 1897; for Populist fusion maneuvers involving Harris, Lewelling, Ryan, and Leedy, among others, see Argersinger, *Populism and Politics*, 52, 127-140, 166-178, 267-269, 279-282, 294; for a discussion of the discontinuity between the People's party and Populism in political rather than legislative behavior, see 140-142, 179-181, 197, 209, 221-222, 231, 235-236, 262-266, 306-310. The Democrats in the legislature had also been nominated more for their electoral appeal than for their political principles. Elected on Populist fusion tickets, they were termed Popocrats and caucused with the Populists. But their actual policy attitudes and voting behavior often placed them at odds with the majority of Populist legislators, demonstrating that fusionists could not be depended upon to support Populist policy proposals.

30. Wynne P. Harrington, "The Populist Party in Kansas," *Collections*

of the Kansas State Historical Society, 16 (Topeka, 1925): 444, and *Kansas Semi-Weekly Capital* (Topeka), October 12, 1897.

CHAPTER 10. NO RIGHTS ON THIS FLOOR

1. Milford W. Howard, *If Christ Came to Congress* (New York, 1964), 4, 17, 20, 294, 337, 359–363. Howard's book, first published in 1894, was one of several that loosely adopted the format of the popular William T. Stead, *If Christ Came to Chicago* (Chicago, 1894), a realistic exposé of Chicago's underworld.

2. Albert Bushnell Hart, "The Speaker as Premier," *Atlantic Monthly* 67 (1891): 380–386; Woodrow Wilson, *Congressional Government* (Boston, 1913), 145; David W. Brady, *Congressional Voting in a Partisan Era* (Lawrence, Kans., 1973), 148, 185–186; Morton Keller, *Affairs of State* (Cambridge, Mass., 1977), 301–304.

3. Brady, *Congressional Voting,* 23, 143; Keller, *Affairs of State,* 299–306; Mary P. Follett, *The Speaker of the House of Representatives* (New York, 1896), 112–121.

4. Keller, *Affairs of State,* 303–304; George H. Haynes, *The Senate of the United States,* 2 vols. (New York, 1960), 1: 284–287, 473–489; David J. Rothman, *Politics and Power: The United States Senate, 1869–1901* (Cambridge, Mass., 1966), 43–72.

5. Margaret S. Thompson has stressed the limitations of roll-call analysis and the value of studying other aspects of congressional operations in *The "Spider Web": Congress and Lobbying in the Age of Grant* (Ithaca, N.Y., 1985), 15–19. The best introduction to the "new institutionalism" in legislative analysis is Ronald D. Hedlund, "Organizational Attributes of Legislatures: Structure, Rules, Norms, Resources," *Legislative Studies Quarterly* 9 (1984): 51–121. For the importance of the "dialectical interplay" between the institutional framework and political actions, see Rogers M. Smith, "Political Jurisprudence, the 'New Institutionalism,' and the Future of Public Law," *American Political Science Review* 82 (1988): 89–108. For an investigation of Populist legislative activity in an institutional setting where roll-call analysis proves valuable, see Peter H. Argersinger, "Populists in Power: Public Policy and Legislative Behavior," *Journal of Interdisciplinary History* 18 (1987): 81–105 (also Chapter 9 of this book).

6. Peter H. Argersinger, *Populism and Politics: William Alfred Peffer and the People's Party* (Lexington, Ky., 1974), 102, 106–108.

7. Ibid., 227–228.

8. *Congressional Record,* 54th Cong., 1st sess., 422–426 (hereafter cited as *CR*).

9. *Baltimore Sun,* December 10, 15, 16, 1891.

10. Ibid., December 15, 16, 1891.

11. *CR,* 54th Cong., 1st sess., 4667, 422–423, 429, and *New York Times,* December 31, 1895, 1.

12. *Baltimore Sun,* December 15, 1891, and *People's Party Paper* (Atlanta), December 31, 1891, January 7, 1892.

13. *CR,* 54th Cong., 1st sess., 577; *Farmers Tribune* (Des Moines), March 24, 1897; *Chicago Tribune,* March 23, 1897, 7.

14. Brady, *Congressional Voting,* 168, 60, and *Farmers Tribune,* April 14, 1897.

15. *New York Times,* April 18, 1897, 3; *Farmers Tribune,* April 28, 1897; *Washington Post,* May 14, 1897.

16. James B. Weaver, *A Call to Action* (Des Moines, 1892), 52–54. For a striking indication of the policy implications of important committee assignments, see Joseph Cooper and Cheryl D. Young, "Bill Introduction in the Nineteenth Century: A Study of Institutional Change," *Legislative Studies Quarterly* 14 (1989): 103, n.9.

17. Brady, *Congressional Voting,* 23; DeAlva S. Alexander, *History and Procedure of the House of Representatives* (Boston, 1916), 58–61; Follett, *Speaker of the House,* 103–104, 115; Albert V. House, Jr., "The Contributions of Samuel J. Randall to the Rules of the National House of Representatives," *American Political Science Review* 29 (1935): 837–841.

18. Weaver, *Call to Action,* 55–61. For the rules on the Monday call and attempts to restrict the influence of individual representatives in the Greenback congresses, see Cooper and Young, "Bill Introduction," 88–89, and Stanley Bach, "Suspension of the Rules, the Order of Business, and the Development of Congressional Procedure," *Legislative Studies Quarterly* 15 (1990): 49–63.

19. *Topeka Advocate,* May 19, 1897, June 29, 1898, and *Washington Post,* May 14, 15, 1897.

20. *CR,* 54th Cong., 1st sess., 316–318.

21. *CR,* 54th Cong., 2d sess., appendix (hereafter cited as app.), 132–133; *CR,* 54th Cong., 1st sess., app., 8; *Farmers Tribune,* April 1, 1896.

22. *Harper's Weekly,* August 12, 1893, 738, and *CR,* 54th Cong., 1st sess., 575.

23. *CR,* 54th Cong., 1st sess., 577–578, and *Chicago Tribune,* January 11, 1896, 9.

24. *Frank Leslie's Illustrated Weekly,* January 23, 1892, 492; *Washington Post,* December 5, 1894, 4; Hortense Marie Harrison, "The Populist Delegation in the Fifty-Second Congress, 1891–1893" (Master's thesis, University of Kansas, 1933); Gene Clanton, " 'Hayseed Socialism' on the Hill: Congressional Populism, 1891–1895," *Western Historical Quarterly* 15 (1984): 139–162.

25. *Washington Post,* December 12, 1894, 4, 7.

26. Thomas E. Watson, *The People's Party Campaign Book, 1892* (Washington, D.C., 1892), 361; Wilson, *Congressional Government,* 69; Alexander, *History and Procedure,* 63–64.

27. *CR*, 52d Cong., 1st sess., 4172.

28. Ibid., 4292, 4432, 4480, 4563, 7081; Harrison, "Populist Delegation," 102; *People's Party Paper*, May 27, 1892.

29. *CR*, 52d Cong., 1st sess., 4799-4800, and Watson, *People's Party Campaign Book*, 361. For the norm of "procedural reciprocity," see Edward V. Schneier, "Norms and Folkways in Congress: How Much Has Actually Changed?" *Congress & the Presidency* 15 (1988): 126-127.

30. *CR*, 54th Cong., 1st sess., 423-424, and 53d Cong., 2d sess., 3610.

31. *CR*, 53d Cong., 2d sess., 3609, and 54th Cong., 1st sess., 424.

32. Alexander, *History and Procedure*, 256, 263, 267; *CR*, 55th Cong., 2d sess., 3390; *Detroit Tribune*, February 26, 1895.

33. *CR*, 55th Cong., 2d sess., 133.

34. Allan G. Bogue, *The Congressman's Civil War* (New York, 1989), 64; *CR*, 53d Cong., 2d sess., 7846, 4442, 7156, 4746, 5500, 4564, 2762, 8109, 4794, 8556, 3840; Harrison, "Populist Delegation," 60-61; U.S. Bureau of Labor, *Report on Slums of Baltimore, Chicago, New York, and Philadelphia* (Washington, D.C., 1894).

35. *CR*, 52d Cong., 1st sess., 6217; 53d Cong., 1st sess., 929; 54th Cong., 1st sess., 184, 3417.

36. *Washington Post*, August 24, 1893, 1, and *CR*, 53d Cong., 1st sess., 669.

37. *CR*, 52d Cong., 1st sess., 5796, 7005, 7025; 54th Cong., 2d sess., 160, 395; 53d Cong., 2d sess., 4591, 7156; Harrison, "Populist Delegation," 73-79.

38. *CR*, 54th Cong., 1st sess., 4081-4083, 4145; 53d Cong., 2d sess., 3810, 3843, 3960-3961, 7236-7237; *New York Times*, April 24, 1896, 2.

39. *CR*, 52d Cong., 1st sess., 3299-3306, 3415-3419. Despite popular belief, perhaps based on the erroneous assertion in Alexander, *History and Procedure*, 152, it was not Henry George's famous single-tax volume, *Progress and Poverty* (New York, 1879), but his tariff reform book, *Protection or Free Trade* (New York, 1892), that was read into the *Record*.

40. *Topeka Advocate*, February 17, 1892.

41. Nelson W. Polsby, "The Institutionalization of the U. S. House of Representatives," *American Political Science Review* 62 (1968): 144-168.

42. Howard, *If Christ Came to Congress*, 95; *Washington Post*, December 8, 12, 1893; *Topeka Advocate*, December 11, 1895; *CR*, 53d Cong., 2d sess., 238-239, 2490, 2584, 3843.

43. *CR*, 52d Cong., 1st sess., 1703; 55th Cong., 2d sess., app., 351; *Washington Post*, May 14, 1897; *Topeka Advocate*, May 19, 1897.

44. *Topeka Advocate*, March 21, 1894, December 23, 1891; Watson, *People's Party Campaign Book*, 216; *CR*, 52d Cong., 1st sess., 6933, 6938-6940.

45. Howard, *If Christ Came to Congress*, 76, 20, 41, 111, 200. For a recent account of the Breckinridge scandal, see James C. Klotter, "Sex, Scandal, and Suffrage in the Gilded Age," *Historian* 42 (1980): 225-243.

46. *CR,* 53d Cong., 2d sess., 436–440.

47. Watson, *People's Party Campaign Book,* 362–363; *Chicago Tribune,* January 13, 1896; *CR,* 54th Cong., 1st sess., 567; *People's Party Paper,* May 6, 1892.

48. *Bradstreet's* 19 (1891): 49, 129; *CR,* 53d Cong., 2d sess., 2833–2835; *New York Times,* March 13, 1894, 2.

49. *CR,* 53d Cong., 1st sess., 1374–1375, 1435; William V. Allen, "How to Purify National Legislation," *North American Review* 159 (1894): 159–164; *Topeka Advocate,* March 31, 1897.

50. *CR,* 53d Cong., 1st sess., 982, and *Washington Post,* December 8, 1893. For modern analyses of the role of lobbyists in the Congress of the late nineteenth century, see Thompson, *"Spider Web,"* and Rothman, *Politics and Power,* 191–220.

51. Robert C. McMath, *Populist Vanguard: A History of the Southern Farmers' Alliance* (Chapel Hill, N.C., 1975), 92–95; *CR,* 55th Cong., 3d sess., 2502; 53d Cong., 2d sess., 5795, 3844, 5833, 8293; Lawrence Goodwyn, *Democratic Promise: The Populist Moment in America* (New York, 1976), 192–193; *Farmers Tribune,* March 31, 1897.

52. *Washington Post,* March 4, 1891, 2. Margaret S. Thompson and Joel H. Silbey correctly call for historians to devote more attention to how members were socialized into the legislative community in their essay, "Research on 19th Century Legislatures: Present Contours and Future Directions," *Legislative Studies Quarterly* 9 (1984): 337. Among political scientists the study of norms is a cottage industry but nearly all work focuses on the period beginning in the 1950s. However, see Dean L. Yarwood, "Norm Observance and Legislative Integration: The U.S. Senate in 1850 and 1860," *Social Science Quarterly* 51 (1970): 57–69; and the suggestive insights in Peter Swenson, "The Influence of Recruitment on the Structure of Power in the U.S. House, 1870–1940," *Legislative Studies Quarterly* 7 (1982): 7–36.

53. *Biographical Directory of the American Congress, 1774–1961* (Washington, D.C., 1961), and *CR,* 55th Cong., 2d sess., app., 131–135. The overall level of prior legislative experience among House members was not calculated in Allan G. Bogue, Jerome M. Clubb, Carroll R. McKibbin, and Santa A. Traugott, "Members of the House of Representatives and the Processes of Modernization, 1789–1960," *Journal of American History* 63 (1976): 275–302, which provided the data used in these paragraphs and in Table 10.1 for the inclusive "all representatives" group.

54. Delloyd John Guth, "Omer Madison Kem: The People's Congressman" (Master's thesis, Creighton University, 1962), 92, 100, 114, 135.

55. Wilson, *Congressional Government,* 62; *CR,* 46th Cong., 2d sess., 925; 55th Cong., 2d sess., 4817, app., 130, 150–151. For a useful survey of the political science literature, see Hedlund, "Organizational Attributes," 52–89.

56. *Topeka Daily Capital,* December 6, 1891; Mittie Y. Scott, "The Life

and Political Career of William Vincent Allen" (Master's thesis, University of Nebraska, 1927), 27, 31–39.

57. *CR*, 52d Cong., 1st sess., 605, 1075; 53d Cong., 2d sess., 2582; 54th Cong., 1st sess., 303; Kirk H. Porter, *National Party Platforms* (New York, 1924), 103; *Washington Post*, March 6, 1894; Howard, *If Christ Came to Congress*, 328.

58. *CR*, 54th Cong., 1st sess., 317, 577.

59. *CR*, 52d Cong., 1st sess., 597–598, and Porter, *National Party Platforms*, 103.

60. *CR*, 52d Cong., 1st sess., 597–598, 656. In the revolt against Speaker Cannon and subsequent rules changes in 1911–1913, the House adopted variants of the Populist proposals. See James Sundquist, *The Decline and Resurgence of Congress* (Washington, D.C., 1981), 167–168.

61. *CR*, 55th Cong., 2d sess., app., 131–135, and 54th Cong., 1st sess., app., 8.

62. Argersinger, "Populists in Power," 99, 101; William A. Peffer, *Populism: Its Rise and Fall* (Lawrence, Kans., 1992), 58, 60, 161–162; Argersinger, *Populism and Politics*, 276–281.

63. *CR*, 55th Cong., 2d sess., 4816–4817, 4824, 2981, 103, 5768, and 55th Cong., 1st sess., 1655.

64. *Farmers Tribune*, May 12, 1897; *CR*, 54th Cong., 1st sess., 4670; 55th Cong., 1st sess., 1926; 55th Cong., 2d sess., 240, 6791.

65. *Farmers Tribune*, April 14, July 14, 1897, and Brady, *Congressional Voting*, 99–100. Brady, the first scholar to note this decline in Populist voting, overstates the situation. Most Populists did continue to vote at least sporadically, and they also continued to meet in regular caucus to make plans.

66. M. C. Scott, "A Congressman and His Constituents: Jerry Simpson and the Big Seventh" (Master's thesis, [Fort Hays] Kansas State College, 1959), 164.

INDEX

50, 68–69, 84, 87, 99–100; defeated for reelection, 26; opposes fusion, 103–104, 108, 125, 243; on party composition, 258n97; and party management, 16, 103–104, 125, 134, 150; senatorial election of, 25, 82–101; supports Omaha Platform, 123

Pence, Lafe, 123

People's party (national): and antifusion laws, 20–21; and ballot reform, 17–18, 35; conflicts with Populism, 10–13, 102, 103–107, 110, 114–115, 117–118, 120, 123–124, 128, 131, 133–135, 150, 211; Cincinnati Conference of, 104; as a coalition, 3–6, 10–11, 23, 24, 87; demise of, 16; and direct legislation, 18, 35; and 1892 election, 9–10; and 1894 election, 122; and 1896 election, 15–16, 127–135; and electoral reform, 17–18; factionalism within, 23, 24–25, 33–34, 121–128, 130–135; and fusion with Democrats in 1896, 15–16, 127–133, 135; and hostility of major parties, 2, 4–6, 8, 18–21; National Committee, 14, 16, 127–129, 130–131, 133; National Convention (1896) of, 129, 132; officials of, promote fusion, 11–16, 121–135; Omaha convention of, 12–13; and popular election of senators, 17, 25, 35; and previous party allegiances, 3–6, 10–11, 14, 34; and prohibition, 6, 24; and proportional representation, 18, 35; and religion, 2; and sectionalism, 4–5, 114; and senatorial elections, 24–30; St. Louis conference of (1894), 123–125; and woman suffrage, 18. *See also under individual states*

Perkins, Bishop W., 55, 85, 238
Peterman, A. L., 162
Peters, Samuel R., 82
Pettigrew, Richard F., 162
Philadelphia Evening Bulletin, 100–101
Phillips, Kirk, 171
Phillips, William, 55
Plumb, Preston B., 41, 60
Polk, L. L., 57, 58, 59, 84, 99, 235
Polsby, Nelson W., 231
Pomeroy, Samuel C., 80
Populism: and distrust of political parties and politicians, 7, 12–13, 22–23, 35, 102, 103–105, 109, 113–120, 124, 133–135; and fusion, xi, 9–16, 102–135, 150; historians' views of, 1, 176–178, 189, 191, 194; as movement, 12, 117–118, 133; and political culture, 2–7; political limits of, 1–

36, 211–212; and religion, 2, 64–79, 260n27, 261n40
Populist Revolt, The (Hicks), 191
Populists: and Congress, x, 26, 27, 34, 104, 213–245; and election of U.S. senators, 24–30, 252n53; legislative activity of, 30–34, 176–212; and lobbyists, 234–235, 244; as political agents, x, 8, 35; and political culture, 2–7. *See also under individual states*
Practical politics, 102–135
Prather, Van B., 43, 103, 107
Pritchard, Jeter, 252n53
Progressivism, 174
Prohibition, 6, 24, 47, 53, 56, 97, 197
Prohibitionists: within the People's party, 4, 24, 53–54, 81, 87, 232, 258n97
Prohibition party, 55, 151; and ballot laws, 160–161, 164
Proportional representation, 18, 35

Railroad commissioners, 45, 195–196, 257n75
Randall, Samuel J., 221, 239
Ranney, Austin, 156
Reed, Thomas B., 213, 214, 219–223
Reed Rules, 214, 223, 224–225
Religion: and Populism, 2, 64–79, 196–197, 200
Representation, 174; as obstacle to third parties, 8–9, 11, 35
Republican-Populists, 5–6, 258n97; alienated by fusion politics, 10, 14, 28, 114, 116–117, 119–120, 162, 173; attitudes toward Democratic party, 3, 10–11, 107, 162; influence of, 81, 87, 88, 95, 97, 100, 108, 161; legislative behavior of, 199
Republicans: campaign tactics against Populists, 5–6, 32, 46–47, 56, 59, 60, 84, 85, 89, 92–93, 100, 152–154, 162–163, 169–170; in Congress, 213–245; and election laws, 18–21, 137, 138, 139–143, 161–165, 166, 169–173, 174–175. *See also under individual states*
Resubmission, 47, 49, 53, 54–55, 56, 60
Rice, John H., 82, 88, 120
Richardson, A. M., 55
Ridgely, Edwin, 227
Rightmire, William F., 40, 50, 54, 57, 254n12
Robinson, Charles: as candidate for governor, 54, 56, 60, 61, 62, 256n64; and fusion, 108–109, 112, 114; senatorial candidacy of, 82, 86
Rogers, John, 23

SOURCE NOTES

I am obliged to the editors and publishers for permission to reprint the following:

Chapters 2 and 4 are reprinted by permission from the *Kansas Historical Quarterly* 33 (Winter 1967): 443–469, and 38 (Spring 1972): 43–64, published by the Kansas State Historical Society.

Chapter 3 is reprinted by permission from *Kansas Quarterly* 1 (Fall 1969): 24–35.

Chapter 5 is adapted and reprinted from Peter H. Argersinger, *Populism and Politics: William Alfred Peffer and the People's Party,* copyright 1974 by the University Press of Kentucky, by permission of the publisher.

Chapter 6 is reprinted by permission from *Mid-America* 63 (January 1981): 18–35.

Chapter 7 is reprinted by permission from *Midwest Review* 5 (1983): 1–19.

Chapter 8 is reprinted by permission from *Agricultural History* 58 (January 1984): 43–58, copyright 1984 by the Agricultural History Society.

Chapters 9 and 10 are reprinted from *The Journal of Interdiscipli-*